Willis Abbot

Battle-Fields and Victory

A narrative of the principle military operations of the Civil War from the accession of Grant to the command of the Union armies to the end of the war

Willis Abbot

Battle-Fields and Victory

A narrative of the principle military operations of the Civil War from the accession of Grant to the command of the Union armies to the end of the war

ISBN/EAN: 9783337411992

Printed in Europe, USA, Canada, Australia, Japan

Cover: Foto ©ninafisch / pixelio.de

More available books at **www.hansebooks.com**

BATTLE-FIELDS AND VICTORY

*A NARRATIVE OF THE PRINCIPAL MILITARY
OPERATIONS OF THE CIVIL WAR*

From the Accession of Grant to the Command of the Union
Armies to the End of the War.

BY

WILLIS J. ABBOT

AUTHOR OF "BLUE JACKETS OF '61," "BLUE JACKETS OF 1812," "BLUE JACKETS OF '76,"
"BATTLE-FIELDS OF '61," "BATTLE-FIELDS AND CAMP-FIRES"

ILLUSTRATED BY W. C. JACKSON

NEW YORK
DODD, MEAD AND COMPANY
PUBLISHERS

CONTENTS.

CHAPTER I.

OPENING OF THE YEAR 1864—THE SOUTH UNCONQUERED BUT LOSING STRENGTH—DEPRECIATION OF CONFEDERATE CURRENCY—THE INVASION OF FLORIDA—KILPATRICK'S CAVALRY RAID—ULRIC DAHLGREN'S DEATH—SHERMAN'S MERIDIAN RAID—FORREST'S FORAYS—HIS VICTORY AT UNION CITY—THE FIGHT AT PADUCAH—THE MASSACRE AT FORT PILLOW, ... 3

CHAPTER II.

THE WAR IN THE SOUTHWEST—RED RIVER EXPEDITION—TAKING FORT DE RUSSY—COTTON SPECULATORS—LOW WATER IN THE RIVER—THE BATTLE OF SABINE CROSS ROADS—ROUT OF THE FEDERALS—GENERAL EMORY'S STAND—BANKS'S RETREAT—LOSS OF THE "EASTPORT"—THE FLEET CAUGHT BY LOW WATER—COLONEL BAILEY'S DAM—THE FLEET SAVED—THE EXPEDITION ABANDONED, ... 24

CHAPTER III.

THE SOUTH NOT SUBJUGATED—PRESIDENT LINCOLN STUDIES THE PROBLEM—ULYSSES S. GRANT COMMISSIONED LIEUTENANT-GENERAL—HIS GRAND STRATEGY—REORGANIZING THE ARMY OF THE POTOMAC—SHERIDAN CALLED TO COMMAND THE CAVALRY—PLANNING THE WILDERNESS CAMPAIGN—THE ARMIES—THE ARMY OF THE POTOMAC MOVES—THE BATTLE IN THE WILDERNESS, ... 42

CHAPTER IV.

AFTER THE BATTLE—"FORWARD BY THE LEFT FLANK"—THE RACE FOR SPOTTSYLVANIA—GENERAL SEDGWICK KILLED—THE ATTACK UPON HANCOCK—THE BURNING WOODS—UPTON'S ASSAULT UPON THE SALIENT—SUCCESS AND FAILURE—"THE BLOODY ANGLE"—THE CONFEDERATES ATTACK IN TURN—A HAND-TO-HAND STRUGGLE, . . . 64

CHAPTER V.

STILL FORWARD—THE CONFEDERATES DISCOURAGED—A TOILSOME MARCH—A FLANK ATTACK—LEE TAKES THE OFFENSIVE—QUARREL BETWEEN SHERIDAN AND MEADE—SHERIDAN'S RAID—IN A TRAP—A PANIC IN RICHMOND—THE ARMY OF THE JAMES—BUTLER'S EXPEDITION—ATTEMPT TO WRECK A RAILROAD—BATTLE OF DRURY'S BLUFF, ... 82

CONTENTS.

CHAPTER VI.

GRANT MOVES AGAIN—LEE FOLLOWS—BATTLE ON THE NORTH ANNA—BURNSIDE'S REPULSE—HANCOCK CROSSES THE RIVER—LEE'S STRONG POSITION—ILLNESS OF THE CONFEDERATE GENERAL—STARVATION IN LEE'S RANKS—THE BATTLES AT COLD HARBOR—CUSTER'S MEN IN ACTION—SHERIDAN'S DEFENSE—HANCOCK'S ATTACK—HEAVY LOSSES OF THE ARMY OF THE POTOMAC—GRANT NOT DISCOURAGED, . . . 105

CHAPTER VII.

IN THE SHENANDOAH VALLEY—SIGEL'S RECORD OF FAILURE—CROOK IN THE KANAWHA VALLEY—BATTLE OF NEW MARKET—VIRGINIA CADETS CALLED TO WAR—THE LEXINGTON MILITARY ACADEMY—THE CALL TO ARMS—THE CADETS IN A CHARGE, . . 127

CHAPTER VIII.

THE WAR IN THE WEST—SHERMAN IN COMMAND—GRANT'S ORDERS—SHERMAN'S PLAN OF CAMPAIGN—HIS SUCCESS AS A RAILROAD MANAGER—THE ARMY IN LIGHT MARCHING ORDER—SHERMAN'S ANTAGONIST—A CAMPAIGN OF STRATEGY—FLANKING JOHNSTON AT RESACA—BATTLE OF DALTON—BATTLE AT RESACA—RAPID RAILROAD BUILDING—A BATTLE PROMISED—PROTEST OF HOOD AND POLK—THE CONFEDERATES RETREAT—NEW HOPE CHURCH—A FIGHT FOR THE COLORS—JOHNSTON'S FABIAN POLICY—GENERAL POLK KILLED—BATTLE OF KENESAW—JOHNSTON RELIEVED, ... 136

CHAPTER IX.

HOOD'S CHARACTER—SHERMAN STILL ADVANCING—BATTLE OF PEACHTREE CREEK—THE FEDERALS TAKEN BY SURPRISE—DEFEAT OF THE CONFEDERATES—FIRST BATTLE OF ATLANTA—DEATH OF MCPHERSON—A FIERCE STRUGGLE—THE CONFEDERATES BEATEN BACK—HOOD RETIRES TO HIS BREASTWORKS—UNION CAVALRY RAIDS—TWO DISASTERS—HOOD'S SECOND SORTIE—ATLANTA EVACUATED—TRIUMPH OF THE FEDERALS 162

CHAPTER X.

GRANT'S MOVEMENT TO THE SOUTH SIDE OF THE JAMES—PANIC IN PETERSBURG AND RICHMOND—GENERAL WISE PREPARES FOR DEFENSE—FAILURE OF GILMORE'S EXPEDITION AGAINST PETERSBURG—SMITH CARRIES THE OUTER WORKS—FAILS TO PRESS HIS ADVANTAGE—BEAUREGARD MOVES TO PETERSBURG—HANCOCK'S WOUND DISABLES HIM—THE CONFEDERATES SURPRISED—SIEGE OF PETERSBURG—THE MINE—WHITE TROOPS OR BLACK?—THE EXPLOSION—THE ATTACK AND BLOODY REPULSE OF THE UNION TROOPS, ... 180

CONTENTS

CHAPTER XI.

IN THE SHENANDOAH VALLEY—BATTLE OF PIEDMONT—DESTRUCTION AT STAUNTON—BRECKENRIDGE ORDERED TO THE VALLEY—HUNTER'S RETREAT FROM LYNCHBURG—EARLY'S MARCH UPON WASHINGTON—EARLY IN FREDERICK—HIS HEAVY REQUISITIONS—PANIC IN WASHINGTON—GENERAL WALLACE INTERPOSES—BATTLE OF THE MONOCACY—EARLY APPROACHES THE CAPITAL—HELP COMES IN TIME—EARLY RETREATS—M'CAUSLAND'S RAID—THE BURNING OF CHAMBERSBURG, ... 199

CHAPTER XII.

EARLY HOLDS HIS GROUND IN THE VALLEY—SHERIDAN SENT AGAINST HIM—THE VALLEY TO BE RAVAGED—THE BATTLE OF WINCHESTER—ROUT OF THE CONFEDERATES—SHERIDAN PURSUES—BATTLE OF TUMBLING RUN—DESOLATION IN THE VALLEY—THE CAVALRY FIGHT—A MYSTERIOUS MESSAGE—SHERIDAN VISITS WASHINGTON—BATTLE OF CEDAR CREEK—THE SURPRISE—SHERIDAN TO THE RESCUE—THE FEDERALS RALLY, 215

CHAPTER XIII.

EXPELLING THE CITIZENS FROM ATLANTA—SAVING ALLATOONA—"HOLD THE FORT"—HOOD MOVING NORTHWARD—PLANNING THE MARCH TO THE SEA—DIFFICULTY OF GETTING PERMISSION—THE GREAT MARCH BEGUN—HAVOC DONE IN ATLANTA—FORAGING—THE NEGROES FOLLOW THE COLUMN—DESTROYING THE RAILROADS—TORPEDOES IN THE ROAD—STORMING FORT M'ALLISTER—SHERMAN VISITS THE FLEET—SAVANNAH TAKEN, ... 235

CHAPTER XIV.

INCIDENTS OF THE WAR—THE STOLEN LOCOMOTIVE—PLAN OF THE RAID—UNEXPECTED DIFFICULTIES—THE BLOCK AT KINGSTON—THE PURSUIT—TENACITY OF THE PURSUERS—TRYING TO BURN A BRIDGE—THE ENGINE ABANDONED—SAD FATE OF THE RAIDERS—GENERAL JOHN MORGAN—REFUSED PERMISSION TO CROSS THE OHIO—HIS DISOBEDIENCE—CROSSING THE OHIO—MORGAN CAPTURED AND HIS COMMAND DISPERSED—THE ESCAPE—THE NEW YORK DRAFT RIOTS—FIGHTING IN THE STREETS, . . . 254

CHAPTER XV.

REPELLING HOOD'S INVASION OF TENNESSEE—BATTLE OF FRANKLIN—THE UNION WORKS CARRIED—GOOD WORK OF THE RESERVES—GENERAL THOMAS DELIBERATE—CLAMOR OF THE COUNTRY—BATTLE OF NASHVILLE—A GREAT CONFEDERATE DISASTER—HOOD'S ARMY DISPERSED—FORT FISHER—ITS VALUE TO THE CONFEDERACY—BUTLER'S POWDER SHIP—THE NAVAL BOMBARDMENT—GENERAL TERRY'S SUCCESSFUL ASSAULT—SHERMAN LEAVES SAVANNAH—HIS NORTHWARD MARCH—BURNING OF COLUMBIA—CHARLESTON EVACUATED, ... 280

CHAPTER XVI

THE END NO LONGER IN DOUBT—PRIVATIONS OF THE CONFEDERATES—PEACE NEGOTIATIONS FAIL—LEE DETERMINES TO ATTACK FORT STEDMAN—THE SURPRISE—CONFEDERATES DRIVEN BACK—DINWIDDIE COURT-HOUSE AND FIVE FORKS—LEE'S LINES PIERCED—UNION VICTORIES ALL ALONG THE LINES—PANIC IN RICHMOND—THE CONFEDERATE CAPITAL ABANDONED—WORK OF THE MOB—RETREAT OF LEE'S ARMY—THE SURRENDER AT APPOMATTOX COURT-HOUSE—GENERAL GRANT'S MAGNANIMITY—THE END OF THE WAR, ... 305

ILLUSTRATIONS.

	PAGE
IN THE WILDERNESS,	FRONTISPIECE
THROUGH THE DAM,	11
BURNING COLUMBIA,	21
DESTROYING A RAILROAD,	31
THE BLOODY ANGLE,	39
IN THE PETERSBURG CRATER,	49
DRAFT RIOTS IN NEW YORK,	59
FORAGING,	77
SHERIDAN AT WINCHESTER,	89
CONTRABANDS IN SHERMAN'S WAKE,	99
LEE AFTER THE SURRENDER,	111
SHERIDAN IN THE SHENANDOAH VALLEY,	123
RESCUING WOUNDED FROM THE BURNING WOODS,	133
SHERIDAN AT FIVE FORKS,	149
REVEILLE,	159
THE WATER CALL,	171
BURNING UNION BREASTWORKS,	191
MASSACRE AT FORT PILLOW,	209
MORGAN'S ESCAPE,	227
THE REWARD OF TREACHERY,	245
THE LOSS OF THE "CRICKET,"	261
HAND TO HAND FIGHT AT ATLANTA,	267
CADETS AT NEW MARKET,	277
WINTER SPORTS IN LEE'S ARMY,	291
HOT WORK AT COLD HARBOR,	301
DEFENDING AN EMBRASURE,	311
THE FIELD HOSPITAL,	321
INCIDENT OF THE RAILWAY RAID,	327

INTRODUCTION.

IN the three volumes of which this is the concluding one I have told for the general reader the story of the military operations of what has been up to this date the most obstinately contested, most colossal, and bloodiest war of modern history. The statistics compiled by government officials show that no less than 313,000 men met death by bullet, shell, saber, or disease while in the army. The loss of the Confederates could have been but little less, and the total of the bloody sacrifice to Mars is unparalleled in the history of war. That this great wound opened in the nation should so soon have healed, and that to-day, but twenty-six years after Lee fired his last gun, the lately severed States should be bound not only by the ties of commerce, but those of social intercourse and brotherly affection as well, is unprecedented. In telling the story of the futile struggle of the Confederacy against the National authority, I have not thought it necessary to depict the men who wore the gray as conscienceless rascals nor contemptible traitors. In that day, when communication between New Orleans and New York was more difficult than it is between the latter port and Liverpool to-day, and when two great and antagonistic systems of labor arrayed the South against the North, it was almost inevitable that perpetual bickering would end in civil war. There are few men who will deny that a high sense of duty, and devotion to what they had been taught to regard as their especial country, contributed as much to filling the ranks of the Confederate army as those of the Union. The author holds that the cause of the South was a bad one, even before the costly court of last resort had pronounced it an untenable one, but he believes that, in setting forth for admiration the deeds of gallantry of the Confederates by the side of those of the National soldiers, he is describing the valor of Americans whose descendants will in any possible war of the future be found following the flag of the undivided nation.

The plan of this work does not include the story of the operations of the navy during the civil war. That will be found in an earlier work entitled " Blue Jackets of '61."

WILLIS J. ABBOT.

Chicago, 1891.

BATTLE-FIELDS AND VICTORY.

CHAPTER I.

OPENING OF THE YEAR 1864—THE SOUTH UNCONQUERED BUT LOSING STRENGTH—DEPRECIATION OF CONFEDERATE CURRENCY—THE INVASION OF FLORIDA—KILPATRICK'S CAVALRY RAID—ULRIC DAHLGREN'S DEATH—SHERMAN'S MERIDIAN RAID—FORREST'S FORAYS—HIS VICTORY AT UNION CITY—THE FIGHT AT PADUCAH—THE MASSACRE AT FORT PILLOW.

ITH all the natural buoyancy of the Southern people, with all their indomitable determination to carry their cause to victory and to recognize no defeat, the coming of the new year (1864) found the Confederacy cheerless and apprehensive of disaster. The soldier seized his musket and rushed into battle with no less enthusiasm than in the palmy days when Lee and "Stonewall" Jackson did about as they chose with the Army of the Potomac, but when the fighting was over, when "the thunder of the captains and the shouting" had ceased, the free parliament about the camp-fire was inclined to take a despairing view of the situation. Indeed, the outlook for the Confederacy was sufficiently gloomy. Foreign intervention in behalf of the South, so confidently expected at the outbreak of the war, had not come; the defeat at Gettysburg settled all that. Nor had the hoped for aid from Southern sympathizers in the North materialized. On the contrary, the autumn elections had resulted in the complete and overwhelming defeat of all candidates who openly opposed the vigorous war policy of President Lincoln. The people of the North were not thinking of abandoning the contest. That was clear enough. When the conscription of 300,000 men in April could be followed by no more serious opposition than a riot among the turbulent denizens of the slums of New York, it was evident that the Confederacy could build no hopes on dissension in the camp of its foes. Meantime, the North was prospering. Trade was active. Money plenty. Never before had fortunes been made so quickly. The gaps in the ranks of the blue-clad soldiery were quickly filled. The expenditures of the government for army supplies were lavish. The comfort of the Northern troops was further enhanced by the labors of the Sanitary Commission, a vast voluntary association which collected and expended nearly five million dollars, and more than fifteen million dollars worth of provisions and clothing in the course of its work. The resources of the government, both of men and of money, were practically unlimited.

It was far different in the South. Its sparsely settled territory could not long meet the heavy demands for more soldiers which the military authorities continually made. In the earliest days of the war the Confederate Congress authorized the drafting of every able-bodied white man between the ages of eighteen and forty-five. After the costly defeat at Gettysburg, the conscription was rigidly enforced, and the privilege so generally enjoyed in the North of buying a "substitute" was denied to conscripts. The land was literally swept clean of able-bodied white men, and the extension of the conscription law to permit the enrollment of boys of sixteen and men of sixty in the reserve or home guard, led General Grant to write that the Confederate authorities "robbed alike the cradle and the grave."

In the depreciation of Confederate currency, too, the soldier of the South could read the story of the government's distress. The paper money turned out by the printing presses at Richmond was accepted at first cheerfully, but as the success of the South seemed more and more questionable, it was regarded with distrust, and taken only at a high rate of discount. When the Confederacy first set up an army and navy of its own, it adopted about the same rate of pay as had been customary in the United States service. Thus in 1861 a brigadier-general who wore the gray drew a salary of $2500 a year, a lieutenant in the navy $1,500, and a private soldier $11 a month. But in 1864, while the ostensible rate of wages was the same, the purchasing power of the paper money in which they were paid had so greatly decreased, that the brigadier-general's pay was equivalent to $8 a month, the lieutenant drew the munificent sum of $4.25 a month, and the private was obliged to meet his personal expenses and perhaps send a little money home out of a monthly stipend equivalent to thirty-three cents. Articles of necessity sold for what seemed like fabulous prices. In Richmond beef, pork, and butter fetched $35 a pound ; common cloth was $60 a yard, shoes $600 to $800 a pair, and a barrel of flour brought $1400. It was not so much that the actual intrinsic value of the goods had increased, though to some extent the blockade had made everything dearer, but the currency had so depreciated that its purchasing power was almost gone. The few who had "hard money," as gold and silver were called, found living never cheaper. The guest at a Richmond hotel who had nothing but Confederate money paid $20 a day, while the sight-seeing Englishman, who had come over on a blockade runner with his pockets full of gold, paid but one dollar.

So the year 1864 opened with the North confident and nerved up to its supreme effort; the South still determined, still defiant, but showing an under-current of distrust of the future which soon developed into despair. Readers of the preceding volume of the series* will recollect the military situation at the close of 1863. The blockade was in its most effective condition. The Atlantic coast, except at Charleston and Wilmington, was practically in the hands of the Federals. Bragg had been driven from

---

* Battle-Fields and Camp Fires ; by Willis J. Abbot. New York : Dodd, Mead & Co.

Chattanooga, and the Mississippi was under national domination from its source to its mouth. But Richmond—the goal of the Army of the Potomac in 1861—was still untaken, and Lee in the East, and Bragg in the West, blocked the pathways of the national armies into the heart of the Confederacy.

Hostilities opened slowly. The seat of war was still in territory sufficiently northern to make campaigning in winter impossible, and January and February passed away without a blow being struck by either of the giant armies. But among some of the smaller detachments there was more activity. Word had come to General Gillmore, who was conducting the Federal siege at Charleston, that Union sentiment was growing in Florida, and that a loyal state government could readily be established there with the aid of but a few bayonets. President Lincoln, on hearing of this, showed great anxiety to thus win one seceding state back to the allegiance it had cast off, and accordingly Gillmore put about 7000 men on a small fleet and went down the coast, landing in Jacksonville, which was found in ruins and deserted by all its white inhabitants. There were few Confederate troops in Florida. The state was far from the seat of war, and the Confederacy needed its men where the fighting was hottest. But such armed Confederates as were within the borders of the state rallied at Olustee, and there encountered the Union forces under General Seymour. It was a battle in the woods. The Confederates had the advantage of position and fought a defensive fight. The Union troops were wearied by a long march over the yielding sands and through the dense tropical jungles of Florida. Yet the fight was a severe one and stubbornly contested. So rapid was the fire that before night fell both parties had exhausted their ammunition. The battle was ended by the retreat of the Federals, leaving five cannon on the field. The loss of the Confederates was 500 men in all. The Union troops lost over 1800. "It was one of the side-shows of the great war," wrote Senator Hawley, who was then a colonel of infantry, "but the loss on the Union side was proportionately about three times as great as at Buena Vista. I suppose it did help to whittle away the great rebellion."

But whatever was the final effect of the battle of Olustee, its first result was to convince General Gillmore that Union sentiment in Florida was a myth, and his troops were soon withdrawn from the state.

The winter of 1863-64 brought to the sorely tried people of Virginia—the great battle-field of the war for the Union—some measure of relief. After the retreat from Gettysburg the Confederates had occupied again their old line along the Rapidan, and there, through the bleak months of winter, the two armies lay in their camps and trenches waiting until spring for the renewal of hostilities. Desperately dull it was. Pitched battles with snow balls, cock-fights, greased pigs and poles, and the like sports were enjoyed on either side of the picket line. Another means of diversion was the regular Friday execution of deserters and bounty-jumpers, for the draft in the North and the rigid conscription in the South were bringing into the armies a class of unwilling recruits, who sought every opportunity to escape. "A gallows and a shooting ground were provided in each corps," writes an officer of the Army of the Potomac, "and scarcely a Friday passed during the winter, while the army lay on Hazel River and in the vicinity of Brandy Station, that some of these deserters did not suffer the death penalty."

Toward the latter part of the winter camp life became unendurably monotonous, and it was with lively satisfaction that the soldiers in the Union camp hailed the news that an expedition was to be dispatched against the Confederate capital. It was on the night of the 28th of February that 4000 cavalry men, led by General Judson Kilpatrick, rode out of the Union lines, their horses' hoofs ringing loud upon the icy ground and their sabers and equipments clinking merrily in the frosty air. The Rapidan was crossed at Ely's Ford. A quick dash of the vanguard, and the Confederate pickets were captured before the alarm could be given. Then on for Richmond by the most direct route. Kilpatrick's plan was an audacious one— such an adventurous project as would have delighted Stuart or Mosby. The main defense of Richmond was Lee's army, intrenched along the Rapidan. This Kilpatrick had flanked, and reaching Spottsylvania Court-house, had between him and the enemy's chief city nothing but a long line of breastworks, empty or insufficiently guarded by untried troops or half armed civilians. Dividing his force into two parts, General Kilpatrick sent Colonel Ulric Dahlgren with 500 men to cross the river and work up toward Richmond on the Southern side. Kilpatrick, with the remainder of the troops, was to proceed to the northern side of the city, and as soon as he could hear the thunder of Dahlgren's guns would make a dash into the streets, effect a junction with Dahlgren, attack Libby prison and liberate the wretched Union captives confined there, and then escape to the Union lines as best they might. It was an adventurous and daring project.

With the main body of the raiders Kilpatrick set out from Spottsylvania at a sharp trot. At Beaver Dam Station he reached the Virginia Central railway, and while his men were engaged in tearing this up and cutting the telegraph wires they were attacked by a force of Confederates under General Bradley T. Johnson. The sharp blare of the bugles and the crack of the rifles called the soldiers from their work of destruction. The skirmish was fierce, but the Confederates soon gave way and fled. The alarm was given now and it behooved Kilpatrick to move quickly, so the smoke of battle had scarcely cleared away when his men were again in the saddle and riding across the country. The telegraph wires had been cut, so the news of their advance could not precede them. At Frederickshall a rich prize was captured. A Confederate court-martial was in session there, and in the midst of its deliberations the Yankee raiders swooped down and captured the whole court—eight commissioned officers in all. And so on toward Richmond the flying column sped, burning bridges, and wrecking railroads in its path, until Tuesday, March 1, found it within five miles of the Confederate capital, and in front of a heavy line of earthworks. The alarm had reached Richmond by this time and the works were manned by invalided soldiers, home guards and clerks from the government offices. Nevertheless they fought well, and their heavy guns were too much for Kilpatrick's light field artillery; so the Federals halted to wait for the welcome sound of Dahlgren's guns to come floating over the city. But though the eager listeners strained every ear, nothing was heard from the southward. After a short delay hope was abandoned and Kilpatrick withdrew his men, the Confederates hanging on the rear and harassing them as they retreated.

Dahlgren had met with fatal ill-fortune on his expedition. Had he left the main body but an hour or two earlier he might have captured General Lee, who, as it was, passed down the Virginia Central railroad but a short time before the raiders crossed his path. At the head of the column rode Dahlgren. By his side was a negro guide who had agreed to lead the expedition to a ford by which the James River could be crossed. The column marched rapidly, for it was essential that the ford should be passed before the enemy could reach it and dispute its passage. But when, after a long ride over lonely roads, the river came in sight, the guide with simulated perplexity declared that he had not found the ford and that he knew not whether to seek it up stream or down. In a moment the men of Dahlgren's command began to suspect the man's good faith. "He is a traitor," was the cry. With ashen lips and stammering tongue the wretch pleaded for mercy, but the enraged troopers, convinced of his guilt, dragged him to the roadside and hanged him to the limb of a tree.

Then the column moved on up the bank of the river, abandoning the original plan of crossing it, as no ford could be found. The canal which skirts the stream was cut in many places, canal-boats laden with grain were destroyed, and the torch was set to several grist-mills and saw-mills. The houses and barns of the people along the line of march were generally left unharmed, but when the boys in blue heard that a particularly spacious barn, with its bins and ricks crammed to overflowing, belonged to Mr. Seddon, the Confederate Secretary of War, the temptation was too great for them, and the structure was soon in flames. By eight o'clock at night the raiders were within five miles of Richmond. For the last two hours they had heard guns, which they took to be Kilpatrick's, from the other side of the city, but before nightfall they died away. Nothing then remained to Dahlgren and his followers but flight. The expedition had failed—failed as did almost every other raid, expedition, or plan of battle which involved a division of the forces into two widely separated parties and a concentration at the sound of the cannon. But Dahlgren was not destined to escape easily from the trap into which he rode so dashingly. In the darkness of the night his force, slender enough at best, was divided. The rear guard of 300 men, under Captain Mitchell, after sharp fighting, made its way through the enemy's lines and finally rejoined Kilpatrick. Dahlgren, with a scant 200 troopers, moved off in another direction and fell into an ambuscade. The first shot fired by the ambushed Confederates killed Dahlgren, and the volley that quickly followed threw the Federal column into the direst confusion. Swarming out from their place of concealment, the graybacks fell fiercely upon the disordered raiders. The Federals were soon put to flight, over one hundred of them remaining prisoners in the hands of the victors. On Dahlgren's body, which was easily recognized by the artificial leg he wore, to replace a limb lost at Gettysburg, the Confederates claimed to have found a paper giving the details of a plan for giving Richmond over to sack, and for the murder of President Davis and his cabinet. The military authorities in the North promptly disavowed all responsibility for this alleged plan, and Dahlgren's friends and associates denounced as forgeries the papers which were published in the Richmond press.

These two ill-fated expeditions then made up the sum and substance of the military movements in the East prior to the coming of spring. In the West, however, General Sherman tried to strike a blow with his cavalry arm, which was parried by the Confederate cavalry leader, Forrest, who dealt a blow in return which proved more effective.

Sherman was at Vicksburg. On a line with Vicksburg, but almost on the eastern boundary of the State, was the town of Meridian. Here two railroads crossed, one running north and south, extending from Mobile into the heart of Tennessee, and the other extending to the eastward into Alabama and Georgia. Railroads were few in the South at that time and the junction had made Meridian an important point. Here the Confederates had erected great warehouses for the storage of provisions and munitions of war. A considerable body of troops, too, was maintained at this point, whence they could be sent speedily by rail north or south, east or west, as the necessity might arise. General Sherman determined to fall upon Meridian, drive away the Confederate garrison, burn the arsenal and

THROUGH THE DAM.

tear up the railroads so as to isolate the different parts of the Confederacy thenceforth. But in addition to accomplishing this he desired to effect the defeat and dispersal of the Confederate cavalry force under General Forrest, which was operating in Northern Mississippi and Southern Tennessee. Forrest was a brave and dashing leader. His men were hardy troopers, used to quick marches and reckless of danger. To crush him and annihilate his command would be a notable victory for the Union cause. Full of this project, Sherman boarded a steamer at Vicksburg and set out for Memphis, where were the headquarters of General W. Sooy Smith, then chief of cavalry in the division of the Mississippi. The river was full of great cakes of floating ice that bumped against the prow of the boat and ground against her sides until those on board feared that she might be sent to the bottom. But Memphis was reached without accident and Sherman and the chief of cavalry were soon in earnest consultation. General Smith was ordered to take the field against Forrest with a force of 7000 men. "You will find General Forrest a daring and able enemy," said General Sherman. "You must be prepared for fierce and sudden attacks. When you have repelled his assault, attack in your turn and put an end to him. This you can do, for you will have 7000 men, while he has but 4000, and my expedition against Meridian will make it impossible for the Confederates to send any reinforcements to his aid." It was agreed that General Smith should start from Memphis on February 1 and march southeast, while Sherman should leave Vicksburg February 3, and march due east. Thus they would effect a junction in the vicinity of Meridian. Sherman then reembarked on the icy river and made his way back to Vicksburg.

Promptly on the appointed day the head of Sherman's column passed out through the chain of earthworks that girdled the landward side of Vicksburg. It was to be an expedition of destruction—a raid. His force of 25,000 men was in light marching order and advanced with such rapidity that the Confederates were driven from the very first, without having time to rally and oppose the advance of the invaders.

Jackson was reached without any fighting, other than slight skirmishing with Polk's cavalry. The ministerial general had but 9000 men in all, so he dared not make a determined stand against Sherman, but fled, without even destroying his pontoon bridge across the Pearl River, whereby the Federal advance was much expedited. From Jackson eastward the path of Sherman's army was marked by a broad belt of ashes and desolation. No public property was spared, nor anything which could be applied to public uses. Mills, railway stations, and rolling stock were burned. Railway tracks were torn up, the ties heaped on roaring fires and the rails heated red-hot and twisted out of shape. Sometimes the soldiers would twine a hot rail about a young tree, making what they facetiously termed "Jeff Davis's neck-ties." To Sherman's lines came escaping slaves in droves, old and young men, women and pickaninnies. Greatly as they impeded the march of the column they were not driven away, partly because the war had now assumed the aspect of a struggle against slavery, and partly because every slave carried away helped to weaken the Confederacy, which had relied upon the blacks to stay on the plantations and raise crops, while the whites went to the front and fought with Lee and Johnston. Moreover, the slaves still further impoverished their masters by taking horses and mules with them when they fled, so that after Sherman's army had passed, most of the plantations in its track were stripped of their live-stock, both cattle and human.

When Meridian was reached its defenders were nowhere to be seen. Sherman took possession and waited for Smith. Days passed without any word coming from the cavalry column. After a week in Meridian, Sherman set the torch to the public buildings and retraced his steps toward Vicksburg. He had taken 400 prisoners, destroyed 150 miles of track, 67 bridges, 20 locomotives and 28 cars; had burned several thousand bales of cotton, a number of steam mills, and over 2,000,000 bushels of corn. Over 1000 Union white refugees and 8000 negroes followed in his wake.

In 1866, the historian Lossing, passing through Meridian, asked the Mayor of the town if Sherman had done the place much injury. "Injury!" was the emphatic reply, "why he took it away with him."

Meanwhile the cavalry column under General Sooy Smith had failed as completely in accomplishing its purpose as Sherman had succeeded in his.

To begin with, General Smith failed to leave Memphis upon the day designated in his orders. The first part of his march was attended by the same scenes that accompanied Sherman's expedition. Cotton was burned, railroads wrecked, and slaves freed. But when still 100 miles from Meridian he encountered Forrest's cavalry. Thinking himself outnumbered he retreated. The Confederates, who really numbered only about 3000, pursued, and at Okolona fell upon the fleeing Federals putting them to rout and capturing five new guns. Thence the blue-coats fled northward in panic, and reached Memphis sorely disheartened and sadly bereft of colors, guns, horses, and men. The disastrous failure of this expedition greatly disappointed General Sherman, who had relied upon Smith to relieve him of the continual annoyance and anxiety which Forrest's skillful and daring raids caused.

The Confederate cavalryman, on his part, did not long rest content with the laurels gained by beating back Smith and his troopers. To his restless and adventurous spirit the briefest inactivity was intolerable. He knew that the Union posts in Western Tennessee along the bank of the Mississippi were now held by garrisons so small as to fairly invite attack. He was not ignorant of the woeful plight in which Smith's cavalry was left by the disastrous expedition against him. Of the 7500 troopers in Smith's cavalry over 5000 were now unhorsed, so that little resistance could be offered to a Confederate cavalry force. Most of Forrest's men were Tennesseans, who would look upon a campaign in their native State as the next thing to a furlough. Influenced by all these considerations, the Confederate leader determined upon an invasion of Tennessee, which should have for its purpose the reduction of the forts on the east bank of the Mississippi held by the Federals. A wiser and far more effective enterprise would have been for Forrest to invade Eastern Tennessee and cut the railroad on which the Union troops at Chattanooga were wholly dependent for their supplies. A railroad torn up requires time for its repair and troops to guard it. Such a blow would have seriously crippled Sherman, and it is said that anticipating and dreading it, he purposely weakened the garrisons in the river forts in order to draw Forrest in that direction.

Forrest's column, stripped to light marching order, is soon in motion.

On the 20th of March he is in Jackson, Miss., and receives a hearty welcome from the people, whose devotion to the Confederacy has been in no wise lessened by the fact that their village has thrice been occupied by Sherman's army and has suffered sorely from pillage and the torch. Without halting, the Confederate column pushes on. At Trenton, a detachment of 600 cavalry men is made from the main body to proceed to Union City, near by, and capture a Federal post there. Within the breastworks at Union City are 500 soldiers at least—more than a match for an attacking party of 600—but Forrest knows the Union commander, Colonel Hawkins, and believes that he will make but a half-hearted resistance. With his 600 men, Colonel Duckworth appears before the works at Union City. His summons to surrender is scornfully refused by the Federals. An assault, though delivered with notable gallantry, is easily repelled; neither party has any artillery, a fact which operates greatly to the detriment of the attacking force. But the musketry fire is rapid and deadly, and Duckworth sees his ranks thinning fast with no apparent weakening of the vigor of the defense. Ceasing the assault, he thinks to employ the name of Forrest to intimidate the Federals. Another demand for a surrender is dispatched, this time in the name of Forrest, who declares that before storming the works he desires to give the garrison a chance to escape useless slaughter. Hawkins is visibly affected and asks to speak to Forrest. Duckworth replies cunningly that the customs of war do not permit an officer of Forrest's rank to stoop to a personal conference with a simple colonel, such as Hawkins, but he himself appearing as Forrest's envoy depicts in vivid phrase the horrors of a capture by storm, and boasts of the strength of Forrest's regiments and the weight of his artillery. Hawkins hesitates, and submits the matter to a council of his officers. A majority favors the continuance of the defense, knowing that before the telegraph line was cut a message had gone north to General Brayman at Cairo, telling of their desperate situation and praying help. But there are timorous ones among them who, in unison with the commander, decide to surrender the fort if the Confederates have any artillery. Forthwith an officer goes to Duckworth's lines, where some ambulances disguised as caissons are shown him. Returning, he reports that the enemy indeed have cannon, and the surrender is speedily consummated. The entire garrison and 300 horses thus fell into the Confederates' hands. When the stars and stripes fell from the staff at Union City, General Brayman, with a whole brigade of Federals, was within six miles of the works hastening to raise the siege.

Forrest, meantime, by marching about twenty-five miles a day, has reached Paducah, on the south bank of the Ohio River, near the spot at which the Tennessee joins it. Here was a considerable force of Union soldiers under command of Colonel Hicks. A defensive earthwork stood not far from the town, but as the place was distant from the seat of war, most of the soldiery had been quartered on the people in the city. Hicks had been prudent, however, and his men had standing orders to muster in the fort at the very first alarm.

So, when a reconnoitering party comes galloping into Paducah on the 25th of March, crying that Forrest is fast coming up the road, the blue-coated soldiery swarm from the houses and make for the fort. Forrest's entry to the city is disputed by a sharp fire of musketry, a devoted rear guard fighting stubbornly in the streets to give their comrades time to gain the shelter of Fort Anderson, and prepare for the coming assault. In Forrest's van is a brigade of Kentuckians commanded by Colonel Thompson. The leader and many of his men are natives of Paducah, and are fired with a fierce determination to drive the Federals from their native city. Charging through the streets they rush pell-mell against the ramparts of the fort. Its defenders have scarce had time to align themselves along the parapets, but they meet the attack boldly and beat back the Southerners with heavy losses. The assailants are preparing for another charge, when they are taken in flank by a fire from two Federal gunboats, the *Frosta* and *Pawpaw*, which lie within easy range on the current of the Ohio River. A solid shot strikes Thompson, killing him instantly, and his men, demoralized by this attack from an unexpected quarter, seek shelter in some neighboring houses, from the tops of which they continue to pour a galling fire upon the defenders of the fort.

Forrest now attempts the expedient which had served Duckworth so well at Union City. A flag of truce is sent forward, bearing a demand for surrender, which closes with the extraordinary threat, "If you surrender you shall be treated as prisoners of war; but if I have to storm your works you may expect no quarter." The usages of civilized war do not justify such a threat, which puts a premium upon poltroonery and rewards gallantry with wholesale murder. In his own behalf General Forrest has pleaded that he only strove to terrify the garrison into a surrender, having no real intention of carrying his bloody threat into execution. But his own soldiers took him seriously, as was demonstrated by their bloody deeds after storming Fort Pillow.

However, in Colonel Hicks the Confederate trooper has an antagonist not to be shaken by threats. "If you want this fort, come and take it," he replies defiantly, and Forrest, not liking the task in hand, concludes that he does not really want it. After holding Paducah several days and plundering the town of everything that could possibly be useful to a cavalry column on the march, he withdraws his men and turns south again.

In Tennessee, on the bank of the Mississippi not far north of Memphis, stands Fort Pillow. Built originally by the Confederates to command the great river, it was a work of no small strength. At the time of Forrest's operations it was but slenderly garrisoned. Scarce 600 men were there to guard the long line of breastworks that extended over hills and across ravines and plateaus. The *personnel* of this garrison was peculiarly irritating to the people of the surrounding country. The two companies of white troops were made up of Tennessee Unionists who, as the majority of the folks thereabouts were of secession proclivities, were regarded as traitors to a lofty and noble cause. The other four companies were colored troops—fugitive slaves from Tennessee and adjacent States, and so long as they remained in the fort they were active in recruiting new members from the slave quarters of the neighboring planters.

Therefore it is that when Forrest reaches Jackson again he is besieged with entreaties from every side, begging him to put the offensive garrison to rout. The proposition is an agreeable one to Forrest, who never remains long idle. On the 12th of April he appears before the fort, his troops wet and muddy from a forty mile march through the rain, over miry roads. But they are full of fight and lose no time in preliminaries. Forrest himself rides forward in the front rank of his skirmishers. Two horses are killed under him, but he escapes unharmed. The Federal commander, Major Booth, is equally gallant but more unfortunate, meeting his death while riding along the line of his outposts. His successor, Major Bradford, withdraws his men to an inner work, having first fired the frame barracks which command it. The garrison is now invested on every side, and Forrest's bugles sound the order to cease firing.

A flag of truce now goes forward to summon the garrison to surrender. Bradford hesitates. His position is desperate enough, but out in the river the gunboat *New Era* is lying, and he thinks that if worst comes to worst, her guns will cover the retreat of his men. Moreover, he sees two more gunboats approaching, and thinks that they bring reinforcements. So the bearers of the flag of truce return to Forrest with the news that the fort will not be surrendered. The Confederates, meantime, have noticed the approach of the two gunboats, and regarding it as a violation of the truce, proceed to openly violate it in their turn, sending troops forward to secure a position in the rear of Fort Pillow.

For a brief space of time all is quiet. It is early springtime. The hillsides are green with the young grass, and the first faint signs of verdure appear on the trees. The great river is turbid and full to the brim with the torrents drained from many a snow-clad hillside of the North. On its tawny breast float the gunboats, heavy, ungraceful, somber black in color, lightened only by the gay hues of the American flag, which floats bravely above each. In this beautiful stage-setting the blackest tragedy of the civil war is about to be enacted—a tragedy unrelieved by any strain of heroism or mercy.

Forrest's bugles ring out again. They sound the charge this time. From every side converging lines of Confederates sweep down upon the earthworks. The struggle is short. Scarcely do the assailants meet with any check, but rush forward, never faltering, and dash over the parapet with wild yells of triumph. The Federals in dismay throw down their arms and flee toward the river's bank, hoping to find shelter under the guns of the *New Era*. But now the detachment of Confederates, that had made its way to the rear of the fort, under cover of the flag of truce, appears and pours its volleys into the disordered mass. There is no longer any attempt at resistance. Everywhere the Federals are begging for quarter. The battle has become a massacre.

Now it is that Forrest's men show that they had taken seriously his threats of wholesale murder for garrisons that dared to offer him resistance. "No quarter!" is the cry. Men begging for their lives are shot down or pierced through and through with bayonets. On the negro soldiers particularly does the bloody rage of the victors expend its fury. Their wounded are dispatched as they lie upon the ground. One wounded man even is foully slain on his pallet in the hospital. In his first report of his victory Forrest writes boastfully of the carnage. "The river was dyed," he says, "with the blood of the slaughtered for two hundred yards. The approximate loss was upward of 500 killed, but few of the officers escaping. My loss was about 20 killed. It is to be hoped that these facts will demonstrate to the Northern people that negro soldiers cannot cope with Southerners."

Having slaked their thirst for blood, the conquerors fall to plundering their captives and the bodies of the dead. Forrest has no intention of occupying the fort, so the prisoners are ordered to fall in and are sent off to Brownsville, under a suitable guard. Some of the Confederate soldiers are set to work to bury the dead—a task which they discharge with indecent haste and infamous cruelty. More than one man sorely wounded, but who has not yet breathed his last, is cast into the common grave with the dead bodies of his former comrades, there to be slowly smothered to death. At least one man was buried alive and dug his way out to make his escape under cover of the night.

Such of the Union wounded as are hurt too severely to be able to march are carried into the frame hospital of the fort. It is For-

BURNING COLUMBIA.

rest's intention to send them off to the *New Era* with a flag of truce, but that vessel steams away, disregarding his signals. With the coming of dawn two more Federal gunboats appear. Before any flag of truce can be displayed, these vessels open fire upon the fort over which the Confederate flag now flies. Forrest is not in the fort and his soldiers, quickly aroused to fury, set fire to the hospitals. Frightful stories are told of the wounded being so fastened to the floors as to be unable to escape from the burning building. But though told under oath before a committee sent by Congress to Fort Pillow to investigate the massacre, it happily appears that these tales are largely false. Nevertheless the hospitals were fired while the wounded were still within them.

In the confusion caused by the bursting of the shells, and the work of removing the wounded from the burning hospitals, some of the negro prisoners still within the fort think they see a favorable opportunity for an attempt to escape. Too late they discover their error. Their watchful guards fire upon them, and not content with stopping them, follow and put them to death. Wounded men are bayoneted, and on a small scale the horrors of the preceding day are re-enacted. At last, one of Forrest's staff officers arriving on the scene, puts an end to the carnage. Such of the Federal wounded as still survive are taken on board the gunboats and Forrest and his men depart, leaving behind them a dismantled fort filled with corpses.

CHAPTER II.

THE WAR IN THE SOUTHWEST—RED RIVER EXPEDITION—TAKING FORT DE RUSSY—COTTON SPECULATORS—LOW WATER IN THE RIVER—THE BATTLE OF SABINE CROSS ROADS—ROUT OF THE FEDERALS—GENERAL EMORY'S STAND—BANKS RETREATS—LOSS OF THE "EASTPORT"—THE FLEET CAUGHT BY LOW WATER—COLONEL BAILEY'S DAM—THE FLEET SAVED—THE EXPEDITION ABANDONED.

IN the extreme Southwest, the very opening days of the year 1864, saw a Union force of no inconsiderable size in the field. The government had long desired to win some notable triumph in Texas. It desired to announce to the people of the North that the Union armies had made a lodgment, and the stars and stripes were floating in every State in the Union. Some progress toward that end had been made in October, 1863, when General Banks landed a force at Brownsville and captured several small Confederate posts in the vicinity. But this exploit did not fully satisfy the authorities at Washington, and on the 4th of January, 1864, General Banks was ordered to take an expedition up the Red River to Shreveport. The troops were to divide into three divisions. Banks, with 17,000 men, was to march overland from New Orleans to Alexandria. Here he was to join a force of

10,000 men, detached from Sherman's army at Vicksburg, and commanded by General A. J. Smith. Admiral Porter, with a fleet of fifteen ironclads and four light vessels, was to convoy the transports which carried Smith's troops up the Red River. When Smith, Banks, and Porter had all effected a junction at Alexandria, they were to proceed to Shreveport, where Steele; who had marched down from Little Rock with 15,000 men, would meet them.

Such was the plan of campaign. It threw to the winds all the fundamental principles of the military art. The Confederates could easily put in the field 25,000 men. They were familiar with the country, well acclimated, and enjoyed the confidence and the affection of the people residing thereabouts. Their scouts and spies were aided in every way by the Louisianians. The best of guides were at their service. The countrymen vied with each other in carrying to the Confederate camp the earliest reports of the movements of the Union army. All this was greatly to the advantage of the Confederates, and made it easy for them to hurl their compact force of 25,000 men against any one of the Union detachments, before the junction which Banks had planned could be effected.

General Banks was not blind to this danger and warned the War Department that a campaign conducted after this plan would end in disaster; but the Washington authorities were obstinate, and the general had no course left to him but to make the best of a very bad enterprise. After the expedition was under way, another element of weakness which Banks had not foreseen was discovered. There were four practically independent commanders—Banks, Smith, Steele, and Porter. Neither one of them had authority to give orders to any of the others. To complete the weakness of the expedition, General Grant succeeded to supreme command of the armies of the United States while it was yet under way, and sent orders that the 10,000 men under Smith must leave Louisiana to rejoin Sherman by the middle of April, whether Shreveport had been taken or not.

The middle of March saw the expedition fairly in the field. Steele sent word from Little Rock that he could do no more than to make a demonstration against Shreveport, because an election was pending in Arkansas, and his troops were needed there to help carry the State for the Union. But Porter's gunboats and the transports which carried Smith's troops were slowly picking their way among the sand banks and snags that obstructed the channel of the Red River, while General Franklin, commanding about 17,000 men from Banks's army, was marching north from New Orleans toward Alexandria, the place of rendezvous.

A little distance below Alexandria the Confederates had built a fort, Fort de Russy, it was called, after the engineer who planned it. It was a formidable work, but poorly provided with guns and sparsely garrisoned. To add to its strength and make an attack by the Union gunboats difficult, if not impossible, the river below the fort was filled with all sorts of devices for obstructing navigation. Into its bed great piles had been driven, and their tops cut off below the surface of the stream. From one bank to the other stretched a massive raft of logs bolted together with railroad iron. All the driftwood, logs, snags, and trees floating down the stream had been caught and held by this raft so that the river for a hundred yards or more up stream was blocked by what lumbermen know as a log jam.

News of the strength of Fort de Russy reached Porter and Smith as they made their way up the river, and they concluded that to take it would be no easy task. It was determined that the troops should be landed, and by making a detour of thirty miles, get in the rear of the fort while the gunboats would attack it in front. So while the troops plodded along the rough and narrow roads, the gunboats brought up before the obstructions in the river and prepared to remove them. The powerful engines and armored rams of the vessels made light work of what at first seemed an impossible task. "A timber hitch with a hawser around a pile, the hawser heads belayed to the bitt heads, and a half a dozen turns back with the wheels, or screw, and the whole thing is done," is the way Porter describes the process, "and in this way a dozen gunboats went to work and in two hours undid the work of many months. The piles were pulled out of the mud faster than dentists pull teeth, and with no complaints from the patient. Then came the rush of the floating logs. We had a short tussle to send them out into the middle of the stream, where they drifted on until they were emptied into the Mississippi, to be carried by that stream down to New Orleans, where they would furnish fuel enough for the poor population of that city for a whole winter."

But the delay at the river barricade, short though it was, was long enough to rob the navy of the glory of taking Fort De Russy. The troops had made a marvelous forced march of thirty-eight miles, and were well inside the parapet of the fort when the *Benton*, the first of the gunboats, appeared upon the scene. For two hours a fierce artillery duel had been maintained between the fort and the Federal forces, and the latter, despairing of the arrival of the navy, had made a charge, General Mower riding at the head of the assaulting column. The Confederates were making a vigorous resistance, when two shots from the bow gun of the *Benton* notified them that they were caught between two fires, and they decamped at once. By their victory the Federals captured ten cannon, 1000 muskets, and 283 prisoners. Their loss was 4 killed and 30 wounded. The Confederate loss was only 9 in all. Properly garrisoned, Fort De Russy would have proved a most formidable obstacle in the path of the national soldiers. So massive were its walls that the detachment left behind by Smith to destroy it was unable to complete the task, and the ruins of the fort still bear witness to what was an engineering triumph, though a military failure.

With De Russy silenced, the army and navy pushed on to Alexandria. The Confederates fled before them and the town was entered without opposition. Three days later the force under General Franklin arrived, and General Banks followed shortly after. With Banks came a horde of cotton speculators, for the expedition, beside its political and military purposes, had its commercial side as well. The cotton mills of New England had shut down for lack of raw material caused by the war and the blockade. The mills of England were in a like plight, and the distress among the operatives thus thrown out of employment was extreme. The cries of distress that arose from the English sufferers were particularly disquieting to the government at Washington. The danger that England might, to relieve the sufferers, seize upon some pretext to interfere in behalf of the Confederacy, break the blockade, and liberate the vast quantity of cotton that was shut up in the South was an ever-present dread to President Lincoln and his advisers. To avert this peril they cast about them for a method of getting the cotton out of the enemy's country without permitting the proceeds to find their way into the Confederate treasury. That the Red River expedition owed its conception in a great part to this desire to get the cotton is beyond question. But this very fact added an element of weakness to a plan of campaign which was faulty from the first. The immense profits of successful cotton speculation seduced officers both of the army and the navy from the straight path of duty. A swarm of speculators hung on the skirts of the column. Admiral Porter himself, declared under oath, that when General Banks arrived at Alexandria to take command of the army he came on a steamer "loaded with cotton speculators, bagging, roping, champagne, and ice." And when, after the expedition had ended in failure, a Congressional committee began an investigation of the ugly rumors concerning it, so many politicians of eminence were found to be mixed up in the cotton speculation scandal that it was thought inexpedient to pursue the matter further.

Upon the arrival of Banks at Alexandria the expedition pushed on up the river, the troops marching by a single road on the southern side. By this time the state of the water in the Red River was beginning to give great uneasiness to Admiral Porter. It was the season of the year when navigation should have been at its best, yet the river stubbornly remained low. Just above Alexandria rapids and a rocky bottom offered a serious obstacle to the progress of the flotilla. The troops could not march without the transports to carry their supplies. The transports dared not press further into the enemy's country without the gunboats to protect them, and the gunboats were too heavy to pass the rapids. For a time it seemed as though the low water—unprecedented in the history of navigation on the Red River extending over half a century—were about to bring the expedition to an inglorious end. But at last the river began to rise. Slowly, inch by inch, it crept up until, by lightening his vessels, Porter managed to drag them above the falls. Then the expedition pushed on toward Shreveport.

But now Banks committed a blunder that was destined to cost him dear. Instead of leading his column along a road near the riverside, where the gunboats could assist in beating back any enemy who might attack, Banks chose a road far distant from the river. Not only did he thus lose the support of the gunboats, but by moving his whole army along a single road he stretched out his column into a long, slender line, the rear of which was a full day's march from the leading regiments. A wagon train twelve miles long was part of the column, necessitating the detail of large detachments as guards and effectually blocking the road to all troops in the rear.

The enemy was not blind to the faults of Banks's order of march. General Taylor, in command of the Confederate troops that blocked the path to Shreveport, retired before the advancing column, skirmishing continually and doing all he could to weary the army, which, encumbered with so heavy a baggage train, was slowly advancing into the snare the Confederates had set for it.

The trap was set near Mansfield. There, where the trees are cut away from the road and a broad clearing stretches along the crest of a slight ridge on either side of the road, General Taylor had drawn up his little army. He had 8800 men all told, and in the column advancing against him there were 25,000 at least. But the manner in which Banks had disposed his troops made it utterly impossible for him to put his whole force into action at once. Taylor knew well enough that he could fall upon and demolish the head of the column before the main body of the Federals could get into the fight. So he formed his line at right angles to the road, shotted his guns, sent his skirmishers into the woods in front, and awaited the attack.

But the attack was slow in coming. The Union cavalry, under General Lee, arrived first on the scene, and quickly discovering the condition of affairs halted to wait for the infantry. Two brigades—2500 men—

came up and were deployed in line of battle, but their commander, General Ransom, well knew that his force was too slender to take the offensive. So he in his turn halted to await the coming of Banks. Word came from that commander in the rear to continue the march toward Mansfield. "You cannot move without bringing on a battle," was the response, and Banks countermanded his order. He knew how perilous it would be to rush into battle with the major part of his command strung out along a narrow winding road.

Taylor was not content to rest quietly within his lines and let Banks bring up all his regiments. He had planned to fight a defensive battle, but as the day wore on with no sign of any attack on the part of the Federals he determined to make the assault himself. It was about four o'clock in the afternoon when the Confederates, responding to Taylor's order to attack all along the line, stepped from the screen of woods that had concealed them and advanced briskly across the open fields. They greatly outnumbered the Federals actually on the field, for Franklin had halted far in the rear, and when frantic messengers came galloping from the front begging him to hasten to the aid of Ransom it was too late. So the blue-clad men who confronted the advancing Confederate host knew well enough that for them there was no chance of victory. When neither side enjoys any advantage of position 2500 men cannot defeat 8500—if all are Americans.

In two parallel lines the men of the South rushed forward, cheering lustily. Most of them were little used to battle, and their officers exposed themselves recklessly, seeking to inspire the men with confidence. The Federals, for their part, reserved their fire until their adversaries were within point blank range, when they let fly a withering volley. Confederate officers fall fast. General Mouton is slain. Four colonels fall. The soldiers, aghast at the carnage, waver and fall back, but are pressed onward by the second line. The Federals load so rapidly and fire with such precision that the assailants on the center and right flank are fain to throw themselves prone upon the earth and seek a shelter from the flying scud of bullets. But over on the left of the Union line the troops are wavering.

DESTROYING A RAILROAD.

There the Federal defense is weakest and the Confederate attack fiercest. Taylor extends his line of battle far beyond the Union flank which is enveloped and begins to crumble away. Lee's dismounted cavalry is cut to pieces and falls back. Nims's battery is imperilled, and the Confederates swoop down upon it before the guns can be dragged away to a place of safety. All along the line regiments begin to fall back. Those that stand firm soon find themselves deserted and in danger of being surrounded, and give way in their turn. Though General Banks plunges into the thickest of the fray, trying to rally his troops, the army is soon thrown into a frantic rout. The narrow forest road is too straitened a channel for the passage of this vast mob of men and horses, guns, wagons, and ambulances. The Confederates press relentlessly upon the rear of the fugitive throng. Ten guns and nearly a thousand men of General Ransom's command are captured. One hundred and fifty-six of Lee's wagons, heavy laden with supplies, fall into the hands of the assailants. The Union officers fight hard to rally their troops, and stem the rushing tide of defeat, but in vain. Their efforts only make them prominent targets for the bullets of the enemy. Generals Franklin and Ransom are wounded, and three colonels on Ransom's staff are killed.

The rout was as sudden as it was complete. An eye witness of the scene thus describes it: "Suddenly there was a rush, a shout, the crashing of trees, the breaking down of rails, the rush and scamper of men. It was as sudden as though a thunderbolt had fallen among us and set the pines on fire. What caused it or when it commenced no one knew. I turned to my companion to inquire the reason of this extraordinary proceeding, but before he had a chance to reply, we found ourselves swallowed up, as it were, in a hissing, seething, bubbling whirlpool of agitated men. We could not avoid the current; we could not stem it: and if we had hoped to live in that mad company we must ride with the rest of them. Our line of battle had given away. General Banks took off his hat and implored his men to remain; his staff officers did the same; but it was of no avail. Then the general drew his saber and tried to rally his men, but they would not listen. Behind him the rebels were shouting and advancing.

Their musket balls filled the air with that strange file-rasping sound that war has made familiar to our fighting men. The teams were abandoned by their drivers, the traces cut, and the animals ridden away by the frightened men. Bareheaded riders rode with agony depicted in their faces, and for at least ten minutes it seemed as though we were going to destruction together."

So in hopeless rout the discomfited Federal army streamed away from the fatal field of Sabine Cross Roads. Intoxicated with triumph, the Confederates pressed hard upon the rear of the fleeing column. Bright visions of the annihilation of the whole Union army and the capture of Porter's fleet danced before their eyes. They forgot that it was only the van of Banks's army that they had overthrown, and they were reckless in their pursuit. But help for the Federals was not far away. Word had reached General Emory of the desperate state of affairs at the front, and he was rushing his fine division forward toward the sound of the cannon. Stragglers began to obstruct his road, but they were pushed to right and left as the solid column marched sturdily onward. When Pleasant Grove, three miles from Sabine Cross Roads, was reached, the throng of fugitives choked the road so that further progress was impossible. Then the troops were deployed to right and left in line of battle. The line was scarcely formed when the main body of Ransom's defeated troops appeared flying before Taylor's triumphant regiment. Emory's line opened to right and left to let them pass, closed again, and greeted the men in gray with a sharp volley and an unyielding wall of cold steel. The Confederates sought to sweep this obstacle out of their path, as they had swept others, but the Federals held their ground stubbornly. Again and again the assailants returned to the charge only to be beaten back. The gallantry on both sides was notable. "Nothing," said General Banks in his report, "could surpass in impetuosity the assault of the enemy but the inflexible steadiness and valor of our troops." After hurling themselves against the Union line, which for the space of an hour and a half withstood their assaults as some granite headland dashes back in spray the waves that break upon it, the Confederates retired sullen and defeated to re-form their ranks and prepare to renew the combat in the morning. But the next day brought no better success to the men in gray. Their numbers were augmented by the arrival of Churchill with about 5000, but these troops were sorely wearied by their long march through difficult country. Yet they were chosen by Taylor to make the principal assault of the day, upon the Union left flank, but were driven back. Then General Mower, who had withstood their attack, charged in turn, drove Churchill from the field and recaptured two cannon which had fallen into the hands of the Confederates in the battle of the previous day. And though General Taylor did his utmost to save the day, the sun went down leaving the Union army victorious. Then there happened a strange thing.

Victorious though he had been, General Banks ordered a retreat during the night. His officers protested, but to no avail. The way to Shreveport lay before him with nothing but a demoralized army to dispute his progress, yet he determined to turn back. Great was the astonishment of the Confederates, who were preparing to fly before their enemy, to find that enemy fleeing before them. Banks with his army proceeded to Grand Ecore on the Red River, and it became tacitly understood in the Union camp that the expedition against Shreveport had been abandoned.

There was no further serious collision of the hostile forces on the Red River. General Kirby Smith took the greater part of Taylor's force off into Arkansas to offer battle to General Steele. So with his reduced force there was nothing left to Taylor but to hang about the banks of the Red River harassing the gunboats whenever one could be caught unprotected by an infantry support. Banks did not stay long at Grand Ecore, but made his way down the river to Alexandria, whither Porter strove to follow him with his gunboats. This was a difficult task, for the water in the Red River was low and falling hourly. Scarcely had the flotilla left Grand Ecore when the *Eastport*, the largest of the ironclads, ran full tilt upon a torpedo and speedily went to the bottom. Porter could not reconcile himself to the loss of one of his finest vessels, so sent to Alexandria for pump boats, by which she was soon pumped out. Progress down the stream was resumed and the voyage was made lively by the Confederates, who swarmed upon the banks, and with field pieces and rifles "peppered" the gunboats and the unarmored transports. The *Eastport*, though raised and repaired, was with difficulty kept afloat. More than once she went to the bottom and was laboriously raised while the Confederates practiced their marksmanship upon those engaged in the task. Finally Porter abandoned all hope of saving her, and fifty barrels of gunpowder, touched off with a slow match, soon completed her destruction.

Soon after the destruction of the *Eastport* the Confederates brought a light battery to the bank and opened fire on the little "tin-clad" *Cricket*, Admiral Porter's flag-ship. The engagement was hot. Twenty cannon were flashing from the shore and the crashing timbers of the gunboat bore eloquent testimony to the Confederate marksmanship. Though under fire only five minutes the vessel was struck thirty-eight times, and out of her crew of fifty twelve were killed and nineteen wounded. A Union transport,—the *Champion*,—heavy laden with runaway slaves, was struck by a shell, which pierced her boiler and filled the decks with scalding steam. Of the 200 blacks on the ill-fated vessel only 15 escaped alive.

Sorely scarred and with decks swept by bullets, the gunboats cautiously made their way down the river to Alexandria, where the rest of the fleet lay at anchor. Here Porter found his officers wearing very long faces. The river had fallen until now jagged rocks reared their peaks above the water everywhere except in a channel scarce twenty feet wide, and which soundings proved to be only three feet deep. Twelve of the squadron lay in the deep water above this barrier, which was known as the "falls." How to get vessels drawing four feet of water through a three-foot channel was a problem that baffled the ingenuity of the navy officers. Porter himself was beaten, and contented himself with heaping maledictions on the river and telegraphing to Grant, beseeching him not to withdraw the troops that alone kept the stranded navy from falling into the hands of the Confederates.

In this emergency an army officer came to the rescue. Lieutenant-

Colonel Bailey, a Wisconsin engineer, suggested that by building a dam across the river below the falls, the water on the falls could be raised sufficiently to allow the vessels to pass. It was with some difficulty that Colonel Bailey obtained permission to make the experiment. The navy officers were slow to concede that any good plan for their deliverance could be conceived by an army officer, so they stood placidly on the decks of their craft and peered over the bulwarks at the spot where a whole army of men was busily engaged in damming the shallow channel of the shrunken Red River.

Three thousand men and 200 teams were employed upon this gigantic piece of engineering. Forests were felled, and houses, barns, sheds, and mills for miles around were torn down to supply lumber for the work. The heavy machinery of sugar houses and cotton gins and presses was seized to supply material for weighting down the ponderous cribs of which the dam was formed. The roads intersecting the neighboring country were cut up by wagons heavy laden with stone gathered for the same purpose. As the dam, building at once from both sides of the stream, began to reach out toward the center of the current, the water rose gradually, and the current rushing through the central gap grew fiercer with each foot of progress. The work went on day and night, and when the glare of great fires on the banks, and torches in the hands of the workers, flashed ruddily upon the black and seething waters, the scene was one of wild picturesqueness. The wing extending from the south bank of the river was built wholly by black troops, and the negroes enlivened their work with their barbaric plantation songs and loud badinage.

Eight days and nights the work went on apace. At last the two wings were brought so near together that two boats loaded with brick and sunk in the center completed the structure. The water rose rapidly, and soon the rocks that had barred the progress of the gunboats down stream were hidden from view. Hope began to rise in the breasts of the sailors. The heavy cannon and the cargoes were sent ashore from the gunboats, which, thus lightened, began the passage of the rapids. This was still no easy task. The channel was narrow and tortuous. The boats could not be given headway, but were kept under control by long cables, made fast now to one bank and then to the other. So slow was the work that when night fell only three of the vessels, the *Fort Hindman*, the *Osage*, and the *Neosho*, had accomplished the passage. The rest remained above the rapids, waiting until daylight should enable them to follow.

There was little sleep in the tents of the Union generals that night. The rising waters were bringing tremendous pressure upon the hastily constructed dam, and Banks, who went down to the river side at midnight, saw that it showed signs of weakening. He notified Porter, who sent word to his captains to be prepared for emergencies. The emergency came, for at daybreak the dam burst just at the center. The two brick-laden barges were swung to right and left as two doors swing open when struck in the center. Admiral Porter stood on the bank and witnessed the disaster. Leaping into his saddle he galloped up to where the main body of the fleet lay at anchor above the rapids.

"Cast off and go down under full head of steam," he cried to the captain of the *Lexington*. The order was obeyed. The vessel plunged into the rapids where the current was now running at full nine miles an hour. All the precautions which had been observed the day before were now thrown to the winds. It was a time for taking desperate chances. As by a miracle the perilous passage was accomplished, but the way opened for the *Lexington* closed behind her, for the water fell so rapidly that none of the other vessels could follow in her wake.

Thousands of men lined the banks of the river when the *Lexington* steamed into the pool above the dam. The whole camp had turned out to see the gunboats shoot through the gap. Amid anxious silence the vessel's prow was turned toward the narrow chasm through which the turbid water was rushing in a veritable cataract. With clear gaze and steady hand the pilot held the boat true on her course. She swept between the wing dams, swayed and rocked a moment as she made the plunge over the three-foot fall, then sped along swiftly and unharmed until she reached the deep and tranquil water below. A mighty cheer arose from the assembled multitude, and Bailey was congratulated on

THE BLOODY ANGLE.

every side for his triumph and the promotion which all knew would surely reward so notable an achievement. The other vessels that floated just above the dam followed quickly in the wake of the *Lexington;* one only, the *Neosho,* whose captain failed to keep her engines going at full speed, suffering any injury.

Six vessels still remained above the rapids, but the partial success so encouraged both soldiers and sailors that little time was spent in effecting their liberation. Wing dams built above the first dam and where the water on the rapids was shallowest soon made the river navigable. The navy by this time had entered upon the work with enthusiasm, and the sailors stripped the ironclads of all their armor except that covering the vital parts, and threw the iron plates into the deepest part of the river. Thus lightened the vessels easily made their way down stream and joined their consorts below.

No time was lost, after this happy deliverance, by either Banks or Porter, in abandoning the Red River. The complete failure of the expedition was admitted, and army and navy made their way back to the shores of the Mississippi, thankful for their escape and feeling that the laborious and disastrous two months' campaign had been foolish in conception and worse than weak in its execution. In it honors were gained by one officer alone, for Lieutenant-Colonel Bailey, who built the dam and saved Porter's fleet, and returned from the Red River country a brigadier-general.

CHAPTER III.

THE SOUTH NOT SUBJUGATED—PRESIDENT LINCOLN STUDIES THE PROBLEM—ULYSSES S. GRANT COMMISSIONED LIEUTENANT-GENERAL — HIS GRAND STRATEGY—REORGANIZING THE ARMY OF THE POTOMAC—SHERIDAN CALLED TO COMMAND THE CAVALRY—PLANNING THE WILDERNESS CAMPAIGN—THE ARMIES—THE ARMY OF THE POTOMAC MOVES — THE BATTLE IN THE WILDERNESS.

THREE years of war had now taxed the energies of the North to the utmost. For three years the tide of young and active men from the fields, factories, and stores had flowed steadily toward the tented plains at the front. The story of battle had become an old one. Scarce a village but harbored two or three crippled veterans. Thousands of houses there were to which war had brought death and sorrow. Yet for all the tremendous outlay of manhood, life, and treasure, the South was not yet subjugated.

President Lincoln saw well enough that there was something wrong somewhere. He was too clearheaded not to understand that the fault did not lie with the rank and file of the Union army. Though not a trained soldier, his natural common sense showed him that what was lacking was a single head for the army; a soldier's mind to plan, and an arm, clothed with needful authority, to execute. At the opening of the war such a post had been filled by General Winfield Scott, but his advanced age had unfitted him for its heavy responsibilities and he soon retired. Then McClellan succeeded, but when he went to take active command of the Army of the Potomac the President relieved him of his duties as general commander of the Union armies. General Halleck followed, but failed to grasp the needs of the military situation. He was always at odds with Mr. Stanton, the secretary of war, and contradictory orders often issued from the offices of the general-in-chief and the war secretary. Nor did Halleck so direct the movements of the armies in the field as to strike blows simultaneously and keep the Confederates engaged all along the line. On the contrary the Army of the Potomac would be passive while the Army of the Cumberland was actively in the field, and thus the Confederates were able to hurry detachments from one part of the country to another, and, despite the fact that the total number of Confederates under arms was greatly inferior to the numbers of the Union army, the former always managed to confront their enemies, at every point threatened, with at least an equal force.

Recognizing the fact that in the lack of an efficient general-in-chief lay the principal weakness of the national military establishment, President Lincoln determined to invest General Ulysses S. Grant with supreme power under the President. Mr. Lincoln had not met the soldier whom he thus honored, but to the man who had anxiously watched over the progress of the war the name and record of Grant were familiar. His capture of Fort Donelson, the way in which he had snatched victory from the jaws of defeat at Shiloh, his dogged and pertinacious siege of Vicksburg, and his brilliant victory at Chattanooga, had earned for him the reputation of having never lost a battle. And so when Congress revived the rank of lieutenant-general and the President nominated and the Senate confirmed the nomination of General Grant for that exalted rank, the whole North applauded the decision and eagerly awaited the first movements which should give a hint of the new commander's ideas concerning the speediest method for putting down the great uprising.

It was on the 9th of March, 1864, that General Grant received his commission of lieutenant-general from the hands of the President in the parlor of the White House. There was no pomp and little ceremony. A few gentlemen gathered together, clad mostly in civilians' clothes. A word or two wishing the new general-in-chief God-speed, and the ceremonial was over. The next day General Grant was in the camp of the Army of the Potomac at Brandy Station, conferring with General Meade. As a result of that conference and of his study of the military problem with which he had to grapple, General Grant determined to fix his headquarters with the Army of the Potomac. The newly appointed commander-in-chief saw that the army of General Lee was the vital point of the Confederate structure. His was the task to demolish that army. Indeed, from the very moment of Grant's accession to supreme command, the Confederate armies, not Confederate capitals or strategic positions, became the objective points of every campaign. To find the enemy and to give him battle was henceforward the purpose of every military movement. The grand strategy which General Grant had planned was, in the main, to keep the Union armies advancing all along the line. Sherman, whom he had determined should succeed him in command of the military division of the Mississippi, was to advance against the army under General Johnston. The Army of the Potomac, which Meade still commanded, should press unrelentingly upon the army of General Lee. General George Crook, in West Virginia, was to advance eastward up the Kanawha Valley, while Sigel traversed the Shenandoah Valley—that highway which so often took Stonewall Jackson within hearing of the church bells of Washington.

Despite a warning letter from his old comrade in arms, Sherman, who besought him to leave the vicinity of Washington and its pestilent proximity to politicians, Grant determined to make his headquarters with the Army of the Potomac. "You may wish an officer who has served with you in the West—Sherman for instance—to take command now of the Army of the Potomac," said General Meade, the victor of Gettysburg, then in command of that army. "You need feel no hesitation in removing me. I will serve wherever I am ordered." Grant declined the offer, retaining General Meade in command. In his "Memoirs" he writes, "This incident gave me even a more favorable opinion of Meade than did his great victory at Gettysburg the July before."

The work of reorganizing the Army of the Potomac, tempering it for the work it had in hand, was pushed with the utmost energy. Soldiers absent on furlough were recalled. Officers who found the hotels of Washington more attractive than the camp were warned that a more soldierly course of conduct would be pleasing to the commander-in-chief. New clothing was issued. Arms and munitions of war went to the front in vast quantities.

Few changes were made by Grant in the *personnel* of the corps of officers. He thought the cavalry arm of service was weak, and sought for a bold and dashing officer who should build it up to the high degree of efficiency for which the Confederate horse had always been notable. For a time he was at a loss.

"Why not try Sheridan?" asked Halleck, to whom he had spoken of his perplexity.

"The very man!" cried Grant. And at once a message went speeding over the wires to the West, where Sheridan was serving, bidding him report for duty with the Army of the Potomac. Already General Sheridan had won a wide reputation as a daring and determined soldier. At Stone River his brigade first checked the victorious advance of the enemy, and when Rosecrans had succeeded in forming his second line Sheridan pointed to his shattered ranks, from which over a thousand good men and true had fallen, and his laconic "Here's all that's left of them," told how hot the fighting had been. At Chickamauga it was Sheridan who first rallied a handful of devoted men at arms about him and forced his way through the enemy to where Thomas, "the Rock," was fighting for time with cool determination. At Missionary Ridge it was Sheridan's men, who, carried away by the fire of battle and the thirst for conquest well implanted within them by their brilliant commander, swarmed up the precipitous steeps and dislodged the enemy from his seemingly impregnable position.

Right well fixed was Sheridan's repute as a soldier. Whether he would develop the qualities of a successful cavalryman was largely a matter of conjecture, but history has shown how well Grant and Halleck judged.

The winter wore on apace and the early Virginia spring came on. The veterans of the two armies that confronted each other along the banks of the Rapidan knew that the end of winter weather meant the beginning of active hostilities again. The hostile pickets who had fallen into ways of friendship and good comradery while ice and snow held the armies tightly fettered, looked with more suspicion upon each other. The spies of Grant and Lee made their perilous expeditions into the antagonistic camps and came out bearing tidings of active preparations for taking the field.

General Grant had determined to lose no time in finding Lee and offering him battle. His intention was fixed to move upon Richmond by Hooker's old route through the Wilderness. It may seem strange that after the disastrous defeat that the Army of the Potomac had sustained in the gloomy thickets of that desolate region of scrub oaks and stunted pines, another Union commander should venture into that maze, the paths of which were so much more familiar to the enemy, and which offered such great advantages to an army acting upon the defensive. But General Grant thought that the Army of the Potomac had never been so handled as to bring out its highest fighting abilities. He knew that his forces greatly outnumbered Lee's, and, moreover, he thought that by a forced march, begun at midnight, he could turn Lee's flank and pass through and out of the Wilderness before his adversary could bring any considerable force to oppose him. And so he pushed forward his preparations, having pontoons built secretly and vast stores of ordnance collected in preparation for the advance, which he had determined should be begun on the 3d of May.

The army which General Grant was about to encounter merits a few words. A very wretched body of men it was, judged by superficial standards. The blockade, the growing destitution of the South, and a most inefficient commissary department had reduced the soldiers of the Army of Northern Virginia to the sorest straits. Falstaff's warriors, that had but a shirt and a half in a whole company, were scarcely worse clad. Their clothing was in tatters—patched, mended, and darned until no trace of the original fabric remained. "A new pair of shoes or an overcoat was a luxury," writes General Law, "and full rations would have astonished the stomachs of Lee's ragged Confederates. But they took their privations cheerfully and complaints were seldom heard. I recall an instance of one hardy fellow whose trousers were literally 'worn to a frazzle,' and would no longer adhere to his legs even by dint of the most persistent patching. Unable to buy, beg, or borrow another pair, he wore instead a pair of thin cotton drawers. By nursing these carefully he managed to get through the winter." For food the luckless graycoats were scarcely better off. But ill-fed and half-clothed as they were, Lee's soldiers were drilled to the highest point of discipline, inured to the hardships of war and the horrors of battle, animated with an untiring enthusiasm, and reposing implicit and unquestioning confidence in their general. The Army of Northern Virginia was a tiger. Though its flanks were gaunt and its coat scarred, it was none the less fierce, sinewy, and cunning. "Lee's army," said a contemporary Northern writer, "is an army of veterans; it is an instrument sharpened to a perfect edge. You turn its flanks—well, its flanks are made to be turned. This effects little or nothing. All that we reckon as gained, therefore, is the loss of life inflicted on the enemy."

A comparison of the numerical strength of the two armies which were about to grapple with each other, is important at this juncture. In the Army of the Potomac on April 30, 1864, equipped and ready for action, were 99,438 men. The Ninth army corps numbering 20,000 more, under the command of General Burnside, joined the Army of the Potomac on the 6th of May, thus swelling the grand total to 120,000 men. To oppose this magnificent army, General Lee had but about 62,000 men. He enjoyed the advantage of position, and of this he skillfully availed himself; but the disparity of numbers was so great that we to-day can see that the contest was hopeless from the start. Lee was not without hope, however. He had fought against heavy odds before. He knew not, though, that he had now to grapple with a soldier of very different caliber from that of those whom he had hitherto met and turned back from the path to Richmond.

On the night of the 3d of May, there was stir in the Union camp. The quartermasters were serving out rations, enough for six days, to each man. The vast caravan of wagons, that when harnessed and on the road stretched out for sixty-five miles, was being packed. About the camp-fires the men were sitting, some writing last letters home, others—new recruits, perhaps—listening to the stories of the veterans who had gone into the Wilderness with Hooker. The cavalry had already left the camp, going out with pontoons to lay bridges at Germania and Ely's fords. The rest of the army was to follow at midnight. The news spread about the camp that the suddenness of the move was due to the hope of the commanding general that a quick start and a forced march would carry the Union army clear through the Wilderness before the Confederates could intercept them in those dreary wilds.

Shortly after midnight the march was begun. All the roads leading to the fords were held by long columns of men trudging wearily along; artillery rumbling over the ground, drawn by long teams of horses; forage wagons and ambulances with their teams of sturdy mules. Torches lighted up the roads, and at the crossing places on the Rapidan great fires blazed upon the banks, illuminating the narrow pontoon bridges so that the wagons might not drive off into the rushing stream. Four thousand wagons are a grievous check to an army trying to move speedily. Grant's train delayed him sorely, so that though he passed the river without encountering any resistance, he was unable to carry out his cherished plan of escaping from the Wilderness before the enemy could offer battle.

Lee, indeed, had heard with grim satisfaction the news that Grant, undaunted by Hooker's fate, was going to brave the perils of the Wilderness. Nothing was further from the mind of the Confederate commander than to attempt to stop the Federals crossing the Rapidan. From the summit of Clark's mountain he had for days been watching every sign of activity in the Union camp, and had warned his officers that the enemy would soon cross at the same fords used by Hooker. It was Lee's fixed

IN THE PETERSBURG CRATER.

intention, so soon as the Federals should be fairly across, to leave his snug earthworks at Mile Run and enter the Wilderness by one of its mazy roads, with which the Confederates alone were familiar, and fall upon the flank of Grant's army. Accordingly, he no sooner heard that the Federals were moving than he put his own columns in motion, and the night of the 4th of May saw vast bodies of armed men pouring from every point of the compass into that dense and gloomy thicket whence had risen once before the roar of musketry, the yells of the charging troops, the screams of the wounded, and all the horrid din of battle.

Toward evening of the 4th, Grant's columns, moving southward, were harassed by a few scattering shots that warned them that the enemy was lying in wait in the woods. The advance was continued with more caution, and word was sent back to General Burnside, with all possible speed, to advance by forced marches until he should come up with the army. The following morning the Confederate pickets were more numerous and still more annoying. Lying hidden in the dense copses, they picked off with unerring aim the Union skirmishers who, because advancing, could not keep themselves concealed. In front of General Warren, the Confederate resistance was particularly stubborn, so that gradually the idea that Lee was retreating, and that the force before them was merely his rear guard, faded from the minds of the Union soldiers. As the roar of battle in Warren's front grew louder and fiercer, General Grant and General Meade galloped to that part of the line. They found the fight well under way. The divisions of Griffin and Robinson were already engaged. Near the center of Warren's line, on the brow of a hill overlooking one of the few clearings in the Wilderness, stood the house of farmer Lacy. There it was that General Stonewall Jackson's right arm had been amputated after the battle of Chancellorsville, and there General Grant chose to make his headquarters. Throughout the battle he remained at this point, judging of the progress of the fight from the reports of his aids, the columns of smoke that rose where the conflict was fiercest, and the noise of the musketry rising and falling as the positions of the combatants changed. Artillery there was but little. The dense undergrowth of the Wilderness did not admit of the passage of heavy guns, nor could they have been used to any advantage had they been placed.

The battle which raged in the cavernous shades of the Wilderness baffles description of its tactical features. It would be too much to say that it was a battle without a plan, but the plans of both Grant and Lee were impeded and wrecked by the difficult nature of the ground. Whole brigades went astray. Colonels were seen leading their regiments into battle by the aid of pocket compasses. Supporting bodies of troops became separated and went into the fight with their flanks exposed, yet in most instances the enemy—equally nonplussed by the character of the battle-field—failed to see and to seize his advantage. It was a battle without coherence or strategy—a battle in the dark. If Von Moltke's dictum, that the operations of the American civil war were but the struggles of two armed mobs, was at all well founded, it was in the case of the battle of the Wilderness. A Southern writer, familiar with the spot in which the battle was fought, says of it: "The country was somber—a land of thicket, jungle, undergrowth, ooze, where men could not see each other twenty yards off, and assaults had to be made by the compass. The fights there were not even as easy as night attacks in open country, for at night you can travel by the stars. Death came unseen; regiments stumbled on each other, and sent swift destruction into each other's ranks guided by the crackling of the bullets. It was not war—military maneuvering; science had as little to do with it as sight. Two wild animals were hunting each other; when they heard each other's steps they sprung and grappled. The conqueror advanced or went elsewhere. In this mournful and desolate thicket did the great campaign of 1864 begin. Here in blind wrestle as at midnight did two hundred thousand men in blue and gray clutch each other—bloodiest and weirdest of encounters. War had nothing like it. The genius of destruction, tired apparently of the old commonplace killing, had invented the 'unseen death.' At five in the morning the opponents closed in, breast to breast, in the thicket. Each had thrown up their slight temporary breastworks of saplings and dirt; beyond this they were unprotected. The question now was which would succeed in driving his adversary from these defenses almost within a few yards of each other, and from behind which crackled the musketry. Never was sight more curious. On the low line of these works, dimly seen in the thicket, rested the muzzles, spouting flame; from the depths rose cheers; charges were made and repulsed, the lines scarcely seeing each other; men fell and writhed and died unseen—their bodies lost in the bushes, their death groans drowned in the steady, continuous, never-ceasing crash."

The battle of the first day in the Wilderness was brief; its stirring incidents few; its results indecisive. Skirmishing began between the hostile forces early in the day, but Longstreet had not come up and Lee held his eager followers in check to await the arrival of his "old war horse" and his division of veterans. Shortly after noon, however, it became impossible to restrain the soldiers on either side. They were done with skirmishing and hot for the battle. Griffin's division became hotly engaged with Jones's brigade of Ewell's corps, and drove it back in confusion. Jones strove manfully to rally his men, but was shot down. Then with yells of defiance other Confederate brigades rushed to the threatened point, and the oncoming of the Federals was stayed. Wright's division of the Union Sixth Corps, which should have gone into action by the side of Griffin, lost its road in the forest, and the Confederates fell on Griffin's exposed flank, forced back his line, and captured two of his guns. Wadsworth's division, too, and McCandless's brigade, mistook their paths and fell into the toils of the vigilant enemy, better acquainted with the mazes of the Wilderness. They escaped only after heavy loss, including a vast number captured by the Confederates.

The fighting was bitter over on the Union left. There Hancock, "the Superb," confronted Hill, one of Lee's most trusted lieutenants. All through the morning, while the skirmishers had been popping away at each other in the open, the main body of the troops of each commander had been busily engaged in building breastworks of logs and stacks of turf. Neither side was in haste to bring on a general engagement. The Confederates were awaiting the arrival of Longstreet, who was still far in the rear, and Hancock wished to complete his defensive works that they might be ready for a refuge in case his advance should be repulsed. Late in the afternoon the advance was begun by Getty's division. Slowly and painfully the soldiers toiled forward through the dense forest, receiving unflinchingly the fire of the enemy, who, still securely sheltered behind his snug breastworks, could aim and fire in almost perfect safety. Birney and Mott came up to the aid of Getty, and the fight soon became very fierce. But a few yards of space separated the foes. The rattle of the musketry was incessant and deafening. Two pieces of artillery, which with infinite labor had been dragged into the midst of the thickets, added their bellowings to the dreadful din, while their shots that enfiladed the enemy's works did great havoc among the Confederates. Until nightfall the battle raged at close quarters in the tangled copses of the stunted pine, sweet gum, scrub oak, and cedar. When it ended the Confederates still held their works, while the Union dead and wounded lay thick on the ground before them.

All that night the relief corps, with torches, went groping about in the underbrush between the lines seeking for the wounded. It was a difficult task, for the bushes closed about a fallen soldier, hiding him from the sight of a searcher only a few feet away. In the tents of the Union generals and about Grant's headquarters there was noise and bustle. A grand attack was to be made the next morning all along the line. Adjutants were writing out the orders for the division commanders, and aides were picking their way through the dark forest, in the black night, delivering them. The telegraph was ticking, too, for General Grant had introduced its use upon the field of battle, and a slender insulated wire reached from his headquarters to the tents of his corps commanders. Spiked poles, driven into the ground, held the wire high above the heads of the marching soldiers. Should it be necessary to change the headquarters the poles had only to be taken down and packed in a cart, the wire rolled neatly on a reel, and the whole telegraph line could move to the front with the army.

BATTLE-FIELDS AND VICTORY.

Fleet couriers went galloping back from the Confederate line that night to where Longstreet had halted far in the rear. They called on him to hasten to the front, for in the morning the battle would burst forth again. No soldier ever responded to a call to battle more readily than Longstreet. No men were ever more ready than his for a forced march to the sound of the cannon. And so they strode along through the night toward Lee's lines, even as on the other side Burnside was pressing forward, that his men might go into the fight shoulder to shoulder with their brethren of the Army of the Potomac.

At five o'clock in the morning the storm of battle burst. The thickets just beginning to put on the soft green hues of spring, the clear light of the early morning, and the birds twittering among the twigs made a picture of peace and beauty destined to be short-lived. The soldiers had received their orders the night before, and when the battle began it was with a crash, and the dogs of war were quickly in full cry. Hancock's line swung forward in magnificent style and with invincible determination. Hill's men in vain endeavored to stem the tide. "Where is Longstreet?" was the cry all along the Confederate right flank, where men were falling and regiments crumbling away before the fury of the assault. For a moment even General Lee's lion heart sank within him, and he sent officers to prepare his baggage trains for a hurried retreat. But Longstreet did not fail him. The news of the peril of Hill's line had no sooner reached him than he put spurs to his horse and called upon his men to take the double-quick. Right nobly they responded, and the long column surged down the plank road toward the sound of the musketry. The thunder of the cadenced tread of thousands of running men rose over the roar of the battle. It was but a short march to the front and soon the regiments were swinging out into line of battle and going into the fight. Lee himself was working among the flying bullets, trying to rally Hill's troops, when Longstreet's fresh regiments came up. A Texas regiment, sweeping by to the charge, cheered lustily for "Marse Robert." The fire of battle blazed fierce within the great Confederate commander, and he spurred his horse and took his place in the charging ranks. A confused medley of cries rose all along the line. "No, No!" "Go back!" "Lee to the rear!" "We won't go in unless you go back." For a moment Lee seemed disinclined to obey the wishes of his men, but when a private dropped from the ranks and, seizing his bridle, turned his horse's head to the rear, he yielded with evident disappointment, and rode off to join General Longstreet.

Sublime, indeed, was the confidence which the Confederates, throughout the war, reposed in their favorite general, and beautiful was the mutual affection so often strikingly manifested by General Lee and his men.

The timely arrival of Longstreet's troops upon the battle-field did its work. The Federal advance was checked and the tide began to set the other way. The Union troops were beaten back to their first line of breastworks, where they maintained themselves stubbornly for a while, but were ultimately dislodged. Gregg's Brigade of Texans was fairly sacrificed by the fury with which it hurled itself against Hancock. Eight hundred men went in on that charge which Lee wished to lead; less than four hundred came out.

Not all of the fighting was in front of Hancock's position. Over on the Union right the gallant troops of Sedgwick and Warren were wasting away in their repeated but fruitless efforts to drive Ewell from the position he had so skillfully fortified, and to which he now so stubbornly clung. As for Burnside, a strange lethargy seemed to have come upon him, which throughout the morning robbed the brilliant forced march, which had brought him to the battle-field in season, of its result. Though more than one command was sent him to relieve Hancock of the brunt of the enemy's attack by taking his troops into action, it was not until late in the day that he obeyed.

But in Hancock's front the fighting was fierce and almost without cessation throughout the day. There Lee himself and Lee's ablest generals, Hill and Longstreet, were pitted against one of the greatest soldiers that the military academy at West Point has ever trained. Soldiers unequaled for steadiness, intelligence, and devotion in all the history of war, were led by officers who knew not how to flinch. It was no time for the niceties of tactics or strategy. Of the 75,000 men engaged in that part of the field, probably not more than a thousand could be seen at one time from any point. But the determination of the charges and the tenacity of the resistance encountered showed that the soldiers were animated by the commanding minds of great leaders. The battle had lulled a little when Hancock's advance had been checked by the impetuous assault which signalized the arrival of the troops of Longstreet on the field. Hancock did not believe that Longstreet's whole force was in his front. His spies and the stories of some prisoners had led him to believe that Longstreet's attack would fall on his left flank, and the roar of the cannon of Stuart and Sheridan, who were fighting in that direction, led him to believe that the expected flank attack was yet to come. Accordingly he redoubled the fury of his attacks upon Hill, who, being now reinforced by all of Longstreet's corps, beat back his assailants with ease. Stanch breastworks of logs protected the Confederates from the fire of their assailants, and as the ground sloped abruptly from the rear of these redoubts the bullets of the Federals flew all too high. Colonel Lyman, who visited the Confederate position after the battle, writes that the saplings and bushes beyond the breastworks were mowed off by the flying missiles at a point a little higher than a man's head, as though they had been hewed down with knives.

While the Union line of battle was thus dashing itself with unavailing fury against the Confederate ramparts, word was brought to General Longstreet that Hancock's left flank was exposed. A flanking party was sent out with the understanding that if it met with success Longstreet and Hill would simultaneously attack in front, thus rolling Hancock up and utterly demolishing him. The plan promised well and for a time seemed probable of fulfillment. The Confederates, concealed by the dense woods, made their way to the Union left unperceived. Three brigades were in the party. Bursting from the woods they fell with impetuosity upon the flank and rear of General Frank's brigade, which was already hotly engaged in front. Taken thus between two fires, Frank's men, who were already nearly out of ammunition, made but a feeble resistance before giving way. Preceded by a swarm of fugitives, the Confederates pressed on and attacked the brigade of General McAllister, who had changed front to meet them. McAllister made a gallant fight, but to no avail. The Confederates had tasted the sweets of victory. They had flanked their enemy in the true way of Stonewall Jackson. They thought the triumph of Chancellorsville was to be repeated. Nothing could stand before them. McAllister gave way and the troops next him became demoralized. General Hancock and his staff, who galloped to the spot on hearing of the danger impending on the left flank, could do nothing. Despair was in the ranks. Rout and panic were spreading. Hancock gave the order to retreat and seek the shelter of the breastworks along the Brock road, there to make a final stand against the gray torrent that threatened to sweep the blue-coats back into the Rapidan.

Disaster had befallen the Federals in Hancock's front as well as on the flank. There General Wadsworth wished a certain regiment to charge across a ravine and carry a Confederate redoubt, which had thus far proved impregnable. Leaping his horse over the breastworks he led the charge himself, but was struck down with a mortal wound while his gallant followers were beaten back.

But now there came to the Confederates, dashing their hopes of victory, a strange mischance, like that which a year before had cost Lee his "right arm"—Stonewall Jackson. General Longstreet, with his staff, riding through the woods to investigate the progress of the flank attack, came suddenly upon a detached body of Confederates. The officers were taken for Federals. A hasty volley was fired and several saddles were emptied. Among those who fell was General Longstreet, not killed, but sorely wounded. In a moment all was confusion in the Confederate lines. The news quickly passed from regiment to regiment that "old Pete" was wounded—wounded as Stonewall Jackson had been by his own men on that fatal field. General Lee galloped quickly to the spot to take command,

DRAFT RIOTS IN NEW YORK.

but the golden moment had passed. The brief panic in the Union lines was ended. No more positions were to be carried by the Confederates in a rush. Hard fighting was to begin again. Perceiving that there was no longer anything to be gained by an immediate attack, General Lee ordered a cessation of the assault, until the confusion which the fall of Longstreet had caused in the Confederate army could be allayed.

It was four o'clock in the afternoon when the broken lines of gray could be discerned from the Federal position approaching again to the assault through the dense undergrowth, and between the thickly growing trees. The sound of the battle, which had for a time been stilled, rose again upon the air, and the watchers on the hillsides, overlooking the Wilderness, saw again the murky clouds of gunpowder smoke rising above the tree tops. This attack fell fiercest on the divisions of Mott and Birney of Hancock's corps. At first the Confederates carried all before them, driving the Federals quickly from their first line of breastworks. But a second line, a little to the rear, afforded a shelter to the dispossessed blue-coats, who, from that point of vantage, aided by two batteries of artillery, poured so deadly a fire upon their assailants that the latter were fain to shelter themselves from it behind the captured redoubt. Then in their turn the Federals sallied out to the charge. A brigade of Gibbon's division, led by Colonel Carroll, attacked the Confederates and fairly drove them from the position they had won. By this time the wooden breastworks had caught fire and were blazing fiercely so that the defenders could not shelter themselves behind them nor could the assailants pass. A lurid wall of smoke and flame separated the warring hosts.'

Just as the sun went down the din of battle burst forth with redoubled vigor on the right of the Union line. There Lee had massed his forces and hoped by weight of men and metal to crush the Federal flank. Led on by General Gordon, the Confederates fell suddenly upon the brigades of Seymour and Shaler who were taken entirely by surprise. The blue-coats thought the battle over and many of them had thrown themselves upon the ground to rest when this unexpected attack startled them. Both of the brigade commanders and a great host of men were captured by the Confederates, and for a time it seemed as though the Union line were shattered. But the exertions of General Sedgwick and the rapid coming on of night robbed the men of the South of the full fruits of their daring attack.

Such, briefly told, were the chief features of the battle of the Wilderness. But while these more salient movements were progressing there was fighting all along the line. Here two hostile breastworks, closely approaching each other, were crested with flame from the guns of a hundred defenders all through the day. There the skirmishers clad in blue or gray were warily picking each other off from behind trees and bushes, and many a poor fellow in this savage sort of warfare fell wounded to the ground, there to slowly starve or bleed to death, missed by his comrades, but untraceable in that vast jungle of stunted vegetation, where perhaps to-day his bones lie slowly moldering in the earth. Toward the latter part of the battle the flaming wadding from the muskets, smoldering cartridges, or bursting shells set fire to the underbrush. Then a new horror was added to the spectacle. From the depths of the thickets came the pleading tones of the wounded beseeching succor. Many were saved— carried out of the flames in the arms of comrades, or swung in blankets lashed to the barrels of muskets. But many—far too many—a piteous, unidentified, unremembered host, lay helpless on the battle-field watching the flames approach, and were freed from their torture at last by the hot blast of the resistless forest fire. How many such there were none can tell. The Wilderness still holds many a grim secret hidden in its gloomy shades.

Heavy indeed was the loss of life in the two days' battle of the Wilderness. In the Army of the Potomac and Burnside's corps the killed were 2265, wounded 10,220, and missing 2902. The loss on the Confederate side cannot be so exactly stated. Doubtless it was far less than that of the Federals, for the Confederates fought chiefly on the defensive. The best authorities place their total loss in the neighborhood of 10,000. But to so slender an army as Lee's this was a crippling blow, and the Confederate must have been blind indeed who could not discern that a few such victories as that of the Wilderness, if purchased at such a price, would leave the Confederacy with no army to fight its battles. Grant's policy of wearing away the enemy's military power by ceaseless and remorseless attrition had begun to tell.

CHAPTER IV.

AFTER THE BATTLE—"FORWARD BY THE LEFT FLANK"—THE RACE FOR SPOTTSYLVANIA—GENERAL SEDGWICK KILLED—THE ATTACK UPON HANCOCK—THE BURNING WOODS—UPTON'S ASSAULT UPON THE SALIENT—SUCCESS AND FAILURE—"THE BLOODY ANGLE"—THE CONFEDERATES ATTACK IN TURN—A HAND-TO-HAND STRUGGLE.

FOR two days the Wilderness had resounded with the thunders of battle from earliest dawn until after night had fallen. But Friday's sun rose over a silent field. The belligerents were there, facing each other grimly over the breastworks, with their dead between them, but neither made any sign of renewing the battle. The Confederates had fought well and effectively, they had blocked their enemy's pathway, they had inflicted upon him a heavy loss; and now they sat in their trenches waiting for Grant to withdraw to reorganize, as had been the custom of commanders of the Army of the Potomac from time immemorial. But Grant had no idea of retreating. It is true that he wisely abandoned all thoughts of driving the Confederates from the position they held in the Wilderness, but he determined to march round their flank and keep on his way to Richmond. Accordingly on the morning of the 7th he prepared a dispatch to

Washington, claiming the Wilderness affair as a victory for the Union cause, and issued orders to his army to take up the march for Spottsylvania court-house in the afternoon. It is difficult to admit the justice of General Grant's claim to victory in the Wilderness battles. Save only the fact that the North could better afford to lose 16,000 men than the South to part with 10,000, the advantage seems to have rested with the Confederates. But Grant's swift determination to continue his advance by the left flank—to go around Lee's position—since he could not go through it—marked a new era in the method of prosecuting the war in Virginia. It was a sore disappointment to the enemy, and it is reported that when one of "Jeb" Stuart's cavalry-men came galloping to Lee with the news that Grant was sending his wounded back to Fredericksburg and was advancing in force upon Spottsylvania court-house, the Virginian turned to his staff with the significant remark, "Gentlemen, the Army of the Potomac has found a head at last."

Some fifteen miles southeast of the Wilderness battle-field, was the little hamlet of Spottsylvania. A wooden court-house with a Grecian portico and plank pillars, a grocery store with the usual drinking shop annex, a roomy, old-fashioned tavern, and a handful of little frame houses made up this dreary little village, whose name was destined to be given to one of the hardest fought battles of the civil war. The military importance of the spot lay in the fact that there roads from every point of the compass met and crossed. It was a position that Grant could scarce afford to lose in the pursuance of his plan for putting himself between Lee's army and Richmond.

Every precaution was taken by General Grant to remove his forces from Lee's front and place them on the road for Spottsylvania without arousing the suspicion of Lee. The troops on the right flank were put in motion first, passing behind the rest of the Union line, which thus served as a screen for their movements. Warren's division was upon the most direct road, and was instructed to make the quickest time possible in its march so as to reach Spottsylvania before the Confederates could take the alarm and occupy the place themselves. But it so happened that Fitz Hugh Lee's cavalry got ahead of Warren, obstructing the road by felling trees, and carrying on a running fight that greatly delayed the Union advance. This enabled a division of Longstreet's corps, marching upon a parallel road, to reach Spottsylvania when it was held only by a few Federal horsemen, who were quickly driven out. When Warren came up, he saw before him the familiar sight of a long line of breastworks displaying the Confederate flag, barring his further progress. He rested on his arms to wait for Hancock, but before the latter's arrival all of Longstreet's corps, and finally the whole of Lee's army poured into Spottsylvania, so that once again the Army of Northern Virginia stood proudly and defiantly between Grant and the Confederate capital.

The country about Spottsylvania is not unlike the Wilderness region, though more plentifully interspersed with clearings which afforded the artillerymen of both armies some opportunity to practice their art. The land lies in ridges, heavily wooded, affording admirable defensive positions. Two rivers, the Po and the Ny, describe tortuous courses toward the southeast, on the west and east sides of the village respectively. A network of roads covered the whole country thereabouts, and a multiplicity of bridges—some of which seem not to have been down on the maps of the Federal engineers—have given rise to a good deal of acrimonious discussion among the Union officers. There is no doubt that the success of the Confederates in first reaching the battlefield was due to a series of accidents which favored them, rather than to any exceptional celerity in their movements.

Sunday morning, May 8, saw the troops—the blue and the gray—swinging into line facing each other. The rifles of the skirmishers, pickets, and sharpshooters rang out sharply upon the warm air, but the great body of the soldiers were busy with the ax and the spade, throwing up those breastworks that in the latter years of the war seemed to rise as by magic wherever an armed body of men halted. There was little fighting that day. Late in the afternoon an assault was made by the Federals but was repulsed. The next day the work of fortifying continued. Both armies seemed loth to come to blows, but the sharpshooters were enterprising and active, especially on the Confederate side. It was by a bullet dispatched on its fatal mission by one of these marksmen that General Sedgwick met his death. The general was superintending the alignment of a body of his troops under a sharp fire. The shrill scream of the minie balls seemed more demoralizing to the men than in many a hot battle, and their heads bobbed involuntarily.

"What, what men!" cried out Sedgwick. "Dodging this way for single bullets! What will you do when they open fire along the whole line? I am ashamed of you. They couldn't hit an elephant at this distance."

For a moment the men straightened up proudly, but a few seconds after a soldier standing near General Sedgwick dodged almost to the ground as a bullet passed close to him with a terrifying whiz. "Why, I am ashamed of you, my man," said Sedgwick, and again he repeated his remark, "They couldn't hit an elephant at that distance." But while the soldier was making his excuses the shrill whistle came again and this time a dull, heavy stroke told that it had found a mark. Those whose gaze was turned toward General Sedgwick were horrified to see the blood gush from his cheek a little below his left eye. With a smile on his face he turned toward his chief-of-staff, tottered an instant, and fell heavily to the ground, carrying down the officer who tried to support him. In a few moments he was no more.

It was determined upon this day that Hancock early on the morrow should make a reconnoisance upon Lee's left, crossing the Po River and turning the enemy's flank. At the crossing place the river flowed deep and black, but scarcely fifty feet wide. Three pontoon bridges were laid and the troops were soon across and moving down the western bank. All seemed to promise well and a position on the enemy's flank and rear was being gained rapidly, when an order came from Meade for Hancock to abandon his operations on that line and return to the main body of the army. An assault was to be made on the Confederate center and Hancock's troops were needed to join in it. This was the reason assigned for abandoning a movement which promised to drive Lee from his position. It seems now to have been an error. Perhaps to Hancock it seemed so then, but, a trained soldier, he accepted unquestioningly the orders of his superior and withdrew his troops across the Po with all possible speed. But the Confederates were now on the alert, and when two of Hancock's three divisions had crossed the river the enemy sallied from their entrenchments and fell furiously upon Barlow's division which alone remained. Though greatly outnumbered, Barlow stood his ground manfully and gave his foes as good as they sent. Twice the Confederates attacked in force and twice they were repulsed. Then Barlow began crossing the river under cover of a heavy artillery fire from the other side, which held the foe in check. Here, as in the Wilderness battles, the woods took fire, and while the fighting troops had more than once to force their way through a fiery barrier, the wounded, lying helpless on the ground beneath, perished miserably in the flames. The retirement of the Federals beyond the river was hailed by the Confederates as a victory, but General Hancock in his report writes, "Had not Barlow's fine division, then in full strength, received imperative orders to withdraw, Heth's division would have had no cause for congratulation." One gun was lost to the Federals during this contest. The horses drawing it took fright, ran away, and the cannon became so tightly wedged between two trees that it could not be dislodged. It was the first gun lost by the Second Corps during the war.

Meantime the contemplated attack on the enemy's right center had been made and failed. General Warren himself, clad in full uniform, led the assault, and strove by voice and deed to urge his soldiers on to victory. But the nature of the field sorely retarded the progress of the storming party. The woods were dense before the enemy's works, and the assailants burst panting from those dense thickets of dead cedars which the shells and canister were searching pitilessly, only to find themselves confronted by a long line of sharp-spiked abatis, beyond which the Confederate guns were roaring and flaming. No company or regimental alignment could be maintained on such difficult ground, and so, though many pressed bravely onward, it was soon a straggling mob and not a disciplined army with which the Confederates had to contend. Nevertheless, some of the brave fellows passed the abatis and reached the redoubt only to die there before the guns of the enemy. Brigadier-general Rice was mortally wounded in this assault. Later in the evening the attack was renewed, but with no more fortunate results. At this time the woods were set on fire, and again the soldiers were forced to see their miserable wounded comrades perish in the flames before their eyes.

Further to the left on the Union line the fighting was still fiercer, and its results equally barren of all save glory. There the Sixth Corps was arrayed—mourning for the recent loss of its gallant commander Sedgwick, and burning to avenge him under its new leader, General Wright. Before the Sixth Corps the Confederate works extended in what is known to military engineers as a salient angle. The west side of this angle, Wright thought afforded a vulnerable point of attack. A storming party was quickly formed: one brigade and four regiments with Colonel Emory Upton in command. To assist and support Upton's attack a division of the Second Corps was ordered to attack on the left.

The fire of a number of Union batteries is now directed upon the threatened point. On all sides batteries can be seen galloping madly across the fields or painfully breaking their way through the thickets to get into positions whence they can pour their missiles into the enemy's salient. While the artillerymen stand to their work, loading and firing with regularity and precision, Upton's men are forming for the charge. In an open field, hidden from the sight of the enemy by a screening thicket of pines and cedars, they form in four ranks; then forward, and pick their way through the forest to its outer edge. The batteries now redouble the fury of their fire. The infantry stands on the alert, for the instant the cannon cease to roar the charge is to begin.

Aides are seen galloping along the line of the artillery. The brazen roar of the canon is stilled. There is an instant of silence, and then a fiercer clamor breaks upon the air as a vast multitude of cheering blue-clad men burst from the edge of the woods and rush toward the

Confederate works. Those grim redoubts are edged with fire immediately, and a spiteful hail of lead beats in the faces of the assailants. But still the blue wave surges onward. Men fall and are trampled under foot by their comrades. The colors drop more than once, but are caught up again and carried on. Now the abatis is reached and torn to pieces by the fierce grip of hundreds of sinewy hands. On, on, and still on, until the foremost are swarming over the breastworks and bayoneting their defenders. There is a hand to hand struggle. Little powder is burned, but the cold steel and the clubbed musket do their deadly work. Many of the Confederates turn to flee. They have a second line of works a few hundred paces to the rear and they strive to reach this shelter. Others, by hundreds, throw down their arms and deliver themselves up. The Federals, determined to make their victory complete, press on and carry the second breastwork as well. They have captured more than a thousand prisoners and many battle flags.

Successful at every point, Colonel Upton now looks for support and reinforcements. None come. He has made a breach in the enemy's line, the sharp edge of the wedge is inserted, and he waits for the heavy blows to be dealt that shall split the enemy in twain. But for some reason, never fully explained, the success gained at the cost of so many gallant lives is not properly followed up. The Confederates are quick to see the peril which Upton's lodgment within their lines threatens. They come in swarms to eject this intruder. Driven away from the second line, they clung stubbornly to the first. In his report Colonel Upton mentions that Captain Burnham of the Forty-third New York was killed between the two lines with two captured Confederate flags in his hands. Finally, however, as darkness came on fast—the assault was not made until after six o'clock in the evening—and as there was no possibility of bringing up other troops to hold the position Upton had so gallantly carried, the order was sent to withdraw, and the captured salient, which had cost so many lives, was abandoned.

The darkness of another night now fell upon this bloody battle-field. Rivers of blood had been poured out. Thousands of lives had been sacrificed. The Confederate lines stood where they had stood when they had first been drawn across Grant's path. Over the log breastworks the Confederate flag was still flying. But the dogged determination of the new commander of the Army of the Potomac was shaken not a whit. In his headquarters he sat, perfecting his plans for continuing the attack on Lee's lines. And early the next morning, when a whole army of dead and wounded men lay about him, he wrote and sent off to Washington this dispatch, the last sentence of which electrified the whole nation.

" We have now ended the sixth day of very heavy fighting. The result is very much in our favor. Our losses have been heavy as well as those of the enemy. I think the loss of the enemy must be greater. We have taken over 5000 prisoners by battle, while he has taken from us but few except stragglers. I am now sending back to Belle Plaine all my wagons for a fresh supply of provisions and *I propose to fight it out on this line if it takes all summer.*"

Two days had now passed since the armies of the Union and the Confederacy had mustered upon the field of Spottsylvania. The Confederates had well occupied the time in perfecting an extended and formidable system of breastworks. In places they had two lines of log redoubts with an abatis, or a forest of trees slashed so as to let the tops fall to the ground without the trunks being entirely severed, obstructing the approach to the foremost one. It was necessary for Grant to attack and carry these formidable works that intercepted him on the path to Richmond. But where should he attack; how tell which was the weakest link in that consummate chain of defense? Everywhere the dense thickets concealed the contour of the Confederate works from the observer on the Union position. The Federal engineers, who stealthily made their way to the front to spy out the enemy's lines, fell victims to the vigilance and skill. of the Confederate sharpshooters, or were captured by their skirmishers. The war balloon had not as yet come into use as a point of vantage whence to study the dispositions of the enemy, and no course remained to the Federals save to push back the enemy's skirmishers, get a hasty glimpse of his works, and retire. This was done at point after point all along the line, and the results, combined with the information volunteered by a few deserters and that painfully extorted from Confederate prisoners, gradually enabled the Union engineers to map with some degree of accuracy the enemy's lines. From the knowledge of the situation thus obtained the Federals reached the conclusion that the point which most invited attack was the apex of that salient angle, the side of which Upton had so gallantly carried. An angle is always regarded as a vulnerable point, because artillery fire from two directions will enfilade the lines of the defenders.

A chill and gusty rain fell throughout the 11th. It often, and indeed generally happened during the war that the day following a battle was rainy—a fact which has led to many interesting speculations as to the possibility of producing rain artificially by concussions and the burning of gunpowder. The rain that fell on the bloody field of Spottsylvania put an end, for the time, to active hostilities. The soldiers crouched about their smoldering camp fires, wrapped in their blankets, and talked of the events of the campaign, and hinted darkly of the possible fatalities in the assault that all knew would be ordered for the morrow. Indeed, preparations for this assault began to be made early in the day. Aides went galloping from one division commander to another carrying orders. General Grant had determined to attack at four o'clock the next morning, they said. Hancock's men—the Second Corps—were to make the main assault at the apex of the salient. The remainder of the army were to attack all along the line, that Lee might not send troops from any point to the aid of those upon whom Hancock's assault was to fall.

When it grew dark, the tread of regiments marching in the rear of the Union lines was heard. Hancock's men were moving to the spot where they were to form for the attack. Along the muddy roads, across the water-logged fields, and under the dripping branches of the forest trees they trudged until they reached the farm of a man named Brown, where they were to be massed until the hour for attacking. A line drawn straight to the southward from Brown's house to the McCool house, which stood inside the Confederate lines, would be just about a mile long and would pass through the vertex of the angle. From the Brown house to the Confederate works extended open fields four hundred yards wide in the narrowest part. This was to be the avenue of attack. In the dark and rainy night the troops made their way to their stations. Not the sharpest-eyed scouts could pierce with their gaze the pitchy darkness. The compass was brought into play, and officers, after striking a match to light up the magnetic needle, led the troops by its guidance. Soon after midnight all were in position. Barlow's division, with regiments formed in close column of attack, was in the center of the open fields, about 1200 yards from the enemy's works. Birney's division, in two deployed lines, was on Barlow's right. Mott was in Birney's rear, with his troops deployed in one long line. Gibbon's division was held in reserve. There, under the dripping, drenching rain they stood in the black night, waiting for the signal to hurl themselves forward upon the works which they knew would be bristling with bayonets and flaming with the flashes of deadly musketry.

General Lee had not been wholly ignorant of the operations going on in his front, but had wholly misconstrued them. His scouts had reported large bodies of Federals in motion and he at once jumped to the conclusion that Grant had begun another flanking movement. In order to have his own army ready to take up the march, he ordered that all cannon posted in places difficult of access should be withdrawn. Under this order all the batteries but two were withdrawn from the salient, and that point weakened just as the Federals were about to assault it. The Confederates were not blind to the fact that the salient invited attack, and they had built a second line of works in its rear to which its defenders might retire in case of an emergency.

Four o'clock came—the hour set by Grant for the attack. The night was still so black that Hancock determined to defer the signal yet a little while. At half past four the signal was given and the men sprang forward like hounds freed from the leash. Pressing rapidly forward, they pass the first hundred yards or so without receiving any fire. Then the Confederate sentries see these ghostly columns advancing upon them out of the night, and their guns ring out an alarm. Instantly the ramparts are ablaze and the assailants answer with undaunted cheers the volleys of the defenders. General Barlow says that his men lost all alignments and pressed on in one solid mass. The Confederate General Johnson says "they came on in great disorder with a narrow front but extending back as far as I could see." Then it was that the Confederates bitterly bewailed the absence of their artillery, which could have poured grape and canister into the assaulting column with murderous effect. One battery indeed—Page's—came galloping back to the scene of action, but it arrived too late for use and just in time to be captured. Before the guns could be unlimbered, the blue-coats were swarming over the ramparts everywhere, their pistols were cracking, their clubbed muskets and keen bayonets doing deadly work. The Confederates were overwhelmed, swept away, surrounded. Some made their way back to the second line of intrenchments. Still more threw down their arms. In less than five minutes the Federals had carried the salient, captured nearly 5000 men, twenty guns with their battery teams, thirty battle flags, and thousands of small arms. The guns were at once turned on the enemy, who were pursued through the woods until the pursuers came face to face with the second Confederate line, which held them in check. The prisoners were sent to the Union rear. Among them were General Johnson and General Steuart. The latter had been a classmate of General Hancock at West Point.

"How are you, Steuart," said Hancock cheerily, as he saw his old friend approaching.

"I am General Steuart of the Confederate army," responded the prisoner haughtily, "and under the circumstances I decline to take your hand."

"Under any other circumstances," said Hancock quietly, "I should not have offered it."

Word had speedily been carried to Lee of the success of Hancock's charge. He saw that his lines had been pierced at a vital point. Either the lost ground must be regained or the whole Confederate position would become untenable. Stripping his trenches everywhere else, he began pouring his troops upon Hancock from every side. Meantime orders had been sent from Meade's headquarters to support Hancock, and the Sixth Corps, with Upton's gallant brigade in the van, rushed to the salient. The clash of arms at this point now became terrific. The Federals were driven out of the salient, but used the breastworks as a protection for themselves. The Confederates trying to drive them away were thus crowded within the arms of a gigantic V, the sides of which spouted fire and lead. Never during the war was the fighting so fierce. Both sides were determined. Neither would yield a jot. So fast fell the dead and wounded that the spot became known in the annals of the civil war as the "bloody angle."

Of the fighting at the bloody angle let some of those who were there tell the story. G. Norton Galloway, one of the Ninety-fifth Pennsylvania, which led Upton's advance, writes thus of the moment when Lee's men came sweeping down to win back the lost salient:

"Under cover of the smoke-laden rain the enemy was pushing large bodies of troops forward, determined at all hazards to regain the lost ground. The smoke, which was dense at first, was intensified by each discharge of artillery to such an extent that the accuracy of our aim became very uncertain; but nevertheless we kept up the fire in the direction of the enemy. Meanwhile they were crawling forward under cover of (the smoke until, reaching a certain point and raising their usual yell, they charged gallantly up to the very muzzles of our pieces and reoccupied the angle.

"Upon reaching the breastworks the Confederates for a few moments had the advantage of us, and made good use of their rifles. Our men went down by the score; all the artillery horses were down; the gallant Upton was the only mounted officer in sight. Hat in hand he bravely cheered his men, and begged them to 'hold this point.' All of his staff had been either killed, wounded, or dismounted.

"At this moment, and while the open ground in rear of the Confederate works was choked with troops, a section of Battery C, Fifth

United States Artillery, under Lieutenant Richard Metcalf, was brought into action and increased the carnage by opening at short range with double charges of canister. This staggered the apparently exultant enemy. In the maze of the moment these guns were run up by hand close to the famous angle, and fired again and again, and they were only abandoned when all the drivers and cannoneers had fallen."

"Our section went into action with twenty-three men and one officer," writes a sergeant who served in Metcalf's battery. "The only ones who came out sound were the lieutenant and myself. Every horse was killed. Seven of the men were killed outright, sixteen wounded; the gun carriages were so cut with bullets as to be of no further service. Twenty-seven balls passed through the lid of the limber-chest while number six was getting out ammunition, and he was wounded in the face and neck by the fragments of wood and lead. The sponge bucket on my gun had thirty-nine holes in it."

The Confederate troops that charged into the salient were under command of General Gordon. Here, as in the Wilderness, General Lee started to lead the charge, but was forced to turn back by the protests of his men. "Go back, General Lee," cried Gordon, seizing his chief's bridle rein, "I will answer for the conduct of my men in this charge." And a great shout of "Lee to the rear!" rose from the tattered ranks that were surging past.

About the "bloody angle" the ground was soaked with rain and blood, and covered with prostrate men. A Confederate officer says in his official report: "The trenches on the right in the bloody angle ran with blood and had to be cleared of the dead bodies more than once." The enemies stood face to face close up to the breastworks on either side, and poured pistol and musket shots into each other at that short range. A major in a New York regiment was shot through the arm and body with a ramrod which some Confederate had neglected to remove from his gun before shooting. The problem of getting ammunition to the fighters in front was no easy one to solve. So rapid was the firing that cartridge boxes were speedily emptied. On the Federal side pack

FORAGING.

mules were driven close up to the line of battle and boxes of ammunition dropped off behind the men in action, where they were opened and distributed by the officers. Captain Fish, of Upton's staff, did gallant work in supplying the Union gunners with ammunition. He rode back and forth between the guns and the caissons with stands of canister under his rubber coat. His tall form, towering above the line of battle as he sat his horse, was a tempting target for the Confederate riflemen, but he showed no sign of fear. "Give it to them, boys; I'll bring you the canister," he cried, and rode to and fro until at last a bullet struck him down with a mortal wound.

"Finding that we were not to be driven back," continues Mr. Galloway, "the Confederates began to use more discretion, exposing themselves but little, using the loopholes in their works to fire through, and at times placing the muzzles of their rifles on the top logs, seizing the trigger and small of the stock, and elevating the breech sufficiently to reach us. Sometimes the enemy's fire would slacken, and the moments would become so monotonous that something had to be done to stir them up. Then some resolute fellow would seize a fence rail or piece of abatis, and creeping close to the breastworks thrust it over among the enemy, and then drop on the ground to avoid the volley that was sure to follow. A daring lieutenant in one of our left companies leaped upon the breastworks, took a rifle that was handed to him, and discharged it among the foe. In like manner he discharged another, and was in the act of firing a third shot when his cap flew up in the air and his body pitched headlong among the enemy." This reckless act of self-sacrifice was imitated more than once. Officers and privates, gray-coat and blue-coat, vied with each other in deeds of desperate valor. It is not often that the fury of a fight stirs a military officer to attempt bits of graphic description in his official report, but the report of Brigadier-General Grant, commanding a Vermont brigade, shows how vividly the scene impressed itself upon the mind of that commander.

"It was not only a desperate struggle," he writes, "but it was literally a hand to hand fight. Nothing but the piled-up logs or breastworks separated the combatants. Our men would reach over the logs and fire into the faces of the enemy; would stab over with their bayonets; many were shot and stabbed through the crevices and holes between the logs; men mounted the works, and, with muskets rapidly handed them, kept up a continuous fire until they were shot down, when others would take their places and continue the deadly work. . . . . Several times during the day the rebels would show a white flag above the works, and when our fire slackened jump over and surrender, and others were crowded down to fill their places. . . . . It was there that the somewhat celebrated tree was cut off by bullets, there that the brush and logs were cut to pieces and whipped into basket stuff . . . . there that the rebel ditches and cross sections were filled with dead men several deep. . . . . I was at the angle the next day. The sight was terrible and sickening, much worse than at Bloody Lane (Antietam). There a great many dead men were lying in the road and across the rails of the torn down fences and out in the corn field; but they were not piled up several deep, and their flesh was not so torn and mangled as at the 'angle.'"

All through the day, under the driving rain, the fight went on at the "angle." Lee could ill afford to lose the men who were falling so fast there, but he dared not attempt to withdraw while daylight lasted. To right and left of the "angle," too, the Federals were delivering blow after blow upon the Confederate lines. No success was won by the assailants on the right, but on the left the breastworks were carried and some guns taken, though the Confederates, rallying, forced the blue-coats out of their lines again. Not until nearly midnight did the thunder of the battle gradually die away, leaving the moans of the wounded and the steady drip, drip of the rain the sole sounds to be heard. After fighting all day for a position of but little serious military importance, General Lee abandoned the salient and withdrew his men to the second line, ready for them in the rear.

Frightful had been the loss on both sides in the sanguinary struggle. The bullets that flew so thick as to cut down a tree twenty-one inches in diameter within the Confederate lines, had slain only too many gallant

Americans, each fighting for the cause he deemed right. The mortality among officers of high rank was greatest among the Confederates—Generals Daniel and Perrin being killed; Walker, Ramseur, and McGowan wounded; while Major-General Johnson and Brigadier Steuart were captured. Among the Federals three generals—Carroll, Wright, and Webb—were wounded. The total number of the killed and wounded on the Union side was 6020. The number missing is reported at 800. The loss to the Confederates was far heavier, but the lack of official records makes any exact statement impossible. A total loss of between 9000 and 10,000 in killed, wounded, and captured is accepted as nearly accurate by the best authorities.

The field of battle presented a frightful spectacle when day broke after the fighting. Everywhere the ground was sodden with the rain and trampled into mire by the feet of the struggling host. Knapsacks, arms, cartridge-cases, accoutrements, and dead and dying men lay on every side. Early in the morning volunteers from the Federal army went out to bury the dead. This is the scene as described by one of the burial party that worked near the "bloody angle." "A momentary gleam of sunshine through the gloom of the sky seemed to add a new horror to the scene. Hundreds of Confederates, dead or dying, lay piled over one another in those pits. The fallen lay three or four deep in some places, and, with but few exceptions, they were shot in and about the head. Arms, accoutrements, ammunition, cannon, shot and shell, and broken foliage were strewn about. With much labor a detail of Union soldiers buried the dead by simply turning the captured breastworks upon them. Thus had these unfortunate victims unwittingly dug their own graves."

CHAPTER V.

STILL FORWARD—THE CONFEDERATES DISCOURAGED—A TOILSOME MARCH—A FLANK ATTACK—LEE TAKES THE OFFENSIVE—QUARREL BETWEEN SHERIDAN AND MEADE—SHERIDAN'S RAID—IN A TRAP—A PANIC IN RICHMOND—THE ARMY OF THE JAMES—BUTLER'S EXPEDITION—ATTEMPT TO WRECK A RAILROAD—BATTLE OF DRURY'S BLUFF.

FORWARD by the left flank!" The order that had passed from division to division in the Union camp after the bloody days in the Wilderness resounded again along the lines after the sanguinary struggle at the salient. General Grant lost no time in repeating the blows under which his antagonist was already showing signs of weakness. He relaxed not at all his pitiless vigilance and energy. He had lost nearly 7000 men in the battle of the 12th. Very well, but the enemy had lost nearly 10,000. Lee's breastworks, still flaunting the stars and bars, barred his path. Then he would go around them, and soon his troops were on the march, passing toward the left flank, there to renew the attack which had proved fruitless on the right. Before the march was begun, a congratulatory address, issued by General Meade, was read to the soldiers of the Army of the Potomac. It recounted the achievements of the army since it had entered the Wilderness, during "eight days and nights almost without intermission, in rain and sunshine." Though there remained hard fighting to be done, the commander encouraged his men with the promise, "We shall soon receive re-enforcements, which the foe cannot expect."

It was that, indeed, which was destined to make all Lee's brilliant strategy and all the gallantry of his soldiers effect nothing in the end. The Army of Northern Virginia could expect no more re-enforcements. The Confederacy was swept clean of its able-bodied male citizens. The losses in battle and the inroads of disease were making gaps in the Confederate lines which never could be filled. "So far as the Confederates were concerned," writes the Confederate, General Law, "it would be idle to deny that they (as well as General Lee himself) were disappointed at the result of their efforts in the Wilderness on the 5th and 6th of May, and that General Grant's constant 'hammering' with his largely superior force had to a certain extent a depressing effect upon both officers and men. 'It's no use killing these fellows; a half-dozen take the place of every one we kill,' was a common remark in our army. We knew that our resources of men were exhausted, and that the vastly greater resources of the Federal government, if brought fully to bear, even in this costly kind of warfare, must wear us out in the end."

The movement to the left, by which General Grant hoped to deal the enemy a crushing blow at a point hitherto unsmitten by battle, was begun by Warren's corps immediately after nightfall of the 13th. A march of some six miles along circuitous and little traveled roads was before them. The rain was falling heavily, soaking the uniforms and knapsacks of the marching men, doubling their weight, and adding greatly to the toil of marching. The mud, troublesome at first, became knee deep after the first three or four regiments had trudged over the road and tramped it into mire. Great fires were built by the roadside to light up the path and give the soldiers a few rays of heat when the frequent halts were ordered. At every cross road men with flaming torches were posted to point out the proper direction. No precaution, indeed, which could possibly expedite or assist the march was neglected. But the obstacles which nature heaped before the advancing column could not be wholly overcome by man. Floundering along in the deep and miry mud, with the rain beating furiously in their faces, and the night so black that the men in the rear rank could not see the backs of those before them, the soldiers made but slow progress. The halts were many, and the ground covered between them but small. Stragglers in great numbers dropped from the ranks and threw themselves on the moist ground before the fires. The plan had been to attack the enemy at four o'clock in the morning, but at six o'clock the weary, wet, mud-stained, and disorganized Fifth Corps was just approaching the spot where the battle was to be fought. With his troops in this condition, General Warren could not hope to make a successful attack upon the enemy's position; therefore the assault was abandoned. The Sixth Corps, which began its march a few hours later than Warren, soon came up, and for a time there was a lively struggle between Upton's brigade—reduced by the hard fighting of the few days previous to a scant 800 men—and the Confederates of Mahone's command, for a hill which commanded all the country round about it. Upton was finally driven off, but General Warren sent General Ayres to recover the position, which was soon accomplished. But the slight advantage thus gained proved of no benefit to the Federals. Lee had discovered their presence upon his right flank, and rushed troops over there to meet this new danger. His breastworks were extended, and cannon withdrawn from his left flank peered through the embrasures at Warren's skirmishers. Had the Federals been able to attack at dawn of the 14th, as contemplated by Grant's original plan, there is every reason to believe that success would have been theirs. But the delay caused by the rain and mud saved Lee's army from a flank attack that might have proved its destruction.

For several days now the two armies rested on their arms. The relief from the strain, which had been constant since Grant entered the Wilderness, was grateful to Federal and Confederate alike. It was at midnight on the 3d of May that Grant had crossed the Rapidan, and not one day had passed since, that the armies had not exchanged shots, and but few days that there had not been fighting all along the lines. With picket duty, the toil of marching and countermarching, and the nervous strain of so many pitched battles, the men—blue and gray—were fairly worn out. Among the Confederates, too, there was great suffering for lack of food. The tacit armistice which succeeded to the terrible fighting at the "bloody angle" brought some measure of rest and recuperation to the wearied bodies and jaded minds of the soldiers, but brought no more rations to fill the empty haversacks of the men who fought with Lee. Yet when the time came for a renewal of the struggle the Confederates sprung to arms with unabated spirit.

On the 17th it was suggested to General Grant that, as Lee had moved a great part of his army to his right flank to meet the threatened attack there by the Fifth and Sixth Corps, his left must be nearly denuded of troops, and a return of those corps to that point would probably take him by surprise. The suggestion was accepted as a good one, and that night the soldiers of Warren's and Wright's corps were retracing their steps over the roads along which they had floundered on the inclement night of the 14th. This time no serious obstacle delayed their march, and at four o'clock in the morning the Confederates standing guard in the line of breastworks behind the fatal salient were startled by the cheer and the rattling fire of rifles that told of a coming attack. The Union artillery, now occupying what had been the original Confederate line of defense, threw its shells over the heads of the advancing Federals and dropped them into the enemy's trenches. The attack was spirited, but the assailants were disappointed in their expectation of taking the enemy by surprise. The Confederates were on the alert, and their rapid and well-delivered fire fell murderously upon the blue-coats, who were painfully picking their way through slashed forrests and over tangled abatis. Though the troops returned to the attack several times with undiminished spirit they were continually repulsed, and Meade at last ordered a cessation of the assault.

General Lee now determined to take the initiative. Ewell's corps was put in motion and sent around Grant's right flank to take the Federals in the rear. Ewell moved expeditiously and passed the fords of the Ny River without attracting attention. With a capable and trustworthy guide he took his column across the fields and along narrow forest roads until the position sought had been gained. The right of the Union army was then held by Tyler's division of heavy artillery. These troops had never before been under fire. Since the beginning of their service they had been inactive in the fortifications that surrounded Washington. Their knowledge of war had been confined to drills and salutes with the great guns. But when Grant began his campaign against Lee, he made it evident that he would never let go his grip upon his adversary long enough for the Confederates to threaten the capital, so that when the fierce fighting in the Wilderness made re-enforcements necessary the Washington forts were stripped of their artillerists, who, to the number of 7000, were sent to the front.

A scattering fire from Tyler's pickets was the first intimation that the Federals had of Ewell's presence in their rear. There was panic for a time in the Union ranks. None could tell how powerful was the force that had thus unexpectedly descended upon them. The drums beating the long roll, the quick cries of the captains forming their companies, the shouts of the teamsters harnessing up the mule teams ready for instant flight should the enemy prove to be in force, mingled with the fire at the front which grew louder and louder as regiment after regiment formed, and swept forward into the fight.

Though new to the excitement and the horror of the battle-field, the men of Tyler's division held their ground well. They bore the brunt of Ewell's attack, repulsed it, and drove the enemy back. The noise of the combat brought the veterans of the Second and Fifth Corps to the ground, and Ewell was soon put to flight. The flanking movement had cost him 900 men and had benefited his cause not in the least.

Let us now, for a time, leave the Army of the Potomac and the Army of Northern Virginia confronting each other in their long redoubts at Spottsylvania, and follow the fortunes of the cavalry corps of the two armies which had been doing some spirited fighting, in the course of a cavalry raid, which was undertaken by the Federal troops under somewhat curious circumstances.

When General Philip Sheridan was summoned from the West to take command of the cavalry of the Army of the Potomac, he entered upon the duties of his office with enthusiasm and with a firm determination to make the cavalry arm of the Union service superior to those bodies of dashing horsemen that under Ashby and Stuart and Forrest had done such gallant service for the Confederacy. Between him and the realization of his ambition Sheridan allowed no man to stand. The story is told of him that when an infantry general, who had a small cavalry regiment for a body guard, sent word to the new cavalry commander that he would like to retain this body of horse, Sheridan responded, "Give my compliments to General —— and say that I have been placed in command of the cavalry of this army, and by —— I want it all."

This spirit of self-assertion led to a scene between Meade and Sheridan just before the battle of Spottsylvania. When Meade arrived at that place he found a body of cavalry there awaiting orders. Meade thereupon ordered the cavalry to hold certain strategic points. Soon after a staff officer from Sheridan came up with orders for the cavalry, but found it already gone. As it turned out Sheridan's orders, if obeyed, would have saved the Union army much hard fighting, and that officer was much aggrieved that his directions should have been forestalled by Meade. An interview between them resulted in a heated argument, which was ended by Sheridan's leaving the room wrathfully with the words, "If I'm permitted to cut loose from this army, I'll draw Stuart after me, and I'll whip him, too. But if you insist on giving the cavalry orders without consulting or notifying me, I will not give another order."

A few hours later Meade reported the quarrel and its attendant circumstances to Grant. The fact that his two trusted lieutenants were at odds did not seem to distress the general. Another thing in the conversation awakened his interest.

"Did he say that he could whip Stuart?" he asked.

"Yes."

"Very well. Then let him go and do it."

Meade returned to his tent and soon issued orders for Sheridan to undertake a cavalry raid. Perhaps he was secretly a little rejoiced that the contumacious cavalryman should thus be forced to substantiate his boast.

The enemy's cavalry was to be the objective point of Sheridan's expedition. Incidently he was to tear up railroads, burn bridges, and inflict all possible damage upon the Confederates; but chiefly he was to "proceed against the enemy's cavalry, and when supplies are exhausted proceed *via* New Market and Green Bay to Haxall's Landing, on the James River, there communicating with General Butler, procure supplies, and returning to this army." This meant a raid right around the rear of Lee's army and close to the outer defenses of Richmond.

"We are going to fight Stuart's cavalry in consequence of a suggestion from me," said Sheridan that night to his division commanders, Gregg, Merritt, and Wilson. "We will give him a fair, square fight. We are strong and I know we can beat him. I shall expect nothing but success."

Preparations for the movement were soon actively under way. All through the camp the troopers were sharpening their sabers, overhauling their equipments, and packing up the three days' rations which had been issued to each man. The command was stripped to light marching order. The ammunition wagons, two ambulances to each division, and a few pack mules made up the entire train. Shortly after sunrise of the 9th of May the clear notes of the bugles rang out on the cool morning air, and the command moved out on the telegraph road. Great clouds of dust rose high in the air above the tree tops, marking the progress of this rushing torrent of horsemen. Ten thousand men were in line. Moving in column of fours along a narrow road, it stretched out over thirteen miles. It was a day's march from the rear guard to the van. A Southern farmer who watched the human torrent passing his farm-house at a brisk trot noted that it took four hours to pass.

SHERIDAN AT WINCHESTER.

Skirmishing with the enemy began as soon as the Union lines were passed, but Sheridan would not permit his march to be delayed, and pressed on, fighting as he went. Late in the afternoon Custer's brigade, which was in the advance, trotted into Beaver Dam Station, on the Virginia Central railway. Two trains stood on the track. The locomotives had steam up ready to start. A crowd of gaping sight-seers, on the edges of which musket barrels glittered plentifully, showed that there was something unusual going on. Without delay the troopers made for the trains. The guards about them fled, leaving behind them their arms. As the men in blue came up around the cars, cheers came from within. It proved that the trains were laden with Union prisoners from the hard fought field of Spottsylvania—378 of them in all—many wounded; and all on their way to the prisons at Richmond. Loud were the cheers of the captives to whom this unexpected succor bringing liberty had come. To rouse the enthusiasm of the cavalrymen the episode was as good as a battle won. Before continuing on their way they set the torch to the trains and to neighboring store buildings that held 1,500,000 rations and a vast quantity of medical stores for Lee's army. By the light of the blazing buildings, detachments of Sheridan's force worked far into the night tearing up the railroad and wrecking the telegraph line.

By this time, however, the Confederate cavalry was hot upon the trail of the invaders. Stuart and his men, elated with the memory of a long series of victories over the Federal cavalry, were eagerly pursuing the blue-clad horsemen, who were manifesting an audacity which the Confederates had not learned to look for among the Union troopers. On the 12th of May—the same day that saw the desperate fighting around the "bloody angle" at Spottsylvania—the hostile bodies of horse clinched in furious combat at Yellow Tavern, only six miles from Richmond. Here Stuart, by able generalship and swift marching, had concentrated all his cavalry and proposed to make a determined stand upon Sheridan's pathway to the Confederate capital. But the battle was brief. The Confederates fought gallantly, but were beaten back. "The disparity of numbers between the opposing forces was very great, to judge from appearances," writes a private of the Sixth Virginia cavalry. "Our men seemed aware of their inferior strength, but were not dismayed. The enemy confidently pressed forward with exultant shouts, delivering tremendous volleys. The Confederates returned their fire with yells of defiance. Stuart, with pistol in hand, shot over the heads of the troops, while with words of cheer he encouraged them. He kept saying 'Steady, men, steady. Give it to them.' Presently he reeled in his saddle. His head was bowed and his hat fell off. He turned and said, as I drew nearer, 'Go and tell General Lee and Dr. Fontaine to come here.' I wheeled at once and went as fast as I could to do his bidding. . . . . When I returned, Stuart had been taken from his horse and was being carried by his men off the field. I saw him put in an ambulance and I followed it close behind. He lay without speaking as it went along, but kept shaking his head with an expression of the deepest disappointment."

The next day Stuart died in Richmond. "I am resigned. God's will be done," were his last words. He was one of the most picturesque and admirable figures among the many gallant men who fought for the "Lost Cause." Those who knew him have never wearied of telling of his lovable traits of character. "Jeb never says 'Go, boys,' but always 'Come, boys,'" was a common saying among his soldiers. Possessing Stonewall Jackson's devotion to duty, genius for discipline, and surpassing executive qualities, his nature was relieved by a sort of boyish gayety which added greatly to his popularity with his troops. He rode into battle with snatches of song upon his lips. Rash he was beyond doubt, fond of leading his command into perilous places, and prone to solitary midnight excursions into the enemy's lines. But under his gray coat there beat the heart of a born soldier. We know that his death was the one that he would have chosen for himself, for a Virginian who rode by his side night and day has told us that as early as 1862, Stuart said, "All that I ask of fate is that I may be killed leading a cavalry charge."

So it was that death came to him, and when the news went forth there were many in the Confederacy who might have said with General Lee when he heard of Stuart's death, "I can scarcely think of him without weeping."

But to return to Sheridan. The death of Stuart and the complete rout of the Confederate cavalry removed the only obstacle that intervened between him and the outworks of Richmond. But nature now took a hand in the defense of the Confederate capital. Rain fell heavily. The roads became miry and the little streams with which that section is plentifully intersected were transformed into torrents. The column continued its advance, but it was no time for rapid marching. The nights were of impenetrable blackness. "It was so dark that we could only follow the cavalry by putting a bugler on a white horse directly in rear of the regiment in front of us, with orders to move on as soon as they did," writes the captain of a battery of artillery that brought up the rear of the column. Once the bugler neglected to give the signal at the end of a long halt and the artillerists suddenly woke up to find themselves alone on a lonely road in the enemy's country. With whip and spur the teams were urged into a gallop and the heavy cannon lumbered along the dark road, now and then exploding a torpedo which the Confederates had planted in the path. At a cross road the battery was met by a man wearing the National uniform, who declared he had been left behind by Sheridan to guide the battery to the remainder of the column. Not until, after much threading of tortuous and muddy roads, the artillerymen of a sudden found themselves right under the guns of the Confederate earthworks, which quickly began to spout fire, did they suspect that they had fallen into the hands of a spy. The false guide paid the penalty of his treachery with his life, but as he had led the blue-coats into the trap none among them knew the way out again. The fire of the Confederates soon slackened, for the night was too dark for it to be effective, and the entrapped artillerymen were left to wonder whether daylight would bring them relief or destruction. Fortunately for them, however, Sheridan had heard the firing and returned. He arrived on the scene at daylight and discovered that his artillery had been caught within the outer line of the enemy's fortifications, and with the bridge that had carried it over a creek now torn up. But Sheridan laughed at all thought of danger. "Why, what do you suppose we have in front of us?" he said to the battery commander, "A lot of department clerks from Richmond, who have been forced into the ranks. I could capture Richmond if I wanted, but I can't hold it; and the prisoners tell me that every house in the suburbs is loopholed and the streets barricaded."

Sheridan did not misjudge the character of the troops that confronted him in the Richmond trenches. His coming had put the Confederate city in a panic. Soldiers there were none save the invalided veterans in the hospitals, and such of these as could handle a musket or wield a sponge-staff were first sent into the city's lines of defense. The governor issued a proclamation announcing that the enemy was at the gates and exhorting all to take up arms for the city's defense. The clerks in the government offices were given guns and led out to the trenches. White-haired men and slender striplings marched side by side in the ranks. Plenty of patriotism and high spirit was there, but a sad lack of the discipline and experience which make troops effective. The Confederate officials knew how weak were their defenders, and President Davis and his Cabinet made preparations for flight in case Sheridan should make a serious attempt to enter the city.

But for the reasons given the Union commander made no attempt to break through the feeble Confederate lines. He fought a sharp battle to extricate his artillery from the predicament into which treachery had led it. Then the command was "forward" and the column of horse took up its march again. Skirting round the city, the bank of the James River was reached at Haxall's Landing. Here General Butler's command was found and a fleet of Union gunboats. After a few days' stop the march was taken up again, and after an uneventful ride across the country the troopers rejoined the Army of the Potomac. "It (the cavalry) had deprived Lee's army for the time being of its eyes and ears," writes General Rodenbough, "damaged his communications, destroyed an immense quantity of supplies, killed the leader of his cavalry, saved to our government the subsistence of ten thousand horses and men for three weeks, perfected the *morale* of the cavalry corps, and produced a moral effect of incalculable benefit to the Union cause. Sheridan's casualties on the raid were 625 men killed or wounded and 300 horses."

Before taking up again the progress of the campaign of the Army of the Potomac, let us go back a little and consider the operations which the Tenth and Eighteenth Corps, under command of General Butler had carried on in co-operation with that army.

In April, 1864, there was gathered at Fortress Monroe an army of some 38,000 men. Many were new recruits. More still were troops drawn from the various forts and posts which the United States had been holding along the Atlantic coast. A great number came from Charleston harbor, where the siege of Fort Sumter and the city had been so long and pertinaciously maintained. With the latter troops came their commander, General Gillmore, who, when he found his regiments were to be taken for active service, wrote to General Grant begging to be allowed to accompany them.

This large body of troops was known collectively as the Army of the James. It was in command of General Butler, who had earned prominence earlier in the war by taking possession of New Orleans after the forts which defended that city had been silenced by Farragut's fleet. Butler had so disposed of his troops as to keep the Confederates continually puzzled as to the direction from which the blow that he was obviously preparing to strike should fall. Part of Butler's troops were at Yorktown, on the path of McClellan's famous Peninsular route to Richmond. The presence of those troops made the Confederates fear that their capital was again to be threatened by the Peninsula, but the fact that the main body of the Federals remained at Fortress Monroe made it still possible for the Union advance to be up the James River to Richmond, or by way of the York River to a junction with the Army of the Potomac. Not all the astuteness of the Confederate spies, whos warmed within Butler's lines, could determine which of these three plans of campaign was to be adopted by the Army of the James.

The solution of the problem came in due time, but it came in the shape of a movement so sudden and expeditious that the Confederates were unable to make any attempt to oppose it. On the 5th of May great fleets of transports lay at anchor in the roadstead off Yorktown and Newport News. On shore all was stirring; the soldiers were breaking camp preparatory to a movement into the heart of the enemy's country. Tents were struck and packed. The ammunition wagons were loaded. Haversacks and knapsacks were overhauled. Officer's servants were rushing round looking for transportation for their masters' baggage. Every now and then the voice of the drum and fife rose above the general din as some transport drew up at the wharf and regiment after regiment marched with brisk step and flying colors through the wrecked camp down to the boat. The troops that had been encamped higher up the Peninsula were already embarked, and the soldiers watched from the decks of their vessels the embarkation of their brothers in arms. Presently the last vessel pushed off from shore. A signal was set at the peak of the general's ship, and soon the prows of the whole fleet were turned up the James River. Then a mighty cry of "On to Richmond" rose from the throats of forty thousand soldiers, for all knew then that they were going to the Confederate capital by the most direct route.

It was an imposing flotilla that spread out over the waters of the broad estuary of the James that bright May day. Five armored vessels were there, one of them a double turreted monitor, sent by the navy to give safe convoy to this grand military expedition. But, saving the men-of-war only, the fleet was a motley collection of worn-out craft. River steamers with their flimsy cabins towering high in air, side-wheel coasting vessels that had been impressed from the routes of marine trade to serve the ends of war, ferry-boats from New York, Philadelphia, and Baltimore, tugs with long trains of canal-boats and barges following in their wake, schooners and sloops, all loaded to the water line with blue-clad soldiery made up this odd armada. General Butler had improvised for himself a sort of volunteer navy, made up of army recruits who had had some nautical experience. A few merchant steamers he had remodeled for gunboats, and put the flotilla under the command of General Graham, an ex-officer of the navy. These vessels took the lead, and as no hostile force was met the whole procession moved in stately fashion up the broad channel of the James to the designated landing point.

Some twenty miles below Richmond the river Appomattox enters the James, which a few miles higher makes a sudden bend and flows in a course parallel to that of its tributary. Between the James and the Appomattox, therefore, there was a neck of land, shaped not unlike a bottle with the point at which the cork should enter, the only part not shut in by running water.

Upon this neck of land Butler's troops were landed and they lost no time in marching to the neck of the bottle and there throwing up breastworks that extended from river to river. Three miles in front of the works ran the railroad between Richmond and Petersburg. This was the great channel through which the Confederate authorities at Richmond drew supplies and re-enforcements from the South. At Petersburg—only eight miles from Butler's line—the road branched in three directions. Over this road at the very moment that Butler was debarking at Bermuda Hundred, Confederate troops by thousands were being drawn to Petersburg. Just before Butler's troops took the field, the feebleness of the Union force at Newberne had tempted General Beauregard to send an expedition to capture that place, which had been in National hands since the first year of the war. But the news of the Butler expedition speedily checked this enterprise, and the troops were sent post-haste to Petersburg, which was too important a railway junction to be sacrificed. Notwithstanding the celerity of their movements, however, the Confederates narrowly escaped being shut out of Petersburg, for a cavalry column sent by Butler from Suffolk, near the mouth of the James, to cut this railroad, reached the lines just after the detachment of Beauregard's troops had passed. Had the cavalrymen been in greater force they might still have accomplished their purpose, but their strength was not sufficient to make it practicable for them to hold the railroad, and they had to burn a bridge or two and retreat. This delayed the movement of the Confederates but a little space, and long before Butler was ready to attack Petersburg in force the town was filled with veterans in gray. We shall see in a later chapter how hard it was for the combined commands of Meade and Butler to drive the enemy from that point of vantage he had so easily won.

Having landed his troops and intrenched his camp, General Butler seemed to have exhausted his energy. It was a moment for promptitude, for immediate offensive operations. The enemy was outnumbered six to one on the day that the Army of the James landed. Every day that now passed without an assault in force was of incalculable benefit to Beauregard, who was gathering troops from all parts of the South and pouring them into Petersburg and Richmond.

When the first blow was struck, it was not Butler who dealt it. On the 15th of May the Union army, which had left its intrenchments in the "bottle" some days before, was arrayed before the Confederate works at Drury's bluff. Its presence there gave great uneasiness to the people of Richmond, who were now beleaguered by two hostile armies, so near that the guns of both could be heard in the streets of the city. General Beauregard had been hastily called from his post at Charleston to undertake the defense of the Confederate capital. President Davis and members of his Cabinet made more than one visit to the earthworks uopn which, with their regiments of gallant soldiers, the people of Richmond relied for protection against the Yankees.

When Butler's movements seemed to indicate that he was about to attack, Beauregard determined to forestall him by leaving his trenches and himself taking the offensive. This he could now do with some chance of success, for Butler's deliberation had given the Confederate general time to replenish his army so that he was now as strong as his adversary. A

CONTRABANDS IN SHERMAN'S WAKE.

reconnoissance made by the Confederates on the night of the 15th hastened their action. They found that the right flank of Butler's line rested, as the military phrase has it, "in the air." A mile of open country intervened between it and the river. A detachment of 150 negro cavalrymen was the sole continuation of the line through this unprotected territory. Beauregard at once issued orders for an attack which should turn and crush this flank, held by General W. F. Smith. He also sent directions to General Whiting at Petersburg to move from the Richmond road and cut off the Union line of retreat to Bermuda Hundred.

The attack was set for the dark hours just before the dawn. The Federals, fearing no activity on the part of their foes, were sleeping heavily. Only the very slightest redoubts of rails and earth protected them. They had expected to fight an offensive battle, and had paid but scant attention to intrenching. General Smith, however, ordered one form of defensive work that proved most effective. His men were sent out along the turnpike that joined Petersburg and Richmond to strip the telegraph line of its wire. Over a mile of this was brought in, and was then interlaced among the stumps and trees before the lines of Brooks's division and part of Weitzel's. Unluckily for the Federals, there was not enough of the wire to set snares for the Confederates all along the line.

A heavy fog settled down upon the earth as the time for the Confederate attack drew near, making the natural darkness of the hour still blacker. When General Smith went out to his picket line at midnight to see that all was well, the moon was shining brightly. Three hours later he was awakened by shots and cries in which the familiar yell of the Confederates rose with such distinctness as to instantly convince the general that his position was being attacked by no small force. Running to the door of his headquarters he found himself in impenetrable darkness. Orderlies were sent away in different directions as fast as they could make their way through the night; one with a message to Gillmore to make an attack in his front, another ordering up the two regiments held in reserve, and a third with orders to the artillerymen to withdraw from the front. The latter message was not delivered, for its bearer was killed before he had discharged his mission, and five of the guns which he had been dispatched to save fell into the hands of the enemy.

Meanwhile the battle was raging furiously. Out of the pitchy blackness of the night and the fog came seven brigades, and fell fiercely upon the three and a half brigades with which Smith was trying to hold a long and difficult line. Heckman received the first shock and was swept away in an instant. The general himself was captured. "As our men pressed forward firing," writes a Confederate artilleryman, "a fine looking man, dressed in a blue coat and high black hat of a Federal officer, was observed mixed up with our troops, shouting at the top of his voice, 'Go in boys! Give 'em h—l!' One of Gracie's men stopped, carefully surveyed the stranger, and said, 'Look hyer, Mister, those clothes don't go well with this crowd. You come along with me. That hat's a beauty. Let's swap.' The prisoner was General Heckman."

Pushing Heckman's brigade before them, the Confederates pressed on through the woods. Victory seemed wholly within their grasp. Smith's right flank was shattered and it seemed as though the victors would soon swing around and take his line in reverse. But at this juncture the two Union regiments that had been held in reserve came up and went spiritedly into action. It was too dark for them to discover the overwhelming force of their antagonists, and they went into the fight with a determination and confidence which might have been lacking had they known how greatly they were outnumbered. The Confederates, for their part, were mystified by this unexpected resistance. Had they been able to discern that there were but two regiments before them they would have crushed them by weight of numbers; but as it was, they became cautious, and for a time the fighting flagged.

The Confederates had not been able to carry all before them at all points on the Union line. Before that part of Weitzel's command which was protected by the network of wire they recoiled sorely shattered. "It was a devilish contrivance, which none but a Yankee could devise," said a Richmond paper of the wire afterward. Rushing onward through the fog, paying little heed to the path over which they were treading, with their eyes fixed upon the Union works, and with no thought in their minds save to carry those works with all possible speed, the assailants fell an easy prey to the snare set for them. The foremost of the line fell headlong over the wires. Those following seeing this, and finding themselves caught about the feet and ankles, hesitated a little. The advance was checked, and on the waving, irresolute line that stood there the Union infantry poured volley after volley at short range so that the gray-clad dead soon lay in heaps above the tangled wires. Nor though they returned again to the charge could the Confederates break through Weitzel's line.

The battle had now raged for some hours. The result of the fighting, though not wholly favorable, was yet in the main satisfactory to Beauregard. His plan of battle was progressing well. The Federal right had been crushed, and he had but to pour more troops into the crater of flaming guns and struggling men to carry all before him. But one detail of the attack was still lacking. Where was Whiting? His duty it was to fall with impetuosity upon the rear of the Federals and cut off their retreat to Bermuda Hundred. His guns should already have been heard, but General Beauregard and Jefferson Davis, who had come down to witness the battle, had long been straining their ears in vain to catch the welcome sound. Aides were sent to Whiting with peremptory commands for him to hasten into action, but still he gave no sign. In their eagerness to catch the first sounds which should tell that Whiting had come, the Confederate President and General pressed forward until they were in range and sight of the Union artillery. A solid shot that cut into the turf before their feet warned them that that was no place for the chief executive of a nation. At last the dull boom of a cannon came floating through the air from the quarter in which Whiting should have been.

"Ah!" said Mr. Davis, "at last!" and a smile spread over his face as in imagination he saw the Union army flanked, taken in the rear, and cut to pieces. But it was a delusive hope. Whiting did not appear, and the victory at Drury's Bluff was won without him.

For a victory it was for the Confederates, though not so sweeping a one as Beauregard had hoped. All day long the tide of battle ebbed and flowed in surges of blood. Strenuously the Federals strove to hold their ground, but fate and the irresistible workings of the rules of strategy were against them. Beauregard had found the weak place in their lines and had massed his troops in the attack at that point. Before sundown Butler had yielded to the inevitable and was in full retreat upon Bermuda Hundred.

"Beauregard's original plan contemplated the aid of a division from Petersburg," writes General Smith. "What changes that might have made in the result had it come on the field opportunely it is not pleasant to contemplate."

But the result as it was was sufficiently disheartening to the Union soldiers. Dead on the field of battle were 390 officers and men. The wounded numbered 1721 and the missing 1390. Five guns and five stands of colors were left in the enemy's hands. The total Confederate loss was 2184.

Beauregard followed fast upon the heels of his antagonist. Butler sought his intrenchments, whereupon the Confederates threw up a line of works confronting him with the flanks resting upon the two rivers. Having a line shorter than the Federal line they effectually prevented Butler from again taking the field. In short they inserted the cork in the famous "bottle," and there Butler remained inactive, until the greater part of his army had been sent away in small detachments to re-enforce the army of the Potomac in its struggle with Lee. It was an inglorious ending to the campaign which had opened with such bright prospect of success.

CHAPTER VI.

GRANT MOVES AGAIN—LEE FOLLOWS—BATTLE ON THE NORTH ANNA—BURNSIDE'S REPULSE—HANCOCK CROSSES THE RIVER—LEE'S STRONG POSITION—ILLNESS OF THE CONFEDERATE GENERAL—STARVATION IN LEE'S RANKS—THE BATTLES AT COLD HARBOR—CUSTER'S MEN IN ACTION—SHERIDAN'S DEFENSE—HANCOCK'S ATTACK—HEAVY LOSSES OF THE ARMY OF THE POTOMAC—GRANT NOT DISCOURAGED.

WE left the two great armies—the chief champions in the fight for and against national unity—confronting each other on the lines at Spottsylvania. There they remained for several days. Each was sorely smitten. Neither was beaten. Neither Federal nor Confederate was dismayed. With vigilant eyes each watched the other's movements, and with cool heads and industrious hands they prepared for the decisive struggle which all knew could not be delayed long.

Grant did not wish to attack Lee again in his breastworks. The immense numerical preponderance of the Union army would be robbed of half of its efficiency if the enemy were permitted to fight behind defensive works. The one advantage gained by the Federals in the bloody fighting at Spottsylvania was the capture of the salient, and this was scarcely an equivalent for the lives lost in storming it, as the Confederates had a second line of works in the rear to which they retired and from which they could not be driven. How to lure them from these works was the problem to the solution of which Grant now devoted his energies.

After studying the problem for some time Grant determined to send one army corps around Lee's right flank toward Richmond. This, he thought, would tempt Lee to leave his works and follow this isolated corps in the hope of crushing it before the remainder of the Union army could come to its assistance. Should Lee take the bait, the rest of Grant's army, which was ready to march on the instant, would follow and fall upon him before he could intrench.

Hancock's corps was chosen to make the movement. Before it moved out from the Union lines at Spottsylvania every possible step was taken to put the whole army in light marching order, so that rapid time might be made upon the road. Over one hundred pieces of artillery, with the caissons and teams, were sent back to Washington. Every wagon and ambulance that could possibly be dispensed with was detached from the army. Eight thousand prisoners were sent to the rear. The field hospitals were disencumbered of twenty thousand sick and wounded men. Heavy re-enforcements, both of veterans and of new recruits, joined the Army of the Potomac, which was thus put in even better condition than it had been in when it first plunged into the gloomy recesses of the Wilderness.

At midnight of the 20th of May Hancock began his march. His route lay to the eastward along roads necessarily tortuous, because only such were chosen as would lead him around the enemy's flank without coming into collision with the gray-clad soldiery. But near Milford a column of troops was met coming from Richmond. The cavalry scouts in the van came galloping in with the alarm. The skirmishers go to the front on a run, and the crackle of the fusillade wakes the echoes of the silent woods, while the artillery gallops across fields to every open spot where a battery can be planted. The roar of battle continues for a time, then dies away. The Confederates have been put to flight, leaving several hundred prisoners in Hancock's hands. It was Pickett's celebrated division of Virginians—the same that made the fierce charge up Cemetery Hill on the last day at Gettysburg—marching to re-enforce Lee.

In the mean time the Confederate commander declined to walk into the trap Grant had set for him. He neither set out in chase of Hancock nor did he sit supinely in his trenches and allow that general to get in his rear. Instead of adopting either course he put his army on the march for a point on the North Anna River which he could easily reach in time to throw up earth-works and once again bar the pathway of the Union army toward Richmond. The more direct routes were at his service, and the knowledge of the topography of the country which his men possessed made this an easy task. The point at which the Federals would have to cross the North Anna River was chosen by Lee as the place at which to make a stand. Here he took up a strong position. His line and the river were like two semicircles, touching each other at one point and then curving away from each other. An enemy trying to assault the Confederates all along their lines would have his own line parted in two places by the river, and would have to cross that stream twice if he desired to re-enforce one of his wings with troops drawn from the other. An assault at the point at which the Confederate line touched the river seemed to promise better for the Federals, and such an assault Burnside was ordered to make.

The North Anna River, at the spot where Lee's lines touched it, was broad and shallow. Its clear waters rippled over a pebbly bottom. "Ox Ford" the spot was called. The ford long used in the pursuit of the ends of peace was now made to serve the purposes of war. Under cover of a sharp artillery fire, which flashed from a half a dozen batteries stationed on the north side of the river, Burnside's men advanced across the fields and through the thicket of trees and shrubs that fringed the edge of the stream. The men in the trenches were vigilant. "Here they come," was the cry. The word of alarm passed up and down the Confederate lines. The cannon were roaring, and the dull yellow smoke of the exploded gunpowder hung heavily over the earthworks. Flying round shot and shells cut through the thickets and mowed down men unseen by the gunners. Canister, grape, and musket balls lashed the surface of the placid little river into foam. It did not take long for Burnside to discover that to cross the river and to carry earthworks held by the veterans of the Army of Northern Virginia was a task beyond his power.

At other points, however, the Federals had effected a crossing. Hancock had crossed at Chesterfield Bridge. Before gaining the bridge he had to drive a detachment of Confederates from their trenches on the north side of the river. How they came to be posted there is inexplicable. They were cut off from all communication with the rest of Lee's army, and seemingly were not a part of his line of defense. But they held their ground well, and pluckily fought their two cannon, upon which was concontrated the fire of five Union batteries. But the defenders were fighting a hopeless fight. "Hancock sent two brigades, Eagan's and Pierce's, to the right and left," says General Grant, "and when properly disposed they charged simultaneously. The bridge was carried quickly, the enemy retreating over it so hastily that many were shoved into the river and some were drowned. Several hundred prisoners were captured."

Warren's division crossed the river at Jericho Ford, on the Confederate left flank. Holding their guns, cartridge-boxes, and haversacks high above their heads, the men waded through water up to their waists while sharpshooters hid in the thickness poured upon them a most galling fire. Such service as this is a great strain upon a soldier's nerves. To be made the target for sharp-shooters, with no means of defending himself and without the excitement of a charge or a pitched battle to buoy him up, is very trying. But Warren's men bore themselves well. The river was crossed and the skirmishers, deploying in the woods, drove off the marksmen who had been so active. Then a pontoon bridge was laid on which the rest of the corps crossed. There was no resistance offered to the crossing, but toward nightfall, just as the wearied Union soldiers were gathering about their camp-fires, to gulp down the hot black coffee and fried bacon that formed their supper, shots rang out on the picket-line, the drums beat the long roll and all sprang to arms. Hill's troops had left their trenches to fall upon Cutler. There was sharp fighting in the few hours of daylight still left, but the Confederates finally retired to their earthworks, none the better off for their attack. Then Cutler's men caught up their picks and shovels and soon had a line of works behind which they could rest in security.

Grant now had placed the two wings of his army on the south side of the North Anna, while his center was still unable to force a passage. His position was a peculiar one. He had, so to speak, driven his army upon a wedge which had split it in twain. Lee's V-shaped lines separated his right wing from his left. The apex of the V, the point which military science would designate for an attack, was covered by the river. "To make a direct attack from either wing would cause a slaughter of our men that even success would not justify," wrote Grant, in the letter in which he announced to Halleck his determination to abandon all idea of offering battle on the North Anna and to once again move by the left flank around Lee's army.

In the course of this letter General Grant expressed his astonishment that Lee had not attacked either wing of his army when it was split up by the North Anna River. This seemed to Grant so glaring a fault upon the part of the Confederate commander that he could only explain it upon the theory that the enemy was already beaten. "Lee's army is really whipped," he wrote. "The prisoners we have taken show it, and the action of his army shows it unmistakably. A battle with them outside of intrenchments cannot be had."

The record of the ensuing twelve months of desperate fighting shows that Grant was seriously mistaken in his estimate of his antagonist's weakness. Many reasons are given for Lee's failure to take the offensive at this moment. Some capable strategists hold that the Confederate general chose the part of wisdom in not attacking either of Grant's wings, because each was so strongly intrenched as to more than make up for any advantage in numbers that the assailants might possess.

No doubt the fact that General Lee was suffering from severe illness while the two armies were upon the banks of the North Anna had something to do with his apparent inactivity. A commander in his tent is never the equal of a general who mingles in the thickest of the fray. Lee was never content to judge of the progress of a battle which he was directing from reports brought to him at headquarters. His martial figure and his good gray horse were always to be seen well up toward the front, and we have noted that on two occasions, at least, only the protests of his soldiers kept him from leading a charge in person.

There is ample evidence to show that Lee intended to strike Grant a heavy blow at the North Anna. "As he lay in his tent," writes Colonel Venable, writing of his great chief's hours of illness, "he would say in his impatience, 'We must strike them! We must never let them pass us again! We must strike them!' He had reports brought to him constantly from the field, but Lee in his tent was not Lee at the front."

Perhaps, too, the sorry condition of the Confederates, so far as food and clothing were concerned, had something to do with Lee's failure to attack. Starvation had become something very real to the luckless veterans in gray. The incompetence of the commissary department was becoming more obvious daily. We have the testimony of a sergeant-major in a Virginia battery that the command marched continuously, day and night, for fifty hours, without food, and that the meal which preceded this prolonged physical strain consisted of three biscuits and one small slice of bacon to each man, while the feast upon which they broke their prolonged fast consisted of just one cracker apiece, without any meat at all. That men could fight upon such a starveling diet seems incredible.

Nevertheless, they did fight, and fought so well that once again General Grant was obliged to abandon his efforts to drive them from their trenches. Putting his army in motion, again by the left flank, he moved away from the North Anna. He had fought no pitched battle there, but the futile attacks upon the enemy's lines and the constant skirmishing that had attended his march from Spottsylvania had cost the Union army about 2000 men—a loss which was about equaled by that of the Confederates.

The next clash of the hostile armies was destined to occur upon ground already historic in the annals of the war. After the usual march by narrow, muddy country roads, with the Confederate cavalry hanging on to the

LEE AFTER THE SURRENDER.

flanks and rear, and every now and then some light battery on a distant hill-top pitching shells into their ranks, the Federals at last reached the point at which they must turn their faces toward Richmond. But there, as at the North Anna and at Spottsylvania, Lee's army barred the way, cool and confident, behind heavy breastworks which had been thrown up while Grant was still upon the march. Behind the earthworks the roofs of Richmond might almost be seen. The sound of the city's bells floated faintly across the intervening forests, and each peal stirred the Southern soldiers to renewed determination and new deeds of daring. They were fighting in defense of their homes now. To them the blue-clad regiments of the Army of the Potomac were invaders, aliens treading upon the soil of Old Virginia—most dearly beloved of all of the States of the South. The Confederate right flank rested upon the Chickahominy River, that stream the sudden rise of which in May of 1862 had so nearly accomplished the complete destruction of the Army of the Potomac. In front of their lines was the little hamlet of Cold Harbor, where McClellan had pitched his headquarters tent two years before, almost to a day. There were veterans in both armies who remembered the incidents of that earlier battle upon this same ground. To the Confederates the remembrance was full of encouragement. It was a recollection of triumph. In Grant's army the thought that another battle was to be fought upon the battle-field of Cold Harbor was not cheering. The veterans of the Army of the Potomac remembered well that McClellan had brought the army to this very spot with but trifling loss, while this new leader who had come out of the West had sacrificed thousands of men to gain no more desirable a position. They knew, too, that the battle that was about to be fought upon this historic field would be fierce and bloody. There could be no more assaulting of breastworks and then moving away by the left flank. The time for flank movements was past. Richmond lay before the Army of the Potomac. Any movement save one directly to the front would be a step away from the Confederate capital. But the pickets could see, out across the clearings before the woods in which they were lurking, the Confederate works—log walls, faced with earth and guarded in front by abatis and slashings, extending far to right and left over hill and valley like a monster serpent. Those who surveyed that scene knew that the task of dislodging the Confederates would be no easy one.

The fighting in the woods and fields around Cold Harbor continued several days. It was begun by Sheridan's cavalry, that led the van of the Federal column in its flanking march from the bank of the North Anna. When about to ford a little creek that flowed across the road along which his column was advancing, Sheridan was saluted by a volley of musketry from a thicket on the further side. A line of skirmishers thrown forward discovered that the troopers of Butler's Confederate cavalry were dismounted and fighting behind strong earthworks. Sheridan brought his guns into action, and dismounting his men sent them into the forest to turn the flank of the enemy. The fight was fierce and long. The Confederates were well intrenched and held their ground manfully. At last Custer's brigade was ordered into action. The troopers dismounted, and armed with their short carbines swept grandly toward the front in columns of platoons. A brass band, playing patriotic airs, marched with them. With a grand rush the Confederate breastworks were carried and a number of their defenders captured. The survivors fled to Cold Harbor, where a larger Confederate force was busily plying the shovel, ax, and pick in building redoubts. The Union cavalry followed fast on the heels of the fugitives and carried the works in which they had taken refuge. Sheridan reported his success to headquarters, but soon determined that he could not hold the position he had won, as the enemy were massing troops in evident preparation for an assault. But just as he was putting his column in motion a courier came galloping with an order from headquarters to " hold Cold Harbor at all hazards." Wearily the troopers returned to the rifle-pits. They had been on duty for eighteen consecutive hours—marching, fighting, and marching again. There was grumbling in plenty as the cavalrymen began their bivouac in the trenches with the certainty of an attack at early dawn before them, but there was but one thought—to hold their ground against any and all odds until the assistance which they knew must be on the road could reach them.

Scarcely had the eastern sky begun to flush with the coming of the sun before the bullets of the Confederate sharp-shooters began humming like bumble bees through the air. The men in the trenches were ready and picked up their arms with alacrity. All night they had been working reversing the redoubts, which had been built by the Confederates to face the other way. By the side of each man was a little pile of cartridges, all ready, that he might load and fire with the greater rapidity. The center of the Union line was held by a New York regiment that was armed with repeating rifles, firing seven shots without reloading—a novelty then and very effective in repelling a charge. Twice the Confederates advanced boldly to the assault. "Hold your fire until they are close upon us," was the order passed along the Union line. Save for the Confederate cheers, there was perfect silence as the gray ranks swept forward to the assault. But when they came within point-blank range of the Union works there was a crash of musketry and the redoubt was hidden in yellow smoke. Cries of agony arose from the ranks of assailants. The charge was checked for a time, and when those unhurt rallied and continued their advance, the repeating rifles in the Union center poured in their rapid and deadly volleys. Though the Confederate loss was heavy their numbers were large and their determination to drive Sheridan from his position indomitable. For four hours the battle raged, but at nine o'clock the head of the column of the Sixth Corps, which had been marching all night, appeared upon the scene, and the hard pressed cavalrymen were relieved. The position at Cold Harbor was thus secured.

Meantime both armies were moving with all possible speed toward Cold Harbor. The hostile lines were now so close together that neither commander could long conceal his intentions from the other, and Grant's every move was met by a counter-move by Lee. There was skirmishing and hard fighting at several points. Two little country churches, Shady Grove and Bethesda, set down in the midst of the forests, were given a fame widely different in its nature from the doctrine of "peace on earth, good will to men" which they represented. Into the details of the almost constant fighting which was attendant upon the transfer of the armies from the banks of the North Anna to the region about Cold Harbor it is unnecessary to enter. Though the total loss was considerable, the skirmishing at no time and at no place rose to the dignity of a battle.

The line which the Army of Northern Virginia took up at Cold Harbor for the protection of Richmond was from three to six miles from the outermost point of the cordon of defensive works that surrounded that city. Between it and the Confederate capital flowed the Chickahominy, now fordable at every point. The left flank of Lee's army rested upon this stream, while the right was enveloped in the densely wooded morasses about the head-waters of several small creeks. In this position the men who had so long baffled every effort of the great and magnificently equipped Army of the Potomac awaited with confidence the coming assault of their enemy.

The first attack was made on the evening of the 2nd of June by the Sixth and the Eighteenth army corps. The latter organization had been withdrawn from the "bottle" at Bermuda Hundred, where it had been useless, and brought to aid the Army of the Potomac. Its march had been long and painful, over glaring, dusty roads, and under a burning sun. By a mistake in the orders it had been sent several miles out of the way, and when it finally, after retracing its steps, arrived at the point on the Union line reserved for it, the men were utterly worn out with their march of over twenty-five miles.

Before the Union army, now arrayed for battle, there extended a clearing for the space of from 300 to 1200 yards. At its further side was a patch of woods, on the edge of which was a line of earthworks held by the enemy. A second redoubt farther to the rear offered a place of retreat for the Confederates, should they be driven from their advance line. The soldiers of Hoke and Anderson held these works and were prepared for the impending assault.

It was six o'clock in the afternoon of June 1 when the men of the Sixth and Eighteenth corps emerged from the woods and began to traverse the field that lay in front of the enemy's position. From the woods in front of them there burst a terrific fire. Bullets hummed angrily through the air. Shells burst above the heads of the attacking troops and solid shot plowed through their ranks. The level clearing over which they had passed was dotted thickly with fallen men. There was little straggling. General Smith says that he met one sergeant of artillery making his way to the rear.

"Where are you going, my man?" asked the General.

"Back to the hill to rally," replied the fugitive, with an approved military salute. But he was not a fair type of the men who made up that long, waving line of blue, that with colors flying and guns flashing was sturdily breasting the storm of missiles and drawing nearer and nearer to the edge of the woods in which the Confederate guns were flashing. At one point only was the Union advance checked. So murderous was the fire that swept through the ranks of Russell's division that to attempt to stem it was madness, and the men were ordered to throw themselves upon the ground for safety. But everywhere else victory rewarded the efforts of the men in blue; they crossed the field, entered the woods, swarmed over the breastworks, and forced the defenders to fly, leaving several hundred prisoners behind. The second line of breastworks, however, received the fugitives and there they rallied, turning upon their pursuers so fierce a fire that the Federals were glad to retire and avail themselves of the shelter of the works they had first carried. There they maintained themselves, although the Confederates made several determined attempts to recapture the position. It had cost the Federals 2000 men to win this slight advantage. Courage and human life were the cheapest things in the Army of the Potomac in the days of the overland campaign to Richmond.

While the Sixth and the Eighteenth corps were thus driving the Confederates, the latter, in their turn, at another part of the field, had taken the offensive. They made repeated attacks upon Warren's front, but were cut to pieces and driven back by murderous discharges of canister, which plowed deep furrows in their ranks. Not all the courage of those battle-scarred veterans, re-enforced by the appeals of their officers, sufficed to plant the Stars and Bars upon the works over which the Stars and Stripes floated so grandly.

By this time the long summer evening was drawing to a close. The sun had set, and the shadows were lighted up fiercely by the flashes of the cannon and the musketry. Gradually the noise of the battle died away. The thunderous roar of the artillery was hushed. The crack of rifles and muskets continued a little longer, but as the night grew darker it too was stilled. The chirping of crickets and the cries of night birds took the place of the harsh sounds of war. The day had been sultry. The soldiers, fagged out by the prolonged nervous strain, wearied by the heat and their exertions, begrimed with dust and gunpowder, threw themselves upon the ground to get a little rest. In the Union ranks it was known that the assault was to be renewed with redoubled energy on the morrow.

During the night some difficulties that delayed the proper disposition of his troops led General Grant to defer the attack until evening. All day the air rung with the explosions of great and small guns. The smell of burning powder was everywhere. All along the lines the pickets, sharp-shooters, and skirmishers were engaged. General Grant says that by this time the noise of firing had become so familiar to his ears that it attracted his attention no more than the sound of footsteps on a busy street arouses the attention of one who lives in it. There was no pitched battle during this day, nothing but a constant interchange of bullets between the lines. All day there was shifting of bodies of troops from one part of the line to another, and great clouds of dust rose high in the air—tell-tale witnesses of the progress of the marching columns. Toward evening a shower came up from the west. The glare of the lightning and the crash of the thunder—heaven's artillery—dwarfed the noise of the firing. The rain fell in sheets, drenching the soldiers, who were wholly without shelter,

A general assault was ordered for the next morning. It was at best a desperate maneuver. The result showed it to be disastrous. But there were reasons other than purely military that led Grant to order the attack. If, after the arduous marching and fighting through the wilderness region he should now turn aside from the very gates of Richmond, the whole country would think that another incompetent or over-cautious commander had been added to the already long list of generals who had failed to lead the Army of the Potomac to victory.

The day of the assault dawned moist and warm. Heavy mists hung over the ground. The soil was wet and spongy. Moisture dropped from the trees and clung to the undergrowth through which the soldiers had to pass. The Federals had been making ready for the assault most of the night. An early breakfast was served out to them—men do not fight well upon empty stomachs. The Confederates, too, were alert. In some inexplicable way tidings of an impending assault always leak out. One of Lee's generals says of this attack, "I was as well satisfied that it would come at dawn as if I had seen General Meade's order directing it."

General Grant's plan of battle contemplated an attack upon the Confederate right and center. The troops of Hancock, Smith, and Wright were to be engaged. The ground over which they had to pass was rugged, cut up by ravines, and thickly spotted with morasses. Dense copses still further impeded the advance of the attacking force, while the enemy had slashed the trees in their front until the way to their intrenchments became almost impassable.

Promptly at the hour set in Grant's order, an artilleryman in the Tenth Massachusetts Battery pulled a lock-string and the report of a signal gun boomed out upon the air. At once the Union lines were put in motion, and, as they appeared emerging from the forest, the Confederates' works blazed with the fires of countless rifles and cannon. There was but little shooting from the ranks of the attacking troops, but the Union artillery in the rear was in full cry, throwing its shells over the heads of the assailants to fall and burst within the enemy's lines.

Hancock's corps was on the extreme left of the Union line. Barlow, Gibbon, and Birney were his division commanders. The two former led the attack, the latter supporting them. Barlow's men advanced in two deployed lines. Their courage and pertinacity were admirable. Struggling through the brushwood, over the rugged ground, and plunging through the morasses, they swept onward in the teeth of a destructive fire. As they came up to the enemy's line, they found the Confederates strongly posted in a sunken road just without their breastworks. The advance was checked for a moment. Heavy volleys were exchanged. But though the Confederates fought hard to hold their ground, the valor and determination of Barlow's troops could not be withstood. Irresistibly they poured over the crest of the works. Most of the defenders fled. Those who strove to prolong the struggle were shot down or captured—several hundred prisoners being thus taken. The captured cannon were turned on their former owners and the gray-coats fairly driven away from this part of their line. Here, then, was a notable success. Lee's line was fairly pierced. Had there been other troops ready to rush into the gap thus opened, the Army of Northern Virginia might have been cut in two. But Barlow's success was not followed up. His own second line failed to come to the assistance of the first. The Confederates, alive to their peril, rushed to drive away the blue-coats who had made a lodgment in their lines. Cannon were run into positions from which they could pour an enfilading fire upon Barlow's troops. Assaulted fiercely in front and on their flanks, with grape and canister tearing through their ranks, the Federals were forced to relinquish the advantage they had won. Slowly and unwillingly they abandoned the captured works and retreated to a spot where a slight rise in the ground afforded them a little shelter. There they halted and maintained themselves against all the assaults of the enemy, digging shallow rifle-pits with their bayonets, tin cups, and canteens, which, split in half, made convenient scoops.

Meanwhile Gibbon, who went into action on the right of Barlow, had fared even worse. The ground over which he had to advance was wellnigh impassable. One vast morass—a lake of thick, tenacious mud—covered all his front. His men struggled bravely to extricate themselves from the bog, while the missiles of the enemy did frightful execution in their ranks. Officers and men fell thick and fast, and though some forced their way through the mire and rushed upon the enemy's works, it was but a small remnant—a pitiful handful easily repulsed.

"One officer alone," writes General McMahon, "the colonel of the 164th New York (Colonel James P. McMahon), seizing the colors of his regiment from the dying color-bearer as he fell, succeeded in reaching the parapet of the enemy's main works, where he planted his colors and fell dead near the ditch, bleeding from many wounds. Seven other colonels of Hancock's command died within those few minutes. No troops could stand against such a fire, and the order to lie down was given all along the line."

No greater success was won by either of the other corps commanders. Everywhere the strength of the Confederate position bade defiance to its assailants. Everywhere the men of the North fell thick and fast before the well-directed fire of troops lodged behind ponderous breastworks.

"Our troops were under arms and waiting," writes General Law, whose command was posted on the right of the Confederate center, " when with the misty light of early morning the scattering fire of our pickets, who now occupied the abandoned works in the angle, announced the beginning of the attack. As the assaulting column swept over the old works, a loud cheer was given, and it rushed on into the marshy ground in the angle. Its front covered little more than the line of my own brigade of less than a thousand men; but line followed line until the space inclosed by the old salient became a mass of writhing humanity, upon which our artillery and musketry played with cruel effect. I had taken position on the slope in rear of the line, and was carefully noting the firing of the men, which soon became so heavy that I feared they would exhaust the cartridges in their boxes before the attack ceased. Sending an order for a supply of ammunition to be brought into the lines, I went down to the trenches to regulate the firing. On my way I met a man belonging to the Fifteenth Alabama regiment of my brigade, running to the rear through the storm of bullets that swept the hill. He had left his hat behind in his retreat, was crying like a big baby, and was the bloodiest man I had ever seen. 'Oh, General,' he blubbered out, ' I am dead! I am killed! Look at this!" showing his wound. Finding it was only a flesh wound, I told him to go on; he was not hurt. He looked at me doubtfully for a second, as if questioning my veracity or my surgical knowledge, I don't know which; then, as if satisfied with my diagnosis, he broke into a broad laugh, and the tears still running down his cheeks, trotted off, the happiest man I saw that day.

"On reaching the trenches I found the men in fine spirits, laughing and talking as they fired. There, too, I could see more plainly the terrible havoc made in the ranks of the assaulting column. I had seen the dreadful carnage in front of Marye's Hill, at Fredericksburg, and on the old "railroad cut," which Jackson's men held at the Second Manassas; but I had seen nothing to exceed this. It was not war; it was murder. When the fight ended more than a thousand men lay in front of our works, either killed or too badly wounded to leave the field. Among them were some who were not hurt, but remained among the dead and wounded rather than take the chances of going back under that merciless fire."

Scarcely ten minutes were required for the assault to be made and repulsed all along the line. The attacking divisions all fell back to cover, and, by an odd coincidence, each of the division commanders sent off a report to headquarters that his attack had failed because the commanders on either side of him had failed to advance, and thus left both his flanks exposed. Curious to discover how it could be that each of the commanders thought his own division the only one that had made the attack, Grant made an investigation and found out that the lines along which the Federals advanced were diverging, so that the further each division advanced the more its flanks were exposed.

There was no second attack of any vigor delivered against the Confederate lines, though orders for a second and a third attack were issued by General Grant. The division commanders had made up their minds that the enemy's position was impregnable, and responded to the orders by having their men open fire from where they stood, or by making isolated and perfunctory assaults at some point at which the Confederate defense seemed weak. Thus the day passed with the two armies confronting each other; the Confederates resting quietly in their trenches, while the Federals, sorely disheartened, made no effort to renew the conflict.

It had been a sorry day for the men of the North. All their courage had availed them nothing. They had been repulsed at every point of

SHERIDAN IN THE SHENANDOAH VALLEY.

attack. Over 1100 of their number lay dead on the field of battle. The wounded numbered 4517. Veterans and raw recruits lay side by side upon the battle-field. General McMahon writes, concerning the scene, "The field in front of us, after the repulse of the main attack, was indeed a sad sight. I remember at one point a mute and pathetic evidence of startling valor. The Second Connecticut Heavy Artillery, a new regiment, eighteen hundred strong, had joined us but a few days before the battle. Its uniform was bright and fresh; therefore its dead were easily distinguishable where they lay. They marked in a dotted line an obtuse angle, covering a wide front, with its apex toward the enemy, and there upon his face, still in death, with his head to the works, lay the colonel, the brave and genial Colonel Elisha S. Kellogg."

It is related by a Southern historian that when General Lee sent a messenger to A. P. Hill, asking the result of the assault on his part of the line, Hill took the officer with him in front of own works, and, pointing to the dead bodies which were literally lying upon each other, said: "Tell General Lee it is the same all along my front."

Heavy indeed had been the loss to the Union army, and no advantage had been won to make recompense for the sacrifice. Disappointment and melancholy forebodings abode with the men of the North that night. Officers of high rank condemned the plan of attack and doubted the wisdom of having attempted it all. The soldiers saw that the blood of thousands of their comrades had been shed for nothing. Grant himself regretted having ordered the attack. Years afterward he wrote, "No advantage whatever was gained to compensate for the heavy losses we sustained. Indeed, the advantages, other than those of relative losses, were on the Confederate side."

It would be idle to deny that this repulse, suffered after thirty days of constant fighting, greatly discouraged the army and the nation. Northern people, as a rule, underestimated the weakening effect of Grant's heavy and repeated blows upon Lee's army. They saw only that, after thirty days of fighting and the loss of over 70,000 men—more able-bodied men than are to be found in a city of 150,000 people—Grant had only succeeded

126   BATTLE-FIELDS AND VICTORY.

in reaching a position which McClellan, years before, had attained with scarcely any loss whatever. And as the army and the people at home pondered upon these things they began to wonder whether the great uprising of the South could ever be quelled. But while the nation doubted, General Grant never faltered, and allowing his men some days to rest after the fatigue of a month of fighting, he sent to Washington for pontoons and ferry-boats, for he had determined to cross the James River and attack Richmond from the South.

CHAPTER VII.

IN THE SHENANDOAH VALLEY—SIGEL'S RECORD OF FAILURE—CROOK IN THE KANAWHA VALLEY—BATTLE OF NEW MARKET—VIRGINIA CADETS CALLED TO WAR—THE LEXINGTON MILITARY ACADEMY—THE CALL TO ARMS—THE CADETS IN A CHARGE.

IT will be remembered that Grant's plan of campaign against the Army of Northern Virginia comprehended a supporting movement by Butler with the Army of the James up that river, and one by Sigel up the Shenandoah Valley, that great highway which more than once led a Confederate host to the very gates of Washington. Of the entire failure of the former expedition we have already spoken; Sigel's campaign deserves scarcely more attention. It was a succession of reverses, suffered, as a rule, at the hands of far inferior forces. The hopes that Grant had builded upon Sigel's expedition as a means of diverting some of Lee's attention from the Army of the Potomac were destined to be shattered. The campaign, which began with fair promise of success, ended in disaster. Just after the bloody and unsuccessful assaults at Spottsylvania, when, if ever, General Grant stood in need of encouraging reports from some of the armies in the field, there came to him this dispatch from Halleck:

Sigel is in full retreat upon Strasburg. He will do nothing but run; never did anything else.

The incidents of Sigel's campaign, save only the battle of New Market, in which the Confederates took into action against him a battalion of slender striplings, cadets from the Virginia Military Academy, merit only a passing mention.

Sigel's plan of campaign contemplated a simultaneous advance of two columns; one under his own command in the Shenandoah Valley, and the other under General George Crook in the Kanawha Valley, and Western Virginia. The slender laurels that were won were gained by the latter commander. Crook's expedition was more in the nature of a raid than a regular military campaign. He had three objects in view. At the little town of Saltville were extensive salt works. Here laborers were working day and night, getting out salt for use in the Confederacy, which, being sorely destitute of saline deposits, had been made to suffer for lack of this necessary condiment. Not far from Saltville was Wytheville, where rich deposits of lead were being worked for the metal which was made up into bullets for the Confederacy. To destroy these two flourishing industries Crook sent out his calvalry under General Averill, while he himself with the remainder of his force moved up the Kanawha Valley for the purpose of cutting the Virginia and Tennessee Railway. This division of his command in the face of the enemy proved unwise. Averill was met at Wytheville by General John Morgan, the famous rough rider of the Confederacy, and driven away, after a sharp fight, without accomplishing his object. But during Averill's absence Crook had encountered General McCausland, who brought a far inferior force into action but was provided with breastworks and a position of such natural advantage as to more than make up for his numerical inferiority. But the spirit of battle burnt fierce in the bosoms of the men who wore the blue that day. They waded a brook, rushed, all dripping, up a steep bank, down which the Confederate fire poured in a flood of lead. They swept over the crest of the earthworks, driving the defenders out in a panic and taking between two and three hundred prisoners. A train of cars came rolling over the road from Saltville bringing reenforcements to the Confederates, but the aid came too late. Crook carried the works, pressed on to the railroad, burned a bridge, tore up several miles of track, and retired.

Meantime Sigel, with a force of about 6500 men, was moving up the Shenandoah Valley, skirmishing, as he advanced, with the puny parties of Confederates who impeded his progress. He met with but little opposition in his march until he drew near the little village of New Market, that stood on the broad and level highway that made the valley such a favorite route for marching bodies of troops. It was at New Market that General Breckenridge, who had charge of the Confederate defense of the Valley, had determined to make a stand, and thither he had dispatched all the troops which he could gather together. There were veterans from the army of Northern Virginia, hardy mountaineers from the craggy heights of the Blue Ridge and the Alleghenies, the "reserve,"—old men mustered from farms and factories, armed with shot-guns and hunting rifles, and a compact well-drilled battalion of 225 cadets—smooth-faced boys, sixteen or seventeen years old, from the Virginia Military Institute at Lexington.

Lexington was the West Point of the South. There Southern boys were bred to the profession of arms. Stonewall Jackson was one of its corps of professors. When the war opened its classes were crowded with gallant, ambitious youths. The necessities of the Confederate army, which forced into its ranks all male citizens above the age of eighteen years, had the effect of closing most of the colleges of the South, but the military school still retained a large class of students between the ages of sixteen and eighteen years. Naturally enough, there burned in the breasts of these lads a fierce desire to follow their elder brothers into the ranks of that army, which, to their eyes, was fighting for the defense of their country and their homes.

Great, then, was the excitement among the cadets when they were roused from their slumbers at dead of night by the resonant rumbling of the long roll. Hurriedly getting into their clothes, they "fell in" and answered to their names. Parade was formed, and in the black night the adjutant read by the fitful glare of a lantern the special orders, which set forth that at six o'clock in the morning the Cadet Corps, provided with three days' rations, should march to the support of Breckenridge at New Market. What shouts went up as the companies broke ranks and the boys scattered to make their preparations for taking the field!

Then came the long march over muddy roads and through streams, the bridges over which had long since been sacrificed to the needs of war. It was a bedraggled but enthusiastic battalion of boys that finally marched into the camp of the veterans, who welcomed them first with lusty cheers, and afterward in a spirit of playfulness by singing "Rock-a-bye Baby" and tenderly inquiring whether they would prefer to have their coffins of rosewood, satin lined. With a queer feeling in their hearts the lads discussed the situation. These bronzed soldiers who jested at death, and who gave no more thought to the battle that was to be fought on the morrow than they would to a day's work in the wheat-fields, opened their eyes to the realities of war. They knew that it was to be no holiday playing at soldiers for them, for General Breckenridge had said, "I do not wish to put the cadets in if I can avoid it, but if occasion calls I shall use them freely."

Sunday morning, May 15, found Breckenridge sending his regiments into battle north of New Market. The guns were flashing and booming amid the graves in the little village church-yard. Sigel's troops were widely scattered. Breckenridge advanced his infantry in solid front: Wharton on the right, Echols to the left, with the cadets in the center. Imboden's cavalry made a detour to take the Federals in the flank. McLaughlin's Union Artillery contested Breckenridge's advance. One of the cadets[1] thus describes the attack upon McLaughlin's guns: "Away off to the right is Luray Gap of the Massanuten range. Our signal corps was telegraphing the position and numbers of the enemy. Our cavalry was mov-

---

[1] J. S. Wise, *Century Magazine*.

ing at a gallop to the cover of the creek, to attempt to flank the town. Echols's brigade was moving from the pike at the double-quick by the right flank, and went into line of battle across the meadows, the left resting on the pike. Out of the orchard and meadow arose puff after puff of blue smoke as our sharp-shooters advanced, the 'pop,' 'pop' of the rifles ringing out exultingly. Thundering down the pike came McLaughlin with his artillery, and, whirling out into the meadows, let fly with all his guns. . . . . Down the green slope we went, answering the wild cry of our comrades as their musketry rattled its opening volleys. In another moment we should expect a pelting rain of lead from the blue line crouching behind a stone wall at the base. Then came a sound more stunning than thunder, that burst directly in my face; lightnings leaped, fire flashed, earth rocked, the sky whirled round, and I stumbled. My gun pitched forward and I fell upon my knees. Sergeant Cabell looked back at me, sternly, pityingly, and called out, 'Close up, men!' as he passed on. I knew no more. When consciousness returned, it was raining in torrents. I was lying on the ground, which was torn and plowed with shell which were still shrieking in the air and bounding on the earth. Poor little Captain Hill was lying near, bathed in blood, with a fearful gash over the temple. Reed, Merritt and another, also badly shot, were near at hand. The battalion was three hundred yards away, clouded in smoke and hotly engaged, and the Federal battery in the grave-yard had fallen back to higher ground."

It was a hot fight that raged around McLaughlin's guns, and the cadets garnered all the laurels that were won in the action. It was a six-gun battery that most annoyed the Confederates, and Colonel Smith's regiment and the cadets were ordered to take it. To get to the guns a deep, rocky gulch, grown up with scrub cedars, thorns, and briers, and filled up with old stumps and rotting logs, must be crossed. Here the veterans of Smith's regiment rested a little, secure from the enemy's fire, but the more agile and ardent cadets floundered through and appeared, all breathless, on the edge of the clearing beyond. This is the scene that followed as described by Cadet Wise:

"As our fellows came on with a dash, the enemy stood his ground most courageously. That battery, now charged with canister and shrapnel, opened upon the cadets with a murderous hail the moment they uncovered. The infantry, lying behind fence-rails piled upon the ground, poured in a steady, deadly fire. At one discharge poor Cabell, our first sergeant, by whose side I had marched so long, fell dead, and by his side Crockett and Jones. A blanket would have covered the three. They were awfully mangled with the canister. A few steps beyond, McDowell, a mere child, sunk to his knees with a bullet through his heart. Atwill, Jefferson, Wheelwright fell upon the greensward and expired; Schrivers's sword-arm dropped helpless to his side, and 'C' company thereby lost her cadet, as well as her professor-captain. The men were falling right and left. The veterans on the right of the cadets seemed to waver. Ship, our commandant, fell wounded. For the first time the cadets seemed irresolute. Some one cried out 'Lie down,' and all obeyed, firing from the knee, all but Evans, the ensign, who was standing bolt upright. Poor Stannard's limbs were torn asunder and he lay there, bleeding to death. Some one cried out 'Fall back and rally on Edgar's battalion.' Several boys moved as if to obey; but Pizzini, orderly of Company 'B,' with his Italian blood at the boiling point, cocked his gun and swore he would shoot the first man who ran. Preston, brave and inspiring, with a smile, lay down upon his only arm, remarking that he would at least save that. Collona, captain of 'D,' was speaking words of encouragement and bidding the boys shoot close. The boys were being decimated; manifestly they must charge or retire; and charge it was. For at that moment, Henry A. Wise, our first captain, beloved of every boy in the command, sprang to his feet, shouted the charge, and led the Cadet Corps forward to the guns. The guns of the battery were served superbly; the musketry fairly rolled. The cadets reached the firm greensward of the farm-yard in which the battery was planted. The Federal infantry begun to break and run behind the buildings. Before the order 'to limber up' could be obeyed, our boys disabled the trails and were close upon the guns; the gunners dropped their sponges and sought safety in flight. Lieutenant Hanna

RESCUING WOUNDED FROM THE BURNING WOODS.

hammered a burly gunner over the head with his cadet sword. Winder Garrett outran another and attacked him with his bayonet. The boys leaped on the guns and the battery was theirs; while Evans was wildly waving the colors from the top of a caisson."

The capture of the battery was the signal for the crumbling away of the entire Union line. When the white banner of the cadets was seen waving above the smoke that hung over the ground where the battery was posted. Echols and Wharton charged Sigel's infantry line and it gave way. From that moment the battle was lost to Sigel, and his men were soon in full retreat. The Confederates pursued hotly until checked by the burning of a bridge by the Union rear-guard.

The loss to the Federals in the battle of New Market amounted to 93 killed, 522 wounded, and 186 captured. The Confederates lost 42 killed, 522 wounded, and 13 missing. Of the 225 cadets who went into the action, 8 were killed and 46 wounded. As the lads had breasted the fiercest fire of the day, they were the heroes of the camp after the action; they mingled with the veterans on terms of perfect equality. There was no more singing of "Rock-a-bye, Baby." Many of the prisoners were Germans, and they looked with wonder upon the boys who had helped to overcome them. "Dem leetle tevils mit der vhite vlag vas doo mutch fur us," said one of the captives. "Dey shoost smash mine head ven I vos cry, 'Zurrender,' all der time."

Of the later operations in the Shenandoah Valley it is unnecessary to speak now. Sigel's failure was followed by his removal, and General Hunter took his place. There was continued skirmishing in the valley, but not until its highway became the channel through which another torrent of gray-clad men poured northward to invade loyal territory did the Shenandoah Valley again draw to itself much attention from those who watched the current of the war.

CHAPTER VIII.

THE WAR IN THE WEST—SHERMAN IN COMMAND—GRANT'S ORDERS—SHERMAN'S PLAN OF CAMPAIGN—HIS SUCCESS AS A RAILROAD MANAGER—THE ARMY IN LIGHT MARCHING ORDER—SHERMAN'S ANTAGONIST—A CAMPAIGN OF STRATEGY—FLANKING JOHNSTON AT RESACA—BATTLE OF DALTON—BATTLE AT RESACA—RAPID RAILROAD BUILDING—A BATTLE PROMISED—PROTEST OF HOOD AND POLK—THE CONFEDERATES' RETREAT—NEW HOPE CHURCH—A FIGHT FOR THE COLORS—JOHNSTON'S FABIAN POLICY—GENERAL POLK KILLED—BATTLE OF KENESAW—JOHNSTON RELIEVED.

THE vastness of the theater of war, and the diverse and varied military movements that were progressing at the same time between the sandy beaches of the Atlantic and the Mississippi River, make it impossible to tell the whole story in chronological order. We can only trace the progress of one campaign of some one of the great armies to a decisive point, and then, going backward a month or two, tell of what the other armies had accomplished during the same period. Having carried Grant through the Wilderness and to his position at Cold Harbor, let us see what the blue-coats in the West were doing, while their brethren of the Army of the Potomac were fighting their thirty days of battle.

The 5th of May, 1864—the day upon which the Army of the Potomac crossed the Rapidan and plunged into the dense thickets of the Wilderness —saw the streets of Chattanooga alive with Union troops marching gayly southward. A long winter of lethargy was past, and the spring campaign was about to open.

It will be remembered that the promotion which put General Grant in command of all the military forces of the United States gave the command of all the troops in the West, and east of the Mississippi River, to Major-General William T. Sherman. Three armies—those of the Ohio, the Cumberland, and the Tennessee—had been consolidated under command of this officer. His total force closely approximated 100,000 men, and he had 254 guns. As with the Army of the Potomac, under Grant's grand strategy, Sherman's chief objective was the army of the enemy directly in his front. This army numbered, according to the Confederate method of computation, 45,000 men, or 55,000 according to the Union method, which counted teamsters, cooks, camp followers, and everybody, as helping to make up the grand total of the army. Yet, the advantage was not so greatly upon Sherman's side as the mere statement of his preponderance of force would seem to imply. He was operating in an enemy's country, where every farmer was almost certainly a spy for the enemy, and not infrequently a guerrilla as well. His base of supplies was at Nashville, and all the articles necessary for the sustenance of 100,000 men and 35,000 beasts of burden had to be brought to him over a single-track railroad, 130 miles long. A Confederate raid or a guerrilla attack which should cut this railroad, would bring almost irreparable disaster upon Sherman's army, and he had, therefore, to detail large bodies of troops to guard it at every threatened point.

According to his usual custom when dealing with subordinate officers whom he could trust, General Grant had given Sherman orders of only a general character. All the details were left to the intelligence of the general in immediate command. These are the words in which Grant outlined the campaign he desired Sherman to undertake: "You, I propose to move against Johnston's army, to break it up, and to get into the interior of the enemy's country as far as you can, inflicting all the damage you can against their war resources. I do not propose to lay down for you a plan of campaign, but simply to lay down the work it is desirable to have done, and leave you free to execute in your own way. Submit to me, however, as early as you can, your plan of operations."

The plan of operations called for was promptly submitted. " I am pushing stores to the front with all possible dispatch," replied Sherman, after a few days, in which he had formulated his general plan of campaign. "It will take us all of April to get in all our furloughed veterans . . . . and to collect provisions and cattle to the line of the Tennessee. . . . . At the signal, to be given by you, Schofield will . . . . drop down to Hiawassee and march on Johnston's right. . . . . Thomas will aim to have 45,000 men of all arms, and move straight on Johnston, wherever he may be, and fight him continuously, persistently, and to the best advantage. . . . . McPherson will have fully 30,000 of the best men in America. He will cross the Tennessee at Decatur, march toward Rome, and feel for Thomas. . . . . Should Johnston fall behind the Chattahoochie, I would feign to the right, but pass to the left, and act on Atlanta, or on its eastern communications, according to developed facts. This is about as far ahead as I feel disposed to look."

The work of "pushing stores to the front," to which Sherman alluded, was one requiring indomitable determination. To transport food and clothing for 100,000 men, and fodder for 35,000 horses and mules, over a single line of railway, was a gigantic task. The road was ill equipped with rolling-stock, and could not supply enough freight cars.

"Seize all the cars and engines that arrive in Nashville from the North," was Sherman's order.

It was done, and the supplies in Nashville were speedily enough moved to Chattanooga. But a new obstacle arose. The president of the road which carried the army's supplies from Louisville to Nashville found his cars mysteriously disappearing, and protested. "We must have our cars and engines back, or we cannot bring your supplies from Louisville to Nashville," he wrote to General Sherman. In reply he was told to seize all the cars that came to Louisville from Cincinnati. This was done, and by this process of robbing Peter to pay Paul, Sherman finally provided his railroad with a sufficient equipment. Cars of all sorts were caught in Sherman's capacious snare, and months later, when he had penetrated to Atlanta, Ga., he was amused to see upon the sides of the freight cars that followed in the wake of his army initials that told that they belonged to some far off New York or New England railway company, that doubtless mourned them as lost.

Next to securing adequate transportation for his supplies, Sherman's greatest task was perhaps the limiting of his troops to such an amount of baggage as was absolutely essential, and the enforcing of that limitation. The lavish commissary of the Federal government had accustomed the Union troops to all the little luxuries which soldiers while on campaign can possibly enjoy. Interminable trains of wagons followed in the rear of every marching army, blocking the roads, and requiring the detail of large bodies of men to guard them. At every halt for the night the soldiers went into camp, pitching their tents and setting up their kitchens. Sherman changed all this. Tents were forbidden except for use as hospitals, and one large tent to each headquarters as an office. Sherman sought no exemption for himself from the rules he had laid down for the government of others. Neither he nor any of his staff had a tent; they slept in the corner of a rail fence with a square of canvas, which any cavalryman could carry strapped to his saddle, for a roof. General Thomas alone, of Sherman's division commanders, successfully evaded the order prohibiting tents. His headquarters was always well supplied with trim canvas houses, while a small wagon train followed his army, and was derisively called by the soldiers "Old Tom's Circus." This infringement of the rule was winked at by Sherman, but in all other cases the tents that were discovered in use were promptly taken from their occupants and turned over to the hospital corps.

The campaign which followed Sherman's departure from Chattanooga was for a long time one of strategy rather than of fighting. Sherman had opposed to him a skillful and a wary antagonist. General Joseph E. Johnston is recognized by military critics as the ablest strategist whom the Confederacy produced. General Johnston was blind neither to his weakness nor to his strength. He recognized the fact that, with a force scarcely half as strong as that of his adversary, he could neither accept nor offer battle outside of his breastworks. But he knew that by holding his men in check he would in time put himself in a position where the Federals would be forced to attack him under conditions which would afford him some chance of victory. One element of Johnston's strength was the fact that he had, in effect, two armies: one an army of veterans with rifles and bayonets, the other an army of slaves with shovels and axes. While the first army was guarding the breastworks in the front the second was throwing up a new line in the rear, and so it came about that Sherman had no sooner turned the flank of the Confederate position that immediately confronted him, than the enemy fell back to a new line of works awaiting them. This maneuver was repeated many times between Chattanooga and Allatoona, for Sherman was not inclined to storm the breastworks that barred his path, while Johnston was even less willing to come out of his works and fight.

The first movement of the campaign was in the nature of a flanking movement. Sherman's army was at Chattanooga. The major portion of Johnston's army was at Dalton, a few miles to the southward. At Tunnel Hill and Buzzard's Roost the Confederates had prepared defensive works that were well-nigh impregnable. All winter they had worked upon them. A stream that flowed in their front had been dammed in several places until it had become a succession of deep ponds. Beyond it stretched long lines of massive earthworks, plentifully studded with guns. To attack these formidable works was a task from which the Federals might well shrink. Fortunately for them a break in the chain of hills, called Snake Creek Gap, and a practicable road running through it, opened a way for a flanking party to reach the enemy's rear. Of the opportunity thus offered, Sherman speedily availed himself. McPherson, with the Army of the Tennessee, plunged into the tortuous defiles of Snake Creek Gap, while the remainder of the Union army pressed Johnston's lines in front sharply, in the hope that, occupied by this attack, he would be blind to McPherson's movement until too late to guard against the peril which threatened his flank. The enthusiasm of the Federal soldiers made of the attack upon the lines at Dalton a veritable battle, although a sharp skirmish was all that Sherman had planned. "The works were found to be very strong," writes General Jacob D. Cox, "and the enemy was not tempted to leave them. Schofield's troops were due east from the crest where Harper was fighting, and from there the view of the combat above was an exciting one. The line of blue coats could be seen among the rocks nearly at right angles with the line of the ridge, the men at the top in silhouette against the sky, close up to the Confederate trenches, where their charges were met with a line of fire before which they recoiled, only to renew the effort, till it became apparent, even to the most daring, that it was useless to lead men against such barriers. The orders were not to waste life in serious assault upon intrenchments, but the zeal of the troops and subordinate commanders turned the intended skirmish into something very like a ranged battle, and the Confederate reports state that five separate and regular assaults were made upon their lines. . . . . During the night the National army rested on its arms, the troops on the mountain sides and crests in line of battle. Rest it could hardly be called, for the surface of the ground was a mass of broken quartz rock, the sharp edges and angles of which had not yielded to weathering, and the bivouac was a rough one."

McPherson's column, meanwhile, had wound along through the gap almost unopposed. For some reason General Johnston had left this highway to his flank and rear undefended, save for a redoubt held by two brigades at its further end. The narrow winding road, and the steep walls of this gorge, into which the sun shone for but an hour or two at noon, afforded excellent opportunities for defensive warfare, but no advantage had been taken of them. When McPherson reached the outlet of the gap and saw the earthworks there looming up before him, he forbore to attack them, thinking that an assault would involve too great a loss of life. Instead of this he took up a position which would insure the keeping of the gap open for the passage of the remainder of the army, and sent word to Sherman. That commander, for his part, was much disappointed by McPherson's failure to attack, and declared that his subordinate's caution had led him to throw away an opportunity for conquest such as comes to a soldier but once in a life-time.

Leaving one corps to engage Johnston in his front, Sherman put the remainder of his army in motion and followed with rapid strides in the path already trod by McPherson. Johnston, ever alert, moved in his turn to meet this flank attack. Howard followed close upon his heels, skirmishing with his rear-guard. At Resaca, where Snake Creek Gap debouches, the Confederate army defiled into trenches awaiting it and was ready for the battle. For three days there was a constant din of war in the fields and woods around Resaca. Sherman had no desire to assault the enemy's intrenchments, but kept up a sufficient show of activity in his front to mask the efforts he was constantly making to turn Johnston's flank. A notable advantage was won by the troops of General Logan's corps, on the right of the Union line. Behind the Confederate ranks at that point flowed Camp Creek, a deep stream inclosed between steep banks. A bridge across the creek was held by the Confederates. Logan saw in this bridge the key to the Confederate position, and ordered its capture. The Federals pressed fiercely forward to the assault and the Confederates fled across the bridge. Before they could destroy it the Union troops followed. Mindful of the value of the position they had won, a part of the Federals began to intrench, while the rest beat back the attacks of the enemy, who tried in vain to regain the ground he had lost. Swiftly a wall of earth and timber rose from the ground. A battery of Union guns dashed across the bridge and went into action behind the new redoubt. Its shells searched out every corner of the Confederate position. General Polk, brought hastily to the scene by the reports of the Union success, saw how important the position was to the safety of the Confederate army and ordered repeated charges, but his troops were repulsed.

It was the one great weakness of Johnston's position at Resaca that he had behind him a river—the Oostenaula—which he had to cross if a retreat should become necessary. A very small body of Sherman's troops, by a movement to the flank and rear, might secure a position on the further bank from which it would be impossible to dislodge them, and where they would effectually cut off his retreat. An added source of weakness was the fact that the railroad bridge, over which came the supplies and re-enforcements for Johnston's army, was now within range of the guns which Logan had planted in the advanced position he had won, and was rapidly going to pieces under their fire. The Confederate commander, ever alert and vigilant, saw his danger and began at once to throw pontoon and trestle bridges across the Oostenaula. Already the Federals had crossed the river on his flank. He sent General Hood to drive them back and, knowing that Sherman would fight hard for the advantage he had won, followed Hood up with re-enforcements drawn from Hardee and Polk. But Sherman's grip upon a position once taken was not lightly loosened. His men met and repelled with unflinching gallantry the repeated attacks of the enemy. A Confederate four-gun battery, which had rashly gone into action unprotected by earthworks, was virtually captured by Union sharpshooters, who picked off the cannoneers before the guns could be served. With all their efforts the Confederates could neither fight the battery nor withdraw it. But they were able to defeat every effort of the Federals to take the guns. Time and again the blue-coats made the attempt but were driven back. Once a Union color-bearer, in the brigade of General Benjamin Harrison (afterward President of the United States), was so chagrined by the Confederate shouts of triumph that he stood alone on the field, waving his flag in defiance. He was quickly shot down. The guns remained on the field surrounded by a group of dead and wounded artillerists until night, when they fell into the hands of the Federals.

Johnston saw that it was now time for him to retreat. A Union force that he could not shake off had effected a lodgment on his flank and was threatening his rear. It is as much the test of good generalship to retreat promptly and in good order, at the proper moment, as it is to advance boldly. "No officer or soldier who ever served under me," writes General Sherman, "will ever question the generalship of Joseph E. Johnston. His retreats were timely, in good order, and he left nothing behind." So it was at Resaca. When the Federals advanced to the attack at sunrise on the 17th, they found the Confederate breastworks empty, and the bridges by which Johnston had crossed the Oostenaula wrapped in roaring flames.

Sherman lost no time in putting his army in pursuit. He accepted Johnston's game and determined to play it to the end. His first task was to repair the railroad bridge that had been burned. This was speedily accomplished. There was with Sherman's army a distinct corps, of about 2000 men, whose especial duty it was to repair wrecked railroads. They had bridge trestles ready made and in waiting, and when the need arose bridged rivers and ravines with a rapidity truly marvelous. It was greatly discouraging to the Confederates to hear the whistle of a train coming from a road which they thought they had permanently wrecked, but long experience made them regard the celerity of the Union repairing corps with some philosophy. Once, when one of the Confederates proposed staying Sherman's progress by blowing up a tunnel, an old campaigner responded, "It's no use, boys, Old Sherman carries duplicate tunnels with him and will replace them as fast as you can blow them up; better save your powder."

It was toward the village of Cassville that Johnston's army now turned its steps. There the Confederate commander had determined to fight a battle. Slaves had been at work preparing defensive works. The engineer officers told General Johnston that the position was a strong one. Sherman, whose advance speedily caught up with the enemy's rear-guard, was convinced that a battle would be fought. He was delighted with the prospect. Weary of marching and strategy, he longed for the clash of arms, and was confident that the victory would rest with him. The stubborn resistance of the Confederate rear-guard first made him believe that a general battle was near at hand, and his surmise was confirmed when the Union scouts came in bringing copies of an order which General Johnston had issued to his troops, announcing that a battle would be fought on the morrow. So eager was Sherman for the fray that he ordered his subordinates not to hesitate to bring on the battle without reference to supports, as he would see to bringing up the necessary re-enforcements in time.

But the Federal commander's hope of bringing his wily foe to battle was destined to disappointment. General Johnston had indeed determined to fight. Polk's corps was deployed on the road along which the Federal column was advancing, with instructions to attack as soon as the blue-coats appeared. Hood was sent by a different road to fall upon the flank of the Union troops. Orders announcing that a battle was to be fought were read to the troops and were hailed with enthusiasm by every regiment. The soldiers were weary of running away and wanted to deal the pursuers a blow. But Hood marched out three miles on the road assigned him and then turned and marched back again, professing to have received information that the Federals were advancing from an entirely different quarter. Though disappointed by the failure of his lieutenant, and utterly denying the sufficiency of the excuse offered, Johnston determined to await the attack of the enemy, since he himself had been balked in his purpose of taking the offensive.

That night there was a council of war at Johnston's headquarters. The lines had been formed and there had been skirmishing along the Confederate front all the afternoon. Polk and Hood warmly contended that the position held by the Confederate army was untenable. The latter spoke freely upon the subject. He declared that a lofty hill in the neighborhood of his command would enable the Federal artillery to enfilade his line. He did not wish to fight in that position. His voice was for battle, but he thought it wiser that he should be given part of Polk's command and be allowed to go out to meet Schofield's corps, which he thought he could speedily demolish.

Johnston was disappointed and angry. He thought that his subordinates had been conspiring to discredit his plans and substitute their own. For Hood's plan of action he had nothing but contempt. As for the plea that the position in which his army was then was untenable, he scoffed at it. But he was not ready to ignore the protests of his two lieutenants. He did not care to go into battle with two of his three corps commanders disaffected. He broke up the conference, saying bitterly, "I am not willing to indulge in a critical battle, with an army much larger than my own, with two of my corps commanders dissatisfied with my plan and unwilling to fight upon the ground which I have chosen or in the position which I have assigned them."

A few minutes later the aides were carrying to the different brigade commanders the order for an immediate retreat, and soon the whole army was in motion, with the soldiers' faces turned once again to the southward. When, with the breaking of day, Sherman's troops moved forward to attack the long lines of breastworks that confronted them, they were empty.

Johnston now turned his steps toward Allatoona pass, a position of great natural strength, whither he no doubt hoped that Sherman would follow him. But just twenty years before this time, Sherman, then a young lieutenant, had traversed the country between Chattanooga and Atlanta, and there still remained with him the remembrance of its general topographical details. He remembered the region about Allatoona as offering almost insurmountable difficulties to an attacking army, and he determined to pass by Johnston's new position and move on to the southward, knowing that his antagonist would have to follow or find himself cut off. To do this was a daring and difficult operation for the Union army. The railroad had to be abandoned altogether. The rations for the army had to be carried in the knapsacks of the men, and the contingency was not improbable that when these were exhausted the troops would have to live upon the country. The army was left utterly dependent upon the country roads, in a region of which there were no trustworthy, or even approximately correct maps to be found. To supply this need the Union engineers were forced to employ the utmost ingenuity. Sketches were made from every commanding hilltop. Every native who was met was questioned as to the lay of the land adjoining and made to mark down on rough maps the location of every house, road, and stream. Reconnoitering parties scattered in every direction, mapping out the country. The rough maps thus prepared were put together and the whole photographed, and copies given out to the different corps commanders. Considering the haste with which these maps were prepared, and the unscientific methods which their makers were forced to employ, the measure of accuracy attained was remarkable. With one of these maps on the ground before him, General Sherman would often spend the greater part of the night planning the route by which the army should move. It was after one of these nights spent in toil that the general fell asleep, leaning against a tree that stood by the side of a road along which a column of soldiers was marching. One of the soldiers, seeing the commander slumbering, said, "A pretty way we are commanded!"

"Stop, my man!" cried Sherman, waking just in time to hear the words, "while you were sleeping last night I was planning for you, sir; and now I was taking a nap."

From his elevated position at Allatoona, Johnston could watch the progress of Sherman's army. In the curling smoke of every camp fire that rose above the fresh foliage of the woods, clothed in their springtime greenery, he had a guide to tell him of the course of his antagonist's march. Quickly discerning the purpose of Sherman's movement, he bestirred himself to defeat it. A few days of quick marching and rapid work with axes and shovels, and a long line of log redoubts and earthworks, plentifully studded with cannon, stretched over hill and dale from Dallas to Marietta, directly across Sherman's path to Atlanta.

On the evening of the 25th of May the region about New Hope Church resounded with the noises of battle—the thunder of the artillery, the sharp and continuous rattle of musketry, the cheers of charging bodies of troops, the yells of defiance, and the cries of wounded men. Nature added her thunder to the general uproar, for during the battle a heavy shower came up; the rain fell in sheets, and the flash of the lightning dimmed the fitful glare of the cannon. Hooker's advance had come upon a line of log breastworks held by the troops of General Hood. The entire Confederate army had not yet come into position, and Hood ordered those of his men who were engaged to make all the noise possible, both in order to give the alarm to the troops still on the road, and in the hopes of deluding the Union troops into overestimating the numbers of their antagonists. It was about six o'clock in the evening when the scattering reports of the skirmishers' rifles gradually swelled into the roar of a pitched battle. Around New Hope Church the cannon were flaming and roaring in the gathering twilight. Far away on the horizon the approaching thunderstorm was flashing and sending on its ominous rumblings to mingle with the general din. Sheltered behind their breastworks the Confederates fought coolly and effectively. They were greatly outnumbered, but one man sheltered behind a redoubt is worth four whose breasts are bared to the pitiless scud of whizzing lead. Yet for two hours the gallant men in blue hurled themselves forward, only to be beaten back, time after time, by the furious fire that beat in their faces from sixteen Confederate cannon, shotted with grape and with canister, and from the muskets of five thousand veteran infantry soldiers. "Again and again Hooker's brave men went forward through the forest, only to run upon log barricades thoroughly manned and protected by well posted artillery," writes General Howard, who commanded the Fourth Army Corps during the Atlanta campaign. "During these charges occurred a thunder-storm, the heaviest shower of the day. . . . . On that terrible night the nearest house to the field was filled with the wounded. Torchlights and candles lighted up dimly the incoming stretchers and the surgeons' tables and instruments. The very woods seemed to moan and groan with the voices of sufferers not yet brought in."

"Hell Hole," the Union soldiers called the spot so pitilessly swept by the Confederate fire, and to many of the poor fellows it proved indeed a place of torment.

The next day was spent by the Union army in intrenching. The experience of years of campaigning had taught the soldiers to throw up earthworks and to slash the trees in their front whenever they halted with an enemy in their front. So expert did they become in this work that less than an hour's labor with axes and spades was enough to enable a regiment to cover its front. By nightfall of the 26th both armies were securely sheltered behind parallel lines of works, so near together that almost every shot at an unprotected enemy took effect, and no officer or soldier could show his head above the redoubt except at the peril of his life.

Upon the day following, the fighting became hot once more. Sherman

SHERIDAN AT FIVE FORKS.

thought to turn Johnston's lines by the right flank, and sent three divisions to make the attempt. The movement, though skillfully planned, was not executed with sufficient secrecy, and the enemy took the alarm. A division was sent to the spot threatened, arriving after the Union scouts, who had been out to reconnoiter preparatory to the attack, had retired. So, when the Union troops plunged into the woods where they expected to encounter little or no resistance, they were met by a withering blast of lead and iron. What they had supposed to be the Confederate flank proved to be only an angle in Johnston's line, and the troops advancing were taken both in front and in flank by the enemy's fire. Yet they persisted in the attack with a gallantry that won applause even from the foe. General Johnston writes: "The Federal formation was so deep that their front did not equal that of our two brigades; consequently those troops were greatly exposed to our musketry—all but the leading troops being on a hill-side facing us. They advanced until their first line was within twenty-five or thirty paces of ours, and fell back only after at least 700 men had fallen dead in their places. When the leading Federal troops paused in their advance, a color-bearer came on and planted his colors eight or ten feet in front of his regiment, but was killed in the act. A soldier who sprang forward to hold up or bear off the colors was shot dead as he seized the staff. Two others who followed successively fell like him, but the fourth bore back the noble emblem. Some time after nightfall the Confederates captured above two hundred prisoners in the hollow before them."

On the day following Johnston in his turn took the offensive, with disastrous results. The Union line was steadily being extended to the left in order to get back to the railroad, which lay a few miles to the eastward. This movement was, of course, easily detected by the enemy, and they began to parallel it by throwing up breastworks and extending their lines to their right. Some movements within the lines of McPherson's command excited the suspicion of the Confederates, and General Hardee was ordered to make a vigorous reconnoissance for the purpose of discovering whether that commander was not withdrawing. There was no lack of vigor in Hardee's movement, and the manner of his reception left him no doubt that, whatever might be McPherson's ultimate intention, the great bulk of the rank and file of the Army of the Tennessee still tenanted the redoubts against which his well-disciplined battalions dashed themselves to pieces in vain. The three brigades of Mississippians that made up Bate's division were the Confederate troops engaged. It was not Bate's intention to attack if it should appear that McPherson's troops were all on the ground. A detachment of Armstrong's cavalry was sent forward, with orders to attempt to thrust itself between the Union cavalry and the flank of Logan's corps. If this could be accomplished it would demonstrate that the National line had been weakened by withdrawals, and at a given signal the Confederates would rush forward to the assault.

Bate's troops were formed in three columns—one brigade to each. It was difficult for the brigade commanders to communicate with each other. While they stood thus under arms, listening breathlessly for the signal, there burst forth from the direction of the Union line a prodigious roar of battle. It was only the thunder of the National guns beating back the too prying Confederate cavalry, but to the waiting brigadiers it sounded like the din of a general engagement. Each of the three—cut off from sight of, or communication with, his comrades in arms—thought that the order for attack had been given and through some mishap had failed to reach him alone. Each thought the other two brigades were engaged, and therefore all three rushed furiously forward to the assault, which they expected to find already begun. A slight success gave them encouragement all too brief. Three guns of an Iowa battery were on the skirmish line unprotected by earthworks, and with no infantry supports. Upon these guns the Confederates descended in a swarm and were speedily in possession of them. The gunners retained presence of mind enough to carry with them their rammers as they fled, thus making the cannon useless for the time. But when, elated with their triumph, the assailants surged on toward the redoubt, behind which the men of Logan's corps lay in wait, there came a roar, a cloud of smoke and ruddy flame, and the ground was covered with men in gray, who went down before the hurtling storm of lead. There was no lack of desperate courage in the ranks of the men who, through their commanders' error, had thus been led into a death trap. Time and again they returned with indomitable pertinacity to the attack, sometimes fighting their way up to the very muzzles of the guns that were so pitilessly mowing them down. But it was courage misplaced, and gallant lives thrown away, for the position could not be carried. After fighting for about half an hour, Bate withdrew his men, leaving many dead upon the field.

Then followed day after day of petty skirmishing. The rifles of the pickets were kept hot by constant shooting, but the great body of both armies was busily engaged in drifting eastward toward the railroad. May expired and June came in, bringing with it weather very different from the traditional summer in the sunny South. A chill wind blew up from the ocean, bearing rain-laden clouds. Day after day the torrents descended until the roads became impassable. None too soon did Sherman once again establish himself on the railroad, and the shrill screech of the locomotive whistle was a cheering sound to his soldiers, who saw in the condition of the roads a terrifying threat of short rations.

Once the position on the railroad was gained the Northern army pressed relentlessly upon its foe. " Not a day, not an hour, not a minute was there a cessation of fire," writes General Sherman. " Our skirmishers were in absolute contact ; the lines of battle and the batteries but little in rear of the skirmishers."

Johnston was forced to abandon one fortified position after another. Sherman would not gratify him by attacking his lines in front. He himself knew too well the value of men in the clean-swept Confederacy to incur the heavy loss which he would certainly suffer if he went out of his works to attack Sherman. There was nothing for him to do but to play a waiting game—give Sherman the greatest possible amount of trouble while losing himself the least possible number of men. This he did with consummate skill.

On the 14th of June the Confederate line extended along the crests of three lofty hills called Lost, Pine, and Kenesaw mountains. From the left flank to the right it measured more than ten miles. With his forces greatly reduced by the fighting of the past thirty days, Johnston could not hold so extended a line, and, in company with Generals Polk and Hardee, he rode over to Pine Mountain to see about withdrawing the troops from that point. With their staffs and the soldiers from the neighboring trenches who gathered about them, the three generals made a conspicuous group on the crest of the mountain. Far away in the valley below, General Sherman noticed the party. By the quick flashes of sunlight that every now and then gleamed from the group he could tell that there were officers there scanning his lines through field-glasses.

"Open fire upon those fellows with one of your batteries and make them keep under cover," said he to General Howard, who stood with him.

"General Thomas has ordered me to be very sparing of my artillery ammunition," replied Howard.

"That as a general rule is all right," returned Sherman, "but I wish to keep up a bold offensive. By using your artillery you make the enemy timid. Let one of your batteries fire three volleys."

The guns of an Indiana battery near by were loaded and aimed, and, as their deep-toned notes boomed out, Sherman rode on, thinking nothing more of the occurrence. Shortly after, however, an orderly came to his headquarters with the news that the Confederate signal flags, which the Union officers had learned to interpret, were waving out from the crest of Pine Mountain to the station at Marietta the message, "Send an ambulance for the body of General Polk." One of the shells that were thrown by the Indiana battery had struck the soldier-bishop in the side, tearing its way through his body and killing him instantly. His loss was greatly deplored in the Southern army, for he was beloved and respected by officers and privates alike. A soldier by education, a graduate of West Point, he had chosen to enter the ministry, and became a bishop in the Episcopal church. But when the war broke out he conceived it to be his duty to cast aside his surplice and take up the sword in the defense of what he considered his country.

Johnston withdrew from Pine Mountain the next day just as Sherman was getting ready to attack it. Soon after he withdrew from Lost Mountain. His entire army was then concentrated upon the lofty crest of Kenesaw, from which he looked down upon the lines of his antagonist. The heavy and incessant rain which had now fallen for nineteen days had forced Sherman to somewhat relax the persistency of his pressure upon the Confederate lines. Yet he gave them but little rest. "I pressed operations with the utmost earnestness," he writes, "aiming always to keep our fortified lines in absolute contact with the enemy, while with the surplus force we felt forward, from one flank or the other, for his line of communication and retreat." Johnston, from his lofty eyrie, could discern these flank movements almost as soon as they were begun. On the 19th of the month he saw that Schofield and a portion of the Twentieth Corps, under Hooker, were threatening his left flank. He determined to meet this movement with so vigorous a counter-attack as to inflict severe damage on the Union army. General Hood's corps was on the Confederate right. Johnston's plan was to withdraw Hood from that position, conduct him swiftly and secretly around the rear of the Confederate position, and have him fall suddenly upon Schofield and Hooker, who would not expect to encounter any very considerable hostile force. The movement was well planned and speedily executed. Hood's troops moved out of their trenches, which were quickly filled by Wheeler's dismounted cavalrymen, who put on a bold front to disguise their slender strength. The march around the rear of the Confederate army was accomplished without delay, and the field of battle was reached at the time set in the plan. Yet the attack failed, and failed disastrously for the Confederates. A lucky accident put Schofield and Hooker on their guard. Several Confederate prisoners were brought in by the Union scouts, who, on being questioned, declared themselves members of Hood's corps. This was significant news. Both the Union generals knew that the night before Hood had been intrenched on the Confederate right. What could have brought him over to the left? What, unless he were planning an attack? With their suspicions thus aroused, the Union commanders plied the prisoners with sharp questions, and soon found out that Hood was indeed in their front, and almost ready to attack them. Then orders were sent out thick and fast. The Federals had been advancing in column along a road, exposed to a flank attack. Quickly they deployed and began throwing up earthworks. The batteries made for the hills and prepared for action. The busy work of forming lines and digging trenches was still proceeding when Hood's attack came, delivered with the fiery dash characteristic of this gallant but reckless commander.

Had Hood's attack been made but an hour earlier, or had the Federals not enjoyed the stroke of good fortune which forewarned them, the result might have been disastrous to Sherman's plans. As it was, the Confederates were repulsed with a loss so heavy that Johnston, in his report, strove to conceal it by cloaking it under the rough estimate of "about one thousand."

Johnston's attempt to force the fighting had thus ended in disaster. Torn and bleeding, his troops again sought shelter behind their works. It now became the turn of Sherman to take the offensive. The prolonged rainy season had produced a feeling of depression among the soldiers. Worse than this, it had converted the roads into quagmires, impassable for wagons, and almost so for columns of troops. Though the railroad brought supplies to Sherman's lines, he found it almost impossible to distribute them to the commands on the extreme flanks. The situation and the temper of his troops would not permit him to dally long with Johnston without bringing on a decisive battle. Accordingly, he determined to make an attack on the morning of the 27th of June. Preparations for the movement were pushed forward swiftly and with the utmost secrecy. In order that the General-in-chief might, so far as possible, supervise the action at every point, the crest of a lofty hill was cleared away, and axmen chopped vistas through the forests to each of the principal points on the Union line. Telegraph wires were strung from all parts of the field to this hill-top, where General Sherman established his headquarters.

At daybreak on the day appointed the Union artillery opened all along the line, and the surrounding hills echoed back the sonorous thunder of the cannon. Secure in their massive works, the Confederates bore the heavy fire with but scanty response. They were veterans, and knew well enough what this cannonade all along the front portended. Their ammunition and their energies were saved to use in the repulse of the infantry attack that they knew was coming. They had not long to wait. About nine o'clock the heads of three attacking columns were discernible pushing their way forward, over swamps and through creeks, past slashed timber, and through dense thickets of underbrush. Upon these columns the Confederates turned their guns, knowing well enough that all other signs of activity in their front were but feints to withdraw their attention from these main attacks. The assailants suffered heavily. Logan's corps encountered both a direct and a flank fire. Seven regimental commanders in his command fell, either dead or wounded. The enemy in his front had a line of strong rifle-pits, which they held until the attacking column was within half pistol-shot, when they rapidly retreated to their principal line. From this refuge Logan in vain strove to drive them, and finally, after suffering frightful loss, was obliged himself to take shelter in the rifle-pits abandoned by the Confederates.

General Thomas's Army of the Cumberland, and particularly the corps of General Palmer, suffered severely in the attack. Their ground was difficult and the resistance they encountered fairly desperate. "Davis's men," writes General Cox, concerning the gallant work of the first division of this corps, "had to pass over rocky and rough ground, part of it covered with forest and tangled with undergrowth. In their enthusiasm they took too rapid a pace at the start, and by the time they had traversed the third of a mile between them and the enemy's works, the men were so blown that they had not the strength called for in the final effort to carry the parapet before them. Colonel Daniel McCook and his second in command, Colonel Hannon, both fell in the assault, and both brigades had a heavy list of casualties among field and company officers, as well as of private soldiers. They reached the trench in front of their objective point, but the narrow front of the column now stood revealed to the enemy, who were able to concentrate upon them also a storm of rifle-balls and canister, which made farther advance impossible. Lying upon the ground, within the range of musket fire from the works, they covered themselves as they could, and finally, by General Thomas's consent, intrenched themselves under a terrible fire, the open ground over which they must retreat making it safer to stay than to return. The cover they were able to make enabled them to hold on till night, and then their works were so strengthened that they were permanently held, though for several days and nights the troops could rest only by sleeping on their arms."

The fate of the attack at other points was but little better. Newton's division found a felled forest with heavy trunks and stumps and the interlaced branches of trees, over which they must struggle before they could reach the enemy's line. In this snare hundreds fell, among them the gallant General Harker. Everywhere along the line, from the right flank to the left, the blue-coats were performing prodigies of valor and suffering frightful loss. Numbers and gallantry were no match for earthworks and gallantry. Sherman learned that lesson well that day at Kenesaw and never forgot it.

Gradually the hopelessness of the attack forced itself upon the mind of the assailants and the effort was abandoned. Night fell with the Confederates still secure in their works. They had lost less than 600 men. Sherman's loss closely approached 3000. "It was the hardest fight of the campaign up to that date," writes Sherman.

Decisive events now followed each other with fairly bewildering rapidity. Twice in the next two weeks Johnston fell back, and the 10th of July found him heavily intrenched behind the Chattahoochie River. Then the settled dislike of Jefferson Davis for General Johnston manifested itself in the sudden dismissal of that officer from his command. "At this critical moment the Confederate Government rendered us valuable service," is the way General Sherman chronicles the fact of his great antagonist's dismissal. "Being dissatisfied with the Fabian policy of General Johnston, it relieved him, and General Hood was substituted to command the Confederate Army." The ostensible cause advanced by President Davis for the removal of Johnston was his failure to defeat or check Sherman's advance. The best military critics, however, have unanimously commended Johnston's course as the most effective one practicable under the circumstances. History has already vindicated General Johnston, and the

REVEILLE.

historians and military critics of the future are likely to adopt the view of General Grant, who writes: "For my own part I think that Johnston's tactics were right. Anything that could have prolonged the war a year beyond the time that it finally did close would probably have exhausted the North to such an extent that they might then have abandoned the contest and agreed to a separation."

CHAPTER IX.

HOOD'S CHARACTER—SHERMAN STILL ADVANCING—BATTLE OF PEACHTREE CREEK—THE FEDERALS TAKEN BY SURPRISE—DEFEAT OF THE CONFEDERATES—FIRST BATTLE OF ATLANTA—DEATH OF M'PHERSON—A FIERCE STRUGGLE—THE CONFEDERATES BEATEN BACK—HOOD RETIRES TO HIS BREASTWORKS—UNION CAVALRY RAIDS—TWO DISASTERS—HOOD'S SECOND SORTIE—ATLANTA EVACUATED—TRIUMPH OF THE FEDERALS.

WHAT is General Hood's character?" asked Sherman of the officers about headquarters, when he heard of the change in the commanding officer of the Confederate Army.

"He is a very brave man, and a rash one," replied General Schofield, who had been with Hood at West Point. "He is the sort of a man to take desperate chances."

"We are likely to have some sharp fighting, then," said Sherman, and he at once sent out to the different corps commanders a warning to be prepared for sudden raids and sorties upon the part of the enemy.

Very accurately had the Union officers estimated the character of their new antagonist and its probable effect upon the future of the campaign.

To one of Hood's disposition the cautious strategy which had enabled Johnston to force Sherman to consume sixty-six days in advancing less than 100 miles was only contemptible. He was for the fight. It did not occur to him that the scarcest article in all the Confederacy now was an able-bodied man not under arms. Johnston had kept this fact well in mind, and had tried in every way to so conduct his defense as to avoid needlessly thinning those already scanty ranks, which could not be replenished. So cautious had been his tactics that in the almost continuous fighting from May 5 to July 4, his total losses were less than 10,000 men, while he inflicted a loss of almost 18,000 upon his adversary. This cautious policy Hood threw to the winds, and, even while the Federal officers were discussing his probable action, he was preparing to leave his secure earthworks and attack the Federals in theirs.

Meantime Sherman had in no way abated his restless activity. A body of 2000 horse had been gathered together from the scattered cavalry detachments in Tennessee and brought to the Union lines before Atlanta by General Rousseau. They had burned cotton and sugar mills, helped themselves liberally to the horses and mules found on the plantations, and wrecked railways by burning the ties and bending the rails out of shape. While the cavalry was thus tearing the enemy's country to pieces, the infantry was pushing stubbornly along toward Atlanta. On the 19th of July the invaders took some positions of notable importance, meeting with such feeble resistance that General Sherman almost concluded that Atlanta would be turned over to him without a battle. General Thomas pushed the Army of the Cumberland across Peachtree Creek. He expected to have his advance stubbornly contested, and made the crossing in order of battle, laying a pontoon bridge for every division. But the enemy seemed blind and deaf to approaching peril, and only a sprinkling fire from skirmishers and sharpshooters annoyed the men of Thomas's command as they strode across the floating bridges and deployed in the fields beyond. In the course of this forward movement a gap two miles wide was opened in the lines of the Union army after the creek had been crossed.

General Hood quickly learned of the gap, which opened a way for him to break up and demolish this wing of the Federal army. He knew that Schofield and McPherson were far away—six miles or more—and that it would be hours before a message could reach them and bring them to the aid of Thomas. He knew that the soldiers of the Army of the Cumberland were advancing, had not yet intrenched, and might be surprised and overwhelmed before any help could reach them.

The troops of Stewart's corps advanced against Newton's line at about four o'clock in the afternoon of July 19. They came rushing down upon the startled blue-coats, shouting madly and creating a tremendous uproar. Newton's men were not yet intrenched. A few companies had little walls of rails and stones piled up in their front, but the shelter afforded was slight. Many of the Federals were at work with their intrenching tools when the storm burst, and had to hastily drop pick, ax, and spade, and catch up their muskets. For a moment it seemed as though the Confederate attack would be wholly successful. Newton's line was thrown into confusion. The assailants turned his flank and pressed upon his rear, while all the time additional lines of men in gray, one after another, like the waves of the ocean breaking on the beach, beat furiously upon his front. Newton's men were veterans, and quickly recovered from their temporary discomfiture. Nobly they held their ground, and shoulder to shoulder opposed a rigid barrier to the rushing tide of Confederates. The flank attack that for a time threatened to roll up the Union line was repelled by the fire of some reserve batteries that General Thomas had posted upon the other side of the creek, covering the tempting gap into which he knew the Confederates would find their way. The shells from these batteries fell thick and fast in the woods where the Confederates were fighting, and speedily drove them away. "It relieved the hitch considerably," said Thomas laconically.

Beaten back from Newton's lines, the Confederates fared no better at any point. Ward, Geary, Williams, and Palmer met and tossed back the oncoming host. At the end of two hours' hard fighting, much of it hand to hand, and all of it done at very close quarters, the Union line still stood firm. The "Rock of Chickamauga" had not allowed the proud title won on another hard-fought field to be wrested from him here.

Withdrawing a little to a sheltered line, the Confederates rested a time preparatory to renewing the assault. Cleburne's division was hastening to their aid, and with this re-enforcement they were confident their purpose could be accomplished. But at this juncture McPherson—from whom Hood had anticipated no interference—created a diversion which saved the day for the Federals. Though too far away to effect a juncture with Thomas, McPherson was in a favorable position for threatening the enemy's works about Atlanta. This he did with such excellent effect that Hood in haste recalled Cleburne and sent him to the spot threatened by Hood. Deprived thus of his expected re-enforcements, Hardee was forced to abandon his contemplated attack.

It had been a disastrous day for the cause of the Confederacy. Hood's losses nearly approached 4000 men. In return for this sacrifice he had gained nothing. He had not driven the Federals back, nor even checked their steady, persistent advance. McPherson's men early the next morning won the crest of a hill from which his Parrott guns could throw shells into the streets of Atlanta. They stormed the earthworks, which were held by Cleburne's veteran troops, and drove them out as though they were but a handful of raw militia. For all his reverses Hood had not even the slight solace of knowing that the enemy had suffered more than he, for it had been the turn of the Union troops this day to fight behind defensive works, and their losses had been comparatively light.

The Confederate general was not dismayed by the disasters that had fallen so heavily upon him. With his army still bleeding from the wounds received at Peachtree Creek, he began planning another attack. First, however, he withdrew his troops from the line of Peachtree Creek to another and stronger line nearer the city. On his heels followed the Federals, who took possession of the works abandoned by Hood, and kept pressing forward in the expectation that the Confederates intended to evacuate the town as well. They were very thoroughly undeceived, however, when they came upon the new line of Confederate works. These were more formidable than any hitherto encountered—massive, well planned, and protected for their entire length by slashings or *chevaux de frise*. Beyond these formidable works the steeples and roofs of Atlanta rose in plain sight. The shells from the cannon posted by McPherson on the hill he had captured were even then falling in the streets of the town, the tall chimney of a large foundry, which had long been engaged in turning out shot and shell for the Confederates, being the artillerists' favorite target.

About noon of the 22d of July, General Sherman and General McPherson were sitting on the front steps of a farmhouse, talking of the chances of battle and of the character of the new commander of the Confederate army. Their horses stood near them in charge of an orderly. McPherson had just come over from his position on the left of the Union line. Sherman had just returned from the front, where he had been with Schofield. It was the day that the enemy's abandonment of the Peachtree Creek line had been discovered, and Sherman had headed his troops in what he expected would be a march directly into the city, until he discovered the new line on which the Confederates were still busily working, with their guns at their elbows, ready for instant action if necessary. Then he rode back to the farmhouse where he met McPherson. With a map spread out before them the two generals were studying the situation of the army. The air was full of the noise of musketry and the heavier peals of the cannon, and occasionally a round shot cut through the foliage of the trees above them. Yet there was no battle in progress. Nothing but the continual exchange of deadly missiles that had been kept up with scarcely any intermission ever since the two armies left Chattanooga. The two officers paid little attention to these sounds, which had become as familiar to their ears as the chirping of crickets to a farmer, or the rattle of wheels to the dweller in a great city. But gradually the noise of battle grew louder. From the east came the roar of musketry, fired not scatteringly but in volleys, and the thunder of cannon, served rapidly.

"That sounds like business," said Sherman. "Where is it?"

Taking a compass from his pocket he listened intently to the sound and soon determined that it came from the direction of the left flank.

McPherson at once apprehended some danger to his command, and, calling for his staff, leaped on his horse and galloped off toward the sound of battle.

"I will send you back word what it is," he cried out to Sherman as he disappeared.

An hour passed. Sherman waited eagerly for McPherson's promised report. At last an aide came galloping up, his horse covered with foam, his face portending that he was the bearer of evil tidings.

"General McPherson has fallen," he cried. "He is either dead or a prisoner, badly wounded, within the enemy's lines."

It was a heavy blow to Sherman. He loved McPherson as a man, and trusted him as an able and courageous commander. But it was no time for giving way to grief. Where McPherson fell, serious danger threatened the Union army.

"Ride fast to Logan," said he to the young officer who had brought the bad news. "Tell him McPherson is dead and that he is the senior officer of the Army of the Tennessee. Tell him to attack the enemy on his flank and give no thought to his rear. I will protect that, and will send reenforcements if needed."

The aide saluted and was off like an arrow.

What then had been the nature of the engagement in which the young commander of the Army of the Tennessee had lost his life?

Word had come to General Hood during the afternoon of the 21st that the left flank of the Union army rested in "air." He saw in this another unexpected but welcome opportunity to strike a blow which might prove decisive. The breastworks, he decided, might be held by the Georgia militia and Stewart's corps, while his own corps, under command of Cheatham, and Hardee's corps, should crush the enemy's flank. Hardee was to move around the exposed flank and fall upon McPherson's rear, while Cheatham attacked in front. The Confederate troops set out at sunset and marched all night to get into favorable positions from which to make the attack.

By one of those fortunate chances which sometimes serve a better purpose than the most elaborately matured plans, the morning of the 22d found the Sixteenth Corps of the Army of the Tennessee marching eastward in the rear of McPherson's line, for the purpose of taking a position on the Union left. Therefore, when, about noon, Hardee's men, thinking that they had reached the Union rear, burst from the woods with frantic yells and poured down upon the Federal picket line, they found themselves confronted by a strong column, which had only to face to the right to be in line of battle to oppose them. The Confederate divisions of Walker and Bate were the assailants in this part of the field. Though disappointed in their hope of carrying everything before them with a rush, they set themselves sternly and grimly to the bloody work that was before them. A wide expanse of open fields extended before them, on the other side of which were the Union divisions of Fuller and Sweeney, well supported by artillery. Despite their most determined efforts, the men in gray could not cross that open clearing, swept as it was by volleys of rifle balls, grape, and canister, all dispatched upon their deadly errands by the sure and practiced hands of veterans. It was the roar of these volleys that had reached the ears of McPherson as he sat with Sherman at the Howard house. When he reached the scene, after sending his wagons away to a safer spot, he found all going well. While giving orders for bringing up the reserves to fill in a dangerous gap in the line, an officer rode up with the news that the enemy was attacking on Blair's flank. Putting spurs to his horse McPherson galloped off toward the spot where this new peril was impending. He chose the road by which the bearer of the news had come to him, but with the advance of the Confederates this road had fallen into their hands, and in a few minutes the Union general and his staff galloped, full tilt, into the midst of Cleburne's skirmishers. The subalterns who followed him wheeled their horses sharply and escaped. McPherson, however, when called upon to surrender, checked his horse, hesitated a moment, then, lifting his hat as though in salute, threw himself flat on his horse and turned to flee. Then a Confederate soldier, taking careful aim, fired, and the gallant McPherson fell. By a strange coincidence the man who shot him also bore the name of McPherson. The riderless horse, with the blood-stained saddle, made its way back to the Union lines, where the news of the fall of the general soon spread. Meantime the Confederates swarmed about his prostrate body, stripping it of everything that was valuable, including a pocket-book in which was a letter from General Sherman outlining the future plan of campaign. The news that this letter had fallen into the hands of the enemy greatly worried Sherman, and it was with much relief that he heard, some hours later, that, by a stroke of extraordinary good fortune, the soldiers of an Illinois regiment had captured the Confederate who had taken the letter and found it still on his person.

While the Confederate divisions of Walker and Bate were being held in check by the stubbornness of the Union defense, Cleburne and Maney were meeting with more success. Their line of march brought them upon the rear of General Blair's left wing, the soldiers of which thus found themselves with their breastworks behind them and nothing between them and the foe. Caught thus in a trap by an enemy in overpowering numbers, many of Smith's men were killed or taken prisoners. There was but one way in which an effective defense could be made, and this was to leap over the breastworks and defend them from the other side. This was done, both by Smith's and Leggett's divisions, and the new line thus formed was taken up and extended by re-enforcements sent forward by Logan. All this was done slowly, for the ground was rugged and covered with a dense undergrowth. The men fought in squads, and sometimes even singly, hand to hand. Muskets were clubbed, the bayonet did its swift and deadly work; sometimes, even, the maddened men grappled and rolled on the ground in the fury of mortal combat. Out of the melee the Federals emerged victorious, for despite their utmost exertions the Confederates failed to carry the position.

It was a moment of vital import to the men of the North, for while they were battling with the soldiers of Cleburne and Maney, General Hood was sending Cheatham to take them in the rear. From his position in a salient of the outer line of the Confederate works about Atlanta, the Confederate commander had watched the course of the battle. He saw

Cleburne's veterans held in check by the vigorous and determined resistance of Smith's men, and he at once sent orders to his old division, now under the command of General Cheatham. The attack was made with spirit. Had it been delivered a little sooner, the left flank of the Union Army would have been caught between two fires and cut to pieces. As it was, Cleburne's veterans had been driven away by the men of Smith's division, who were now ready to give their attention to this new attack. Again they leaped over the breastworks and faced about to meet and repel the danger that threatened them from the rear. With courage undaunted, with zeal in no way exhausted by their long struggle against heavy odds, they plied their ramrods, making ready for the withering volley with which they would greet the foe when his long, irregular lines should come within effective range. The great guns were already at work, throwing their shells into the distant masses of men. Cheatham's troops came on gallantly, though the shells were tearing great gaps in their ranks and they knew that the long line of earthworks on the crest of the hill would spout flame and deadly rifle-balls as soon as they had drawn a little nearer. But when the musketry did burst out like a crash of thunder, the Confederates went down in platoons like grain before the cradle of the reaper. The artillery-men let their shells lie, and loaded their guns with grape and canister, which did deadly work in the advancing regiments. The hill was not half-way scaled when the Confederates gave up the effort and fell back in confusion.

But now Cleburne's men, smarting under their defeat, sprang from the thickets and reopened the attack from the opposite direction. It was a blunder, perhaps an unavoidable one, but nevertheless a serious and costly error, that led Cleburne and Cheatham to make their attacks alternately, when, by attacking at the same moment, they would have had the enemy between two fires. As it was the Federals again changed front, sought the other side of their works, and once more sent Cleburne's troops in shattered and bleeding masses to the rear.

Now for a time the battle lagged, but it was only to give the assailants time to reform their broken lines, fill their empty cartridge-boxes, and pre-

THE WATER CALL.

pare for the assault again. This time Hardee was to attack from the south and Cheatham from the north and west. The Federals, with swift and trained intelligence, penetrated the plan of the enemy and, grasping their shovels and axes, speedily had a line of earthworks completed, extending from the flank of the works that they had been defending, at a right angle. Thus protected on both fronts they awaited with calm confidence and determination the expected assault.

In front of Smith's line was a large, square house. Earlier in the action Colonel Jones, whose regiment had been stationed near the spot, had asked leave to burn it, declaring that it hid the movements of the Confederates. Permission was refused him, however, and later in the battle the defenders of the hill had ample reason for regretting that Jones had been unable to do as he wished. When Cheatham's second advance was begun, Confederate sharpshooters filled the house, which overlooked the Union lines. From the upper windows they sent their unerring bullets straight to the mark. The four-gun battery of De Gres, which was posted near by, was made entirely useless, for the sharpshooters picked off the gunners so fast that the cannon could not be served. Nor was this all, for behind the house and its outbuildings a brigade of Confederates was massing, ready for the charge. When all was ready, and the guns were silent, surrounded each by its artillerists, lying dead and wounded on the ground, the troops in ambush rushed out with a cheer. In an instant they were in possession of the guns. They turned these upon the Union line, against which the assailants now rushed with redoubled fury. All was swept away before this irresistible flood of shouting men. Smith and Wood were driven from their trenches. The Confederate banners were everywhere waving in triumph. Wood hastened to Sherman for orders for his guidance in this moment when all seemed lost. De Gres was there, telling with tears in his eyes of the loss of his guns, which had been famous in the Union army since the day of Shiloh. On the battle-field, where the guns were roaring and the shells and bullets whistling, Logan was galloping along the line of the Fifteenth Corps, his hat in his hand, his long black hair streaming in the winds, his eyes blazing with the fire of battle.

"Remember McPherson," he cried. "Let us avenge him! Don't disgrace the name of the Fifteenth Corps."

It was indeed a critical moment. The Confederates had pierced the Union line. They had captured Federal cannon, and turned them against their former owners. They held a section of the Federal works, and a large number of the blue-coated troops were in full retreat. Had Hardee but have attacked at the same moment with Cheatham, there is little doubt that the rout would have spread and the victory would have rested with the men of the South. But the two commanders were far apart. Messages passed but slowly between them, and before Hardee came into action the Federals had rallied and were already wresting back from Cheatham the ground he had so gallantly won. General Sherman ordered Schofield to mass all his artillery on a hill, whence it could pour its deadly volleys into Cheatham's ranks. Then Wood's brigade rallied, made a short half-wheel, and came down upon Cheatham's flank. Smarting under their recent defeat, fired with a fierce determination to regain their lost honor, the men of Wood's command fought with invincible valor and irresistible determination. Their cheers rang loud above the roar of the battle. As they rushed ferociously upon the enemy, the tattered gray lines, already sadly demoralized by the rapid and effective volleys of grape and canister with which Schofield's artillery was pelting them, gave way in dismay. De Gres's lost guns were recaptured, and all save one, which had exploded in the enemy's hands, were turned again against those troops whom they had been for years pursuing with deadly missiles. The Confederates had long since ceased to advance; they were now in full retreat. A brief rally was made at the breastworks, which they strove to hold in reverse against the victorious flood of blue. They were soon dispossessed, and before long Hood, gazing through his field-glasses, suffered the mortification of seeing his finest troops, shattered and beaten, drifting back from the crest of a hill which they had fairly won, only to be no less fairly driven away.

The crisis was now past for the Federals. The attacks of Hardee and Cleburne, that followed shortly after Cheatham's repulse, were met and repelled with comparative ease. A new north and south line had been formed, so that the enemy could no longer direct his assaults against the rear of the Fifteenth Corps. The confusion that followed the sudden death of McPherson had been allayed, and Logan now held firmly the guiding-reins of the Army of the Tennessee.

As the sun sank slowly in the west and the shadows lengthened, the struggles of the Confederates became less vigorous. Their attacks were less frequent and lacked the enthusiasm which they had manifested earlier in the day. It had become evident to the humblest of Hood's men-at-arms that the day had gone against them—that for all their displays of courage and their generous sacrifice of life there was no reward. Gradually they discontinued their efforts, until at last the sounds of battle died away, save that now and then some gun boomed out, throwing shells into the rear of a retreating Confederate column; or the sound of a few rapidly exchanged volleys told that the rear-guard of one of the retiring columns had halted and faced about to beat back a too pertinacious pursuer.

It had been a costly day's work for Hood. He had lost not less than 10,000 men. In front of one division of the Seventeenth Army Corps 1000 dead Confederates were found by their comrades, who came with a flag of truce. Before Logan's corps lay 700, and elsewhere on the field 1500 more. Two thousand Confederate prisoners were taken, over half of whom were wounded. The total loss to the National forces was 3521 in killed, wounded, and missing. It was a tremendous, an irrevocable disaster, which Hood's second effort to depart from the cautious tactics of his predecessor in command had brought upon the Confederacy.

The events of the next six weeks may be briefly passed over. Hood retired to his breastworks around Atlanta. They were among the most impressive examples of defensive works to be seen during that colossal war, in which Vicksburg, Petersburg, and even less famous positions were fortified in a manner that fairly eclipsed the historic Sebastopol. The Confederate military engineers were masters of their art. Their plans were executed by gangs of slaves, who dug while the white men fought.

Sherman had no desire to hurl his army against those impenetrable walls of logs and earth, behind which Hood's veterans sat grimly waiting. He tried plan after plan to lure Hood out of his refuge. A cavalry raid was first planned. General Stoneman and General McCook were sent out with a body of horsemen, with the purpose in view of tearing up the railroad by which the Confederates were drawing supplies and men from Alabama. Stoneman had about 5000 men; McCook 4000. They started from opposite flanks of the Federal army, and were to effect a junction beyond Atlanta and push on to Andersonville, where was that gloomy prison pen in which 32,000 Union prisoners of war, half-clothed and half-starved, were huddled together, all unsheltered, upon a swampy tract of land that scarce gave room for one-third of their number. The expedition ended disastrously. The two wings failed to come together. General McCook, after tearing up a section of track, destroying a vast quantity of railway rolling-stock, and taking 400 prisoners, found himself surrounded, and only escaped with the loss of his prisoners and 600 of his own men beside. Stoneman met with even more ill-fortune. He, too, did havoc with the Confederate railway connections, burning a bridge, destroying seventeen locomotives and a great number of cars. But while he was engaged in his work of destruction, General Hood was telegraphing in every direction for troops. When forty miles from Andersonville, Stoneman found himself surrounded. After a sharp battle he and 700 of his troopers were captured, while many more of his men fell into the enemy's hands as they strove to make their way back to the Union lines.

The attempt to free the prisoners cooped up at Andersonville thus ended in complete failure. But it was as well, after all, that neither McCook nor Stoneman had come within sight of that dismal stockade, within which loyal Union men were herded like cattle. The intelligence of the raid and its purpose had reached the Confederate commander at the prison camp. In an order, for which his memory will ever be execrated, this officer, General Winder, said: "The officers on duty, and in charge of the battery of Florida artillery, will, on receiving notice that the enemy has approached within seven miles of this post, open fire on the stockade with grape-shot, without reference to the situation beyond this line of defense."

Meantime Sherman and Hood had clashed again. The Union general, finding that the Confederates still blocked his path, despite their losses in the battle of the 22d, began once again his favorite flanking maneuvers. The Army of the Tennessee, to the command of which Howard had succeeded, was sent around to the southwest side of the city to cut Hood's railroad connections. On the 28th of the month Howard and Sherman were riding along in the rear of Logan's troops, which were moving into their new position. The fire of the skirmishers was rapidly growing fiercer, and occasionally the rush of round shot through the air and tree-tops was heard. Howard sniffed the battle from afar.

"General Hood will attack me here," said he.

"I guess not," replied Sherman lightly; "he will hardly try it again."

Nevertheless, Howard was right, and it was soon evident that Hood meant to fight. Logan's men had no defensive works, and it was too late to build any. A few fence-rails, loosely piled up, behind which they fought, kneeling or lying down, were their sole protection. Hood's men charged fiercely from the forest, but were steadily met and repulsed. A few of the enemy's regiments passed beyond Logan's right flank, but were met by some Union troops, armed with repeating rifles, and beaten back. Before this movement was met the appearance of the enemy on their flank caused some little panic in the Union lines, and one officer ran to Sherman with the despairing cry, "You've made a mistake in McPherson's successor! Everything is going to pieces!"

"Is General Howard there?" asked Sherman calmly.

"Yes, I suppose he is."

"Well, I'll wait until I hear from him before I take any action."

Sherman's confidence was well founded. Six of the Confederate assaults, delivered in swift succession, were repulsed, and then they came no more. How many Confederates fell cannot be exactly told. Over 600 of their dead were buried by Logan's men, however. The men of the Fifteenth Corps, speaking of the battle, says General Sherman "spoke of it as the easiest thing in the world; that in fact it was a common slaughter of the enemy; they pointed out where the rebel lines had been, and how they themselves had fired deliberately, had shot down their antagonists, whose bodies still lay unburied, and marked plainly their lines of battle, which must have halted within easy musket-range of our men, who were partially protected by their improvised lines of logs and fence-rails."

There now followed a period of comparative quiet. Hood had had his fill of attacking Sherman, and clung stubbornly to his breastworks. His men, too, though their courage and their discipline made them respond quickly enough to every call to action, were disgusted with the rashness which hurled them against a foe well hidden behind breastworks.

"Well, Johnny, how many of you are there left?" asked a Union picket, soon after the affair at Ezra church.

"Oh, about enough for another killing," grimly and rather ruefully responded the Confederate addressed.

Sherman brought up his heavy siege-guns and began bombarding the town. The great shells fell in every quarter of the city. Conflagrations started by the bursting missiles swept away whole blocks. The women and children took refuge in cellars, or in holes dug in their gardens and roofed over with boards and earth. "One thing is certain, whether we get inside of Atlanta or not, it will be a used-up community when we get through with it," was Sherman's promise to Halleck.

Meantime the Union commander, by moving around to the southern side of the city, cutting railroad lines, and sometimes exposing a single division to attack as a tempting bait, strove to lure the Confederates from their refuge. In this he failed. Jefferson Davis, who had removed Johnston for his caution, had warned Hood against making any further attacks. Not until the 1st of September did the ancient antagonists meet again in pitched battle, at Jonesboro. There the Confederates were again signally defeated.

The next day a courier came galloping to Sherman with a message from General Slocum, who had been left in the trenches before Atlanta. It gave the tidings that the city had been evacuated, that Slocum had marched in without a fight, and was then in possession. When General Thomas heard the news he snapped his fingers, whistled, and almost danced with joy. The soldiers sang, cheered, and fired salutes. A courier was sent back to the nearest telegraph station to dispatch the good news to President Lincoln. "Atlanta is ours and fairly won," was the way in which Sherman announced his victory. The bells at Washington were rung and the cannon fired, while General Grant, to whom the tidings came as he was patiently besieging Lee at Petersburg, ordered that his triumphal salute should be fired "with *shotted* guns from every battery bearing on the enemy."

CHAPTER X.

GRANT'S MOVEMENT TO THE SOUTH SIDE OF THE JAMES—PANIC IN PETERSBURG AND RICHMOND—GENERAL WISE PREPARES FOR DEFENSE—FAILURE OF GILLMORE'S EXPEDITION AGAINST PETERSBURG—SMITH CARRIES THE OUTER WORKS—FAILS TO PRESS HIS ADVANTAGE—BEAUREGARD MOVES TO PETERSBURG—HANCOCK'S WOUND DISABLES HIM—THE CONFEDERATES SURPRISED—SIEGE OF PETERSBURG—THE MINE—WHITE TROOPS OR BLACK?—THE EXPLOSION—THE ATTACK AND BLOODY REPULSE OF THE UNION TROOPS.

THE summer of 1864, that was spent by General Sherman in doggedly fighting his way into Atlanta, was passed by the Army of the Potomac in a no less tedious effort to take the little Virginia city of Petersburg, which, by virtue of its position upon the railroads, was really the key to Richmond.

Grant, after the battle of Cold Harbor, gave his battle-scarred veterans but brief rest. He had determined early in the campaign that the way to attack Richmond was from the south, and even while the battles of Spottsylvania and Cold Harbor were being fought, a great fleet of steamers, schooners, sloops, canal-boats, barges, and pontoons was moving from Washington toward the point at which Grant proposed to cross the James River. It was a difficult task that Grant had set himself. To withdraw an army, everywhere in contact with the enemy's lines, move it fifty miles and take it across two rivers, one of them a broad, navigable stream, is enough to tax the resources of the ablest general. Yet it was accomplished without disaster and even without serious hindrance. A line of intrenchments protected the flank of the Union army throughout its march ; two stone-laden barges, sunk in the channel of the river just below Richmond, effectually prevented the Confederate ironclads from descending the stream to interfere with the crossing; while a spirited cavalry demonstration on the right flank diverted Lee's attention from the true purpose of the Army of the Potomac.

The army moved on the 12th of June, and soon had safely passed the James. Picturesque and wonderful was the scene at the crossing. The river there is seven hundred yards wide, and its tawny current was spanned by a pontoon-bridge, over which an interminable procession of marching troops, rumbling artillery, and white-topped army wagons was unceasingly passing. The day was bright and clear and the sunlight danced on the waves, sparkled brightly on the polished barrels of fifty thousand muskets, and was reflected in dazzling flashes from the shining brass cannon. Above the bridge several sullen-looking gun-boats lay at anchor, ready to fend off any attack by water; while below, steam craft of every style of naval architecture were puffing to and fro, ferrying across the troops for which the bridge did not afford a broad enough pathway. In that wild and little-settled region, with the woods growing thick to the very banks of the river, this tremendous concentration of military power, this restless and intelligent activity, seemed to illustrate most vividly the resistless force that had been enlisted in the effort to crush out all armed resistance to the national government.

General Lee was strangely blind to this movement of his determined antagonist. Not until three days after Grant had left his front did the Army of Northern Virginia take up the march for Petersburg in its turn. Meantime the Confederate control of that town had been placed in serious jeopardy more than once. It is difficult to understand, when the importance of the position is considered, why it was that the Confederates left it so long inadequately defended, and why the Federals were so slow in taking advantage of the enemy's error.

On the 9th of June Petersburg was held only by the brigade of General Wise, about 2000 strong. Great was the consternation then of the citizens, and of General Beauregard, who was holding Butler pent-up at Bermuda Hundred, to learn that a Federal force about 4500 strong was on its way to attack the town. Beauregard sent Wise 600 men, under command of General Dearing, and telegraphed frequent and importunate requests to Richmond for more troops. But there was a panic in Richmond then, and his entreaties were ignored. Wise, for his part, pluckily set to work to make the best of the resources at hand. Fortunately for him the town was well provided with defensive works—at that time there was scarcely a strategic position in all the South that was not walled and fortified, ready for any emergency. Into the trenches Wise sent his regular troops and the "home guards"—the latter made up of boys too young for service in the army, and old men, gray-haired and decrepit. Still, great gaps appeared in his line of defense. He went to the hospital and pressed into service all the invalided soldiers whose condition permitted them to carry guns. Thence to the jails, where he threw open the doors, put muskets in the hands of the prisoners, and bade them fight for their liberty. Then he went back to the breastworks to await the attack, hoping only that he might hold the Federals in check until help from Richmond could reach him.

The national forces were in two divisions; 3000 infantry under General Gillmore and 1500 cavalry under General Kautz. They had hoped to take the enemy by surprise, but the bridge across the Appomattox had not been muffled, and the clatter of Kautz's horses' hoofs, as the cavalry crossed, could be heard for miles, and put the enemy on his guard. When Gillmore arrived and saw Wise's troops snugly ensconced behind their earthworks, he concluded that he was not strong enough to attack, and accordingly retired without a fight. Kautz was more determined. Attacking the works on the southern side of the city, he carried them one after the other. Then he fought his way into the heart of the city, driving several hundred of the Confederates, mostly militia, before him. But it was one thing to enter a town of 18,000 people and another to hold it. He could hear nothing from Gillmore, and he knew well enough that no re-enforcements were at hand. So after a brief stay in the city he withdrew.

Once again did the Federals have the town of Petersburg—the capture of which was destined to cost them many good and gallant men and months of weary waiting—within their grasp, but lost it through a blunder.

On the 15th of June the division of General W. F. Smith was before the Petersburg works, which were still but slenderly manned. How meager was the force before him Smith did not know. Had he but been aware of the great opportunity that lay open to his grasp, he might have gone over the breastworks and into the town with but little loss. But he saw cannon peering through the embrasures. There were men to man them, and infantrymen to support them, he knew. But how many? To discover this he spent the greater part of the day in a careful reconnoissance. Not until the sun went down did he conclude that it was safe to hazard an attack. Then he ordered his guns brought up and a fierce artillery fire concentrated upon the point at which he intended to attack. But some one had concluded that there would be no active hostilities that night, and the artillery horses had been unharnessed and taken to the rear to water. Before they could be brought up and the guns put into position an hour had elapsed. Then the cannon burst into full cry and their great bolts beat against the earthen walls, behind which crouched only a handful of Confederates. When the cannonade stopped to let the long waving lines of blue go sweeping to the front, there was scarcely any resistance offered. The loss that befell the Union forces was chiefly in the ranks of a brigade of colored troops, then under fire for the first time. The black men—but lately released from the thralldom of the slave-driver—proved their manhood well. They swarmed over the crest of the works, ahead even of their white comrades in arms. They laid hold upon four cannon that the Confederates had abandoned in their flight, wheeled them about, and turned their fire upon the retreating columns of the foe. Everywhere victory followed the battle-flags of the men in blue. Five redans, sixteen pieces of artillery, and more than 300 prisoners were taken. It needed but that the advantage thus gained should be vigorously pressed for Petersburg to drop into the hands of Smith.

Meantime re-enforcements were coming to the aid of the Federal commander. Hancock, with his famous Second Army Corps, was on the march for Petersburg. Blundering orders, based upon an incorrect map, had misled him, or he would have been by Smith's side early in the day. As it was, two of his divisions came into an effective supporting position while the attack was still under way. Their arrival was known to Smith, who, with their aid, could readily have swept away the Confederates. Instead of this he ordered the newly arrived troops to relieve his own soldiers in the captured redoubts. It was a bright moonlight night. Smith's troops had marched barely six miles and had done but little fighting. The enemy's force was insignificant, even when the advantage it possessed in being protected by earthworks was considered. Yet the night passed without an attack, and the Federals had permitted another golden opportunity to pass.

Confederate troops now began pouring into the defensive works at Petersburg. Hoke's division, after a forced march of eighteen miles from Drury's Bluff, began arriving at about nine o'clock at night. As fast as the regiments came in the men were given intrenching tools and set to work throwing up a new line of works between the town and the redans which had been captured by the Federals earlier in the night. Troops came from Beauregard, too, for that general had concluded that it was wiser to save Petersburg than to hold the line of earthworks by the aid of which he kept Butler bottled up at Bermuda Hundred. Leaving 1000 men to guard his line, he moved all the remainder of his force to Petersburg. His ruse, however, was speedily discovered. Lieutenant-Colonel Greeley, in command of a Connecticut regiment at Bermuda Hundred, thought he discerned signs of a movement within the Confederate lines. Creeping forward on his hands and knees, hidden from the gaze of the enemy's pickets by the long grass, but in imminent danger of detection every moment, he learned that his suspicions were well founded. Soon after he swooped down on the breastworks, capturing them and Beauregard's rearguard. But in the mean time the former defenders of those works had reached Petersburg and were busily preparing for the battle of the morrow.

In the morning Hancock succeeded to the command of the Federal forces before Petersburg and issued his orders for an early attack. Directly in front of his lines the enemy's works were still held by only a slender force, though no doubt the Confederates were prepared to rush additional troops to the defense of any threatened point. Yet there is every reason to believe that the Petersburg lines could have been pierced had Hancock's orders been vigorously and promptly carried out. But a shot that had been fired at Gettysburg a year before now came between Hancock and victory. The wound which he had received on that famous field had never fully healed. The six weeks of marching and fighting, amid the pelting rain, had caused it to give the general much trouble, which on this day of battle culminated in such fearful agony that he was forced to lie on a sick bed instead of directing in person the movements of his troops. Thus deprived of the trained and determined mind that had long guided and animated them, the men of the Second Corps moved but laggingly. The assault that should have been made at daybreak did not take place until half the morning had passed. The redoubt that might have been readily entered at the earlier hour spouted flame and hot lead at the later. One redan was taken and then, for a time, comparative quiet rested upon the battle-field.

At sundown the din of battle began again. Meade had arrived and taken command. Hancock had yielded place to begin a furlough of ten days. With Meade had come the Ninth Corps, and there were now 50,000 blue-clad men-at-arms upon the field. The assault was made about six o'clock, and was received with gallantry by the enemy. For a time the Union line wavered between success and failure, but finally succeeded in driving the Confederates from one of their advanced works, which was quickly intrenched against them. Here the men of the Second Corps proceeded to make themselves comfortable for the night—opening their haversacks and devouring their rations with appetites in no way dulled by the knowledge that the moon was shining brightly, so that the night would bring them no respite from fighting. And, indeed, the whole night was passed in attacking the enemy and in repelling in turn the spirited assaults with which he retaliated.

At dawn, on the morning of the 17th, Potter's division of the Ninth Corps carried in a brilliant fashion the Confederate redans and lines that crested a ridge on which stood the Shand farm-house. Four guns, five stands of colors, 600 prisoners, and 1500 stands of arms were captured in this assault. The brilliancy of the attack was greatly enhanced by the difficult nature of the ground, which was steep in slope and obstructed by slashed pine timber. The assault was a complete surprise to the Confederates. "I spent the entire night in moving my troops through the felled timber, getting them in proper position, and preparing for the attack," writes General Griffin, who led the assault. "We were so near the enemy that all our movements had to be made with the utmost care and caution; canteens were placed in knapsacks to prevent rattling, and all commands were given in whispers. I formed my brigade in two lines. . . . . Colonel Curtin formed his in the same way. . . . . My orders were not to fire a shot, but to depend wholly on the bayonet in carrying the lines.

"Just as the dawn began to light up the east I gave the command, 'Forward.' It was passed along the lines in whispers; the men sprang to their feet and both brigades moved forward at once in well-formed lines, sweeping directly over the enemy's lines, taking them completely by surprise, and carrying all before us. One gunner saw us approaching and fired his piece. That was all we heard from them, and almost the only shot fired on either side. The rebels were asleep, with their arms in their hands, and many of them sprang up and ran away as we came over. Others surrendered without resistance. We swept their line for a mile from where my right rested, gathering in prisoners and abandoned arms and equipments all the way."

For the next thirty-six hours the fighting before Petersburg went on without intermission. Beauregard was standing at bay before a vastly superior force. Lee still lagged in sending him aid. Not an hour passed that his lines were not in peril at some point from an assaulting column of Federals. Meade knew how weak, in point of numbers, was the force by which he was opposed, and spared no effort to pierce the lines that barred his path to Petersburg. Some successes he achieved, while he met with some reverses. Before a few redoubts his troops were driven back across fields covered thickly with their own dead and wounded. Some redoubts were taken, only to be recaptured by the enemy. Others were captured and held. But Beauregard, when driven from one line, had another ready to fall behind, between the Federals and the town, and when the sun went down, on the night of the 18th, the defenses of Petersburg seemed as powerful as ever. By that time, too, the heads of Lee's columns were entering the town. The time for taking Petersburg by assault was past, and General Grant ordered the Union troops into cover, to rest from the exertions that were over, that they might be ready for those yet to come. Already, in the struggle for the Confederate stronghold, 10,586 had been lost, of whom 1298 had been killed and 7474 wounded. The Confederate loss has never been reported, but was doubtless heavy, though not so great as that of the Federals.

Grant now settled down and began a regular siege of Petersburg. His troops were kept busy throwing up new works, mounting siege-guns and mortars, and digging the parallels and approaches which were to lead them near enough to the Confederate works to make an attack effective. Lee met this threatened danger in kind, strengthening his works, laying out new lines of defense and taking precautions against every possible form of attack. He was holding Petersburg under orders, not of his own judgment. His own clear military insight had told him that Richmond was doomed as soon as Grant put his army south of the James, thereby getting into a position whence he could at his leisure cut the railroads that connected the Confederate capital with the South. It is said that Lee warmly urged the evacuation of Richmond, but Jefferson Davis would not listen to the suggestion, and commanded that the Army of Northern Virginia should continue, at Petersburg, the stubborn defense that it had so long maintained in the region between the Rapidan and the James.

As Lee had anticipated, Grant's first act, when he had fairly established his army in the trenches before Petersburg, was to send a column to cut the Confederate railway communications. The Weldon railway was the one first marked for destruction, but the disposition of the troops employed gave the Confederates an opportunity, of which they speedily availed themselves, to strike an effective blow at their persistent foe. The divisions of Birney and Wright were sent by Meade to cut the Weldon road, but through some blunder on the part of these generals a gap was left between the two divisions. This was quickly known within the Confederate lines, and A. P. Hill's men sallied out and drove straight into the gap. There was but little fighting. The Federals, taken by surprise and demoralized by the sudden appearance of the enemy on their flank, threw down their guns and fled. In Gibbon's division whole regiments were captured, with their flags. A battery of four guns was abandoned to the enemy, who lost no time in turning it against the Northern ranks. Though Gibbon made a strenuous effort to recover his position, he was beaten back. The railroad was for the time saved to the Confederates, who came out of the affair elated with triumph and boasting the capture of four cannon, several stands of colors, and 1700 prisoners.

For a time now the chief activity of the Union troops was centered upon the repeated efforts that were made to destroy the railroads at every vulnerable point. But behind the ponderous walls of earth that now sheltered Grant's army, an undertaking, startling in its conception and gigantic in its proportions, was slowly being pushed to completion.

After the assaults of the 17th and 18th of June had fixed the extreme points at which the Union lines could be maintained, the Ninth Corps was left within 130 yards of the Confederate works. In that corps was a regiment 400 strong, recruited mostly among the coal miners of Pennsylvania. Its commander, Colonel Henry Pleasants, who before entering the army had been a mining engineer, became impressed with the idea that it would be an easy task to tunnel under the enemy's works, dig chambers there, fill them with powder, and at the proper time blow the whole Confederate redoubt into the air, and through the gap thus made thrust a column of troops that would tear Lee's entire system of defense to pieces. His plan met Burnside's approval, and he began work.

Colonel Pleasants soon found that it was a difficult task that he had set himself. He had first to survey carefully the ground between the enemy's works and his own, while the rifle-balls of the Confederate sharpshooters whizzed dangerously near the old-fashioned theodolite through which he was peering. He discovered too that, while he had permission to undertake the work, his superior officers, with the exception of General Burnside, regarded it as a piece of folly, and left him severely to his own resources. His mining tools had to be extemporized. Cracker boxes, bound with hoop-iron, were used to carry out the dirt, which was dumped at the mouth of the tunnel and kept carefully covered with brush lest some keen-sighted Confederate, descrying the growing mound of fresh earth, should suspect the subterranean attack that threatened their lines. Despite this caution, however, the enemy did discover what was being done. At first they began to meet it by sinking a counter-mine, but this was abandoned for lack of tools. Beauregard then contented himself with building a second line of works in the rear of that which he expected to be blown up, and studding it thickly with cannon trained so as to pour a concentrated fire upon the breach that would be made. Then the Confederate commander removed all save a few troops from the threatened redoubt and calmly awaited the earthquake.

For nearly a month the men of Pleasants's regiment burrowed in the earth. The tunnel in which they were working was scarcely five feet high, and the miners had to wield their tools lying down or stooped over in an awkward and wearisome posture. The difficult and tedious task of carrying out the excavated earth, a bushel at a time, in cracker boxes, still further protracted the labor. Still, some progress was made. After four weeks of work the men in the mine could tell by the vibrations of the walls of their gallery that the enemy's heavy guns were at work directly above their heads. Sometimes, indeed, when the artillery duel was at its fiercest, the earth shook so that the diggers expected that at any moment their tunnel might cave in and bury them deep beneath the battle-field. At last, however, the work was completed, and without any mishap. The subterranean chambers were charged with 8000 pounds of gunpowder in kegs, connected by a long continuous fuse. All was made ready to touch off this artificial volcano over which the Confederates were sleeping.

A discussion now arose over the choice of troops to lead the assault into the crater when the mine should be sprung. General Burnside urged the employment of negro troops. He believed that the white soldiers had been so long accustomed to fighting behind breastworks that they had lost the dash and enthusiasm necessary for a forlorn hope. Meade, however, was averse to the employment of colored troops in this service. The negro was at that time a subject of bitter controversy, and Meade feared that he would be charged with pushing the black troops to the front to get them killed. Therefore he ordered that a white division of the Ninth Corps should make the attack, leaving it to Burnside to choose which of his three divisions should be employed. This Burnside did by permitting his division commanders to draw lots for the perilous honor, which fell to General Ledlie.

At 3.30 o'clock in the morning of July 27 the Federal troops were drawn up in line waiting for the roar of the explosion, which would be the signal for the attack. A long delay occurred, which could not be explained until two plucky soldiers volunteered to enter the mine and discover its cause. They found that the fuse had gone out. Quickly relighting it, they made their way with all possible speed to the surface of the earth again. The minutes passed slowly while the dull red spark underground was crawling along the fuse to the first keg of powder. Suddenly a cry rose from the assembled host of soldiers. Before their straining eyes a great block of the Confederate works rose bodily, high in air, spread out like a tree at the top, and fell back in fragments with a roar that could be heard miles away. Fire and smoke shot upward with this column, and flames played weirdly about its crest, seventy-five or one hundred feet in air. Men, cannon, gun-

BURNING UNION BREASTWORKS IN THE WILDERNESS.

carriages, sand-bags, earth, in masses as large as a small house, and the finest floating dust, all rose with this terrible fountain. The ground shook as with an earthquake, throwing down many of the men in blue that stood gazing. It seemed as though the flying débris would fall within the Union lines, and many of the ranks that were formed for the assault were broken in the panic.

It was time now for the assault. The columns of blue should already have been pushing their way toward the smoking crater. But an odd oversight delayed the attack. In the midst of their planning to get into the enemy's works it had never occurred to the Federals that they would find difficulty in getting out of their own. But now that the time had come to charge, they suddenly discovered that they were in deep trenches with lofty ramparts before them unprovided with sally-ports or means for climbing over. But the men extemporized ladders by thrusting bayonets between the logs and holding them while others used them as steps, by the aid of which they scaled the redoubt. Then, hastily forming on the colors, they rushed forward to the crater.

"Little did these men anticipate what they would see on arriving there," writes Major Powell.[1] "An enormous hole in the ground, about 30 feet deep, 60 feet wide, and 170 feet long, filled with dust, great blocks of clay, guns, broken carriages, projecting timbers and men buried in various ways— some up to their necks, others to their waists, and some with only their feet and legs protruding from the earth. One of these near me was pulled out, and proved to be a second lieutenant of the battery which had been blown up. The fresh air revived him, and he was soon able to walk and talk. He was very grateful, and said that he was asleep when the explosion took place, and only awoke to find himself wriggling up in the air; then a few seconds afterward he found himself descending, and soon lost consciousness.

"The whole scene of the explosion struck every one dumb with astonishment as we arrived at the crest of the débris. It was impossible for the

---

[1] "Battles and Leaders of the Civil War."

troops of the second brigade to move forward in line, as they had advanced; and owing to the broken state they were in, every man crowding up to look into the hole, and being pressed by the first brigade, which was immediately in the rear, it was equally impossible to move by the flank, by any command, around the crater. Before the brigade commanders could realize the situation, the two brigades became irretrievably mixed, in the desire to look into the hole."

Meantime the Confederates had recovered from the panic that had spread through their ranks at the moment of the explosion. In the fresh line of works that Beauregard had constructed in the rear of that wrecked by the explosion, they were returning to their guns. The trenches to the right and left of the crater were still held by the enemy, and as the Federal troops swept forward to assault the frowning redoubt in their front, they were thrown into confusion by a murderous fire poured into their backs by this force left on their flank and rear. Though they bore themselves gallantly and cut to pieces the South Carolina infantry that tried to make a stand in the crater, the assailants were not long in discovering that they had thrust themselves into a trap from which they were not likely to escape unscathed. To add to the perplexities of their position the division commander, General Ledlie, instead of accompanying his troops in their charge, had remained behind snugly sheltered in a bomb-proof. He could neither see the progress of his troops nor correct their errors. Had a competent commander been on the ground the enemy would no doubt have been driven from the trenches, which were open and exposed to a flank attack. But no one had authority to deviate from the plan of attack as ordered, which was to press straight ahead and carry the enemy's new line. To do this in the teeth of a galling fire from an enemy in front well covered by earthworks, while artillery on distant knobs and hills was throwing shells into their midst, and several infantry regiments were firing volleys into their backs, was more than the men of Ledlie's division could accomplish. Baffled and badly cut up, they fell back. Only in the crater could they find any shelter, and even that was but partial. The men clung to the precipitous sides of the pit, digging their toes or heels into the clay, or thrusting in their bayonets and clinging to them. Even then many were shot, and he who was hit by a musket-ball rolled helpless to the bottom of the chasm. More troops kept pouring in, for despite the messages describing the hopelessness of the situation that were sent him, General Ledlie, from his secure retreat in the bomb-proof, demanded that the original plan should be carried out, and sent additional regiments to maneuver in a place already overcrowded by those that were there. The enemy's fire was increasing in rapidity and effect continually, and as the crater became more crowded almost every shot found its mark. The thud of the bullet striking into human flesh, the cries of the wounded and the noise of heavy bodies rolling down the steep sides of the pit were sounds of momentary occurrence.

In the midst of the most frightful scenes, some ludicrous incident impresses itself upon the minds of the spectators because of its very incongruity. The veterans who lived through that bloody day in the Petersburg crater and have told of their experience, all mention the disaster that befell General Bartlett. Earlier in the war this veteran soldier had lost a leg, which he had replaced with a cork one and rejoined the army. Soon after the troops sought refuge in the crater the thud of a striking shot was heard and the general was seen to totter and fall. His friends sprang to his side and picked him up, when he cried out:

"Put me anywhere where I can sit down."

"But you are badly wounded, General, aren't you?" asked one of his supporters.

"My leg is all shattered to pieces," he replied.

"Then you can't sit down. You must be carried to the rear."

"Oh, no!" exclaimed the general. "It's only my cork leg."

Two hours had passed from the time of the springing of the mine, when General Burnside ordered the division of colored troops into action. Some prisoners had told that officer that the enemy had no works in the rear of the one that Ledlie's division was then assaulting, and that they had already begun to retreat when Ledlie's men broke and fled. Thinking then that it needed only that a heavier force should be employed in the attack,

Burnside ordered Ferraro to put in his negro soldiers. But the same causes that had made the earlier attack a failure defeated this. Ferraro sought out Ledlie in his bomb-proof and sat there with him, leaving his troops to advance without their commander. His men found difficulty in getting out of their works, and finally emerged by twos and threes. Once they were out and aligned for the charge, they showed the greatest valor. Coming to the crater they saw that it was already too crowded, and swerving to the right they swept on around it toward the lofty line of earthworks from which the storm of leaden balls was beating in their faces. It was here that one of the colored sergeants—a huge, muscular fellow, stripped to the waist, with his bare skin shining like polished ebony—was seen to grasp one of his comrades by the collar and throw him over into the trenches. "None o' yer skulkin', now!" shouted the black Hercules to the luckless private, whom he had detected in an attempt to edge away into the comparatively safe recesses of the crater.

The arrival of the colored troops did not change the situation in any way for the better. Though they fought gallantly and took some prisoners and a flag in a hand-to-hand conflict with a party of the enemy that tried to make a stand outside of the breastworks, they were unable to take the decisive position against which they had been sent. Torn by a furious artillery fire that fell upon them from both flanks, and the steady and merciless volleys of the Confederate infantry in their front, the black troops gradually lost their organization and began to go to pieces. In their retreat most of them made for the Union lines, which they had left so full of hope and high ambition. Some, however, turned their steps toward the crater, there to swell the exhausted, cowering throng of soldiers who preferred to crouch half-sheltered there rather than brave the perils of a retreat to the Union lines across ground swept by the fire of the foe.

The morning was now more than half spent and the sun stood high in the heavens. Its burning rays poured down pitilessly upon the fainting, bleeding crowd in the fatal pit. No air was stirring. The wounded were crying aloud for water and trying to moisten their dry and cracking lips with their parched tongues. The blood of the injured, trickling down the steep sides of the hollow, had collected in little pools on the bottom of hard red clay. The field before the crater, which division after division had vainly attempted to cross, was covered with the killed and wounded, both black and white, lying so thick, says Major Henzton, "that one disposed to be so inhuman might have reached the works without stepping on the ground."

A report of the agonizing condition of these troops had been carried to Meade, and he, with General Grant's acquiescence, had directed Burnside to abandon the offensive and to withdraw his troops from the crater whenever that could be done safely. But Burnside dared not permit his men to retire while the field over which they had to pass was swept by the enemy's guns. Such a retreat he feared would become a rout, and the enemy, leaping from his intrenchments, might follow the frantic throng of demoralized men into the Union work sand endanger the whole army. If there had been intrenching tools at hand the men in the crater might have dug a covered way in which to retreat, but none were to be found.

Matters were now coming rapidly to a crisis. The Confederates, not content with the results of their fire upon the men in the crater, were preparing to sally out and attack them. Their preparations were made in full view of those upon whom the blow was to fall, but out of sight of the artillerymen in the Union trenches. Accordingly the attacking force formed without any interruption, and sallying forth, swarmed over the crest and down the sides of the crater. When the Confederates appeared the Union guns opened fire, but it was then too late. In a few moments the enemy was fiercely assailing the unhappy Federals, who, wearied by long exertions, and crowded together in that infernal pit of death, could offer but a feeble resistance. About 87 officers, among them General Bartlett with his shattered cork leg, fell into the hands of the enemy, together with 1652 men. The remainder fled to the Union lines, while the Confederates soon sought their stronghold again.

So ended in complete and mortifying failure the battle of the Petersburg crater. It had brought to the Union army nothing but disgrace, suffering, and death. The days of planning and working that had preceded it were but labor thrown away. The loss to the Union army had been, according to General Meade's report, 4400 men, of these over 400 being killed. The Confederate loss cannot be accurately determined, but was somewhat less, although there were 300 men in the exploded redoubt, most of whom must have perished.

A competent military authority has described this battle as "the most discreditable to the Northern arms of all the battles of the war." General Grant says of it: "The effort was a stupendous failure. It cost us about 4000 men, mostly, however, captured; and all due to inefficiency on the part of the corps commander and the incompetency of the division commander who was sent to lead the assault." So great was the outcry both in the army and out of it over this affair, in which an attacking force found as much trouble in getting out of its own works as in getting into the enemy's, and in which the commanders of a storming party lurked behind in bomb-proofs, that a special court of inquiry and a Congressional investigating committee took the matter up. The character of their findings was such that General Ledlie soon after resigned from the army, while General Burnside, at his own request, was relieved of his command.

CHAPTER XI.

IN THE SHENANDOAH VALLEY—BATTLE OF PIEDMONT—DESTRUCTION AT STAUNTON—BRECKENRIDGE ORDERED TO THE VALLEY—HUNTER'S RETREAT FROM LYNCHBURG—EARLY'S MARCH UPON WASHINGTON—EARLY IN FREDERICK—HIS HEAVY REQUISITIONS—PANIC IN WASHINGTON—GENERAL WALLACE INTERPOSES—BATTLE OF THE MONOCACY—EARLY APPROACHES THE CAPITAL—HELP COMES IN TIME—EARLY RETREATS—M'CAUSLAND'S RAID—THE BURNING OF CHAMBERSBURG.

A WEEK after the battle of New Market, in which the Confederate cadets so signally distinguished themselves, General Sigel was relieved from the command of the Union forces in the Shenandoah Valley, and was replaced by General Hunter. The new commander moved with celerity, fought his troops hard and won a succession of victories, none of them in the first importance in itself, but all of which, when taken together, summed up a very considerable total of effective blows at Confederate supremacy in the valley.

Pushing along the level roads of that beautiful dale, his foragers bringing in for the support of his soldiers the produce of those fertile farms that had so long contributed bountifully of their richness to the Confederate granaries, Hunter came to Piedmont. Here the Confederate General William E. Jones barred his path. The Southern troops were ready for the battle. Behind their breastworks they listened to the stirring strains of "Dixie" and the "Marseillaise," played by a regimental band, while their commander rode along the lines urging them to fight well and beat back the Northern invaders. The battle that followed was brief but decisive. The Confederates were cut to pieces. Their loss was over 1000. Their leader was slain. The shattered remnant of his army went drifting up the valley, spreading on every hand the dire tidings of defeat.

Hunter pushed on to Staunton, where he was joined by Crook and Averill. The total Federal force by this concentration was increased to about 18,000. The stop at Staunton was long enough to permit of the destruction of the depot, woolen factory, government stables, steam mill, wagon shops, warehouses, three miles of railroad and $400,000 worth of commissary stores belonging to the Confederate war department. Among the spoil of war was a great quantity of shoes, with which Crook and Averill shod their men, who were barefoot after much marching.

Leaving Staunton, the Union columns marched toward Lynchburg by four parallel roads. No more formidable force was in their immediate front than a flying battalion of sharpshooters, who burned bridges and harassed the Federals from the farther side of every stream. At Lexington a stop was made. Some cadets, too young to accompany the battalion that had taken the field with Imboden, fired from the windows of the Institute at the marching column. For this the torch was set to the college buildings and they were soon in ruins. The residence of ex-Governor Letcher, near by, met a like fate, because some of Hunter's scouts discovered a proclamation, signed by Letcher, advising the people of the Valley to rise and carry on a guerrilla warfare against the Federals. The sight of these blazing edifices seemed to stimulate Hunter's appetite for destruction, for he ordered that the buildings of Washington University should also be burned. But some of his officers, who knew that the college owed its existence to the First President, the great American whom later Americans, North and South, love to honor, protected against this, and the buildings were spared. Yet the Union soldiers could not refrain from pulling down a statue of Washington that stood in the college hall and carrying it off to Wheeling.

It would have been better for Hunter had he pushed straight on to Lynchburg, his objective point, instead of dallying to ply the torch among the public buildings of Lexington. Time was an important factor in the success of his enterprise then, though just how vitally important Hunter could scarcely have been expected to know. Lee had received early tidings of the disaster at Piedmont, and knew that the next move of the Federals would be the siege of Lynchburg, an important point in the strategic surroundings of Richmond. With scarce a moment's delay he sent off Breckenridge to hold the threatened town. Breckenridge had been in the Shenandoah Valley only a few weeks before, when his troops had beaten Sigel at New Market. As it had long been the custom of Union commanders in the Valley to lapse into a long period of inactivity after a defeat, Lee had felt safe in calling Breckenridge to his side at Richmond. But the swiftness with which Hunter regained the ground lost by Sigel convinced the Confederate general that a new head was in control of the movements of the Union armies, and he hastily dispatched Breckenridge to the threatened point, following him a short time later by the division of General Early.

Breckenridge reached Lynchburg but a few hours before Hunter's skirmishers appeared. The march of the Union columns over the lofty crest of the Blue Ridge had been slow and toilsome. McCausland's Confederate sharpshooters, who had opposed their advance ever since the battle of Piedmont, harassed them greatly as they plodded through the narrow defiles and along the tortuous roads that wound in and out among the crags of this wild and rugged spur of the Alleghenies. This gave Breckenridge time to prepare defensive works at Lynchburg, and by the time Hunter's full force came up the Confederates, though greatly outnumbered, were at least fairly prepared to hold their ground until Early could come up. That commander, for his part, had marched swifty and reached the threatened town before Hunter had attacked it. While the Union troops were erecting breastworks before the city they could hear the cheers of the inhabitants as they hailed the arrival of Early's veterans. The battle that was fought the next day was begun by the Confederates, who charged Hunter's works. Though the charge was repulsed and the works held, the Federal commander saw that the time for the capture of Lynchburg had passed, and determined to retreat. Far from his base of supplies, with no railroad in his rear, he was beginning to find the problem of feeding his men difficult of solution. He had not ammunition enough for a pitched battle. To stand still and starve, to fight without powder or shot, or to take to his heels were the only courses left to him. Therefore the Confederates awoke morning to find the Union trenches empty.

Hunter's retreat was made with headlong speed, not so much because of fear of the enemy as for the purpose of getting to his supplies at the earliest moment. His hard bread had given out. His daily ration of flour to each man was but six ounces. Beef was the chief food of the soldiers, the cattle being driven along with the flying column and slaughtered when the troops halted at night. Once during the march no rations at all were issued for forty-eight hours. The men grew gaunt and wolfish. The short rations that began on the 18th were continued until the 27th, when Gauley Bridge was reached, where a train loaded with 70,000 rations of hardtack, sugar, coffee, and bacon awaited the famished soldiers. There was but little fighting on the way. Once the cavalry of McCausland swooped down upon the reserve artillery train, which was without proper escort, and began to shoot the horses and destroy the caissons and limbers. Troops from the rear hastened to the rescue, but McCausland made his escape with three guns, while five more had to be abandoned for lack of horses to drag them. The disabled caissons and limbers too had to be left behind.

In making his escape, Hunter chose to turn his steps down the Kanawha Valley toward the Ohio. This left the broad pathway of the Shenandoah Valley, leading northward, open. Early's troops were the men of Stonewall Jackson's old division, the wiry "Foot Cavalry" that had so often found the valley the road to victory. There was now no armed force between them and the Potomac River. There was practically no serious obstacle between them and the Federal capital. It was with a burst of enthusiasm that the grizzled veterans hailed the announcement that their steps were to be turned northward and that once again, after so many months of defensive fighting, the theater of war was to be shifted from the battle-scarred territory of Virginia to the placid and unvexed fields of the North.

When Lee detached Early from the forces in Richmond and sent him to snatch Lynchburg from Hunter's clutches, he had ordered that general, after disposing of Hunter, to move down the Shenandoah Valley, cross the Potomac, and threaten Washington and Baltimore. Early suggested that he might do more than threaten Washington—that with swift action and a fair amount of good fortune he might perchance even marshal his regiments in the streets of the national capital. But this Lee declared would be impossible. It would be enough for him if the vigor of his trusted lieutenant's march and operations in the vicinity of Washington should so alarm the Federal war officials as to force Grant to withdraw some of the troops then engaged in hemming in the Confederates at Petersburg with a circle of steel and of iron.

Therefore, after the retreat of Hunter had cleared the valley of all hostile troops, Early turned the heads of his columns to the north. Twelve days later he began the crossing of the Potomac, after having burned a vast quantity of army stores belonging to the Federals, at Harper's Ferry. There was delay in marshaling the Union forces to meet him. The War Department gave but little attention to the reports of the officers in command at Harper's Ferry, and on the night of the 3d of July, when the Confederates were fighting Sigel within a half a day's march of the Potomac, General Grant wrote Halleck that Early had returned to Richmond. Two days later the farmers of Maryland and Pennsylvania were fleeing from their homes in dread of the invaders. Wagons loaded down with household goods of every description, some of which it would baffle the most rapacious trooper to carry away, crowded the roads, making for places of safety. McCausland's cavalrymen were in Hagerstown, where they collected a tribute of $20,000. The main body of the Confederates was moving eastward over South Mountain, where a battle had been fought just before the bloody day of Antietam.

In Washington there was some slight alarm, but the officials at the War Department scoffed at any thought of serious danger. "It is only one of the Confederate raiding parties," they said. "It will be sent flying back to the place whence it came long before it can put Washington in any jeopardy."

Grant, who had become alive to the gravity of the situation, offered to send Halleck an army corps for the defense of the capital. But Halleck replied that a division of dismounted cavalry would do. Luckily for the people of Washington, and the honor of the national capital, Grant concluded to be on the safe side, and sent half of the Sixth Corps along with the cavalry.

Dawn of the 8th of July saw Early's tattered regiments marching into the little town of Frederick, where Stonewall Jackson had been before them in 1862. Among Early's battle-scarred veterans there were some who had marched through the broad and dusty streets of the Maryland city on that earlier campaign, and they hailed the villagers, who stood open-mouthed upon this sudden irruption of a hostile army, with familiar gibes and shouts of " Here we are again! Ain't you glad to see us?"

The townspeople, for their part, were in no way pleased. They thought the war had gone from their neighborhood. Its echoes had for so long resounded from the far-off fields of Virginia, growing more and more distant every week, that they thought that no more Confederates would be seen north of the Potomac, except as prisoners. The situation was not made more agreeable when General Early summoned the chief men of the city to his headquarters and demanded of them a tribute of $200,000, which was paid.

Thus far the Confederates had encountered no serious resistance. Their progress had been in the nature of a triumphal march. There had been in their front nothing but raw, undisciplined forces which fled at their approach. They had now reached a point their presence in which was an equal menace to two great cities. Frederick is at the apex of a triangle, with Washington and Baltimore equidistant from it and connected with it by straight and level roads. Upon which city did the Confederates purpose to descend? None could answer this question, and panic seized upon both towns. In Baltimore the bells were rung to summon the citizens to a meeting to discuss ways and means for defending the city. Banks sent their treasure North for safe keeping, and wealthy citizens sought anxiously for hiding-places for their plate and jewels. In Washington the excitement was at fever heat. President Lincoln had already called upon the governors of Pennsylvania, New York, and Massachusetts for 100-day volunteers for the defense of the national capital. The department clerks were already enrolled and helped to man the cordon of forts by which Washington was surrounded.

Meantime there confronted Early, at the banks of the Monocacy River, a few miles east of Frederick, an army of about 9000 Federal soldiers under command of General Lew Wallace. The Confederates had scarcely begun to ascend the western slope of South Mountain when Wallace, hastily gathering together all the regular troops from the forts around Baltimore and from their posts along the railroads, together with all the Home Guards militia and 100-day men that he could find, had rushed forward to secure this position, which covered the roads to Baltimore and Washington both. On the very day that the Confederates entered Frederick, Wallace's force was increased by the timely arrival of Ricketts's division, which had been sent by Grant from the lines before Petersburg.

With his slender force Wallace could hardly hope to win a victory. He was fighting for time—time to allow the troops that he knew were on the way from Petersburg to reach Washington. His main line of defense was behind the Monocacy River, with Tyler's motley forces holding his right wing, while Ricketts's veterans were on the left, which Wallace felt sure would be the point attacked by the enemy. A heavy body of skirmishers was left on the west bank of the river, with orders to oppose and delay the enemy's advance until the last moment possible, and then retreat, burning the bridge behind them.

The sun had scarcely risen on the morning of the 9th when Early's men came pouring out of Fredericksburg ready for battle. In appearance they were a sorry crew. They were gaunt with long-suffered privations and continual marching, and clad in clothes stripped from the backs of captives, or taken from the shelves of the stores in Frederick. So many blue uniforms were in their ranks that the unschooled soldiers in Tyler's command at first hesitated to fire upon them, thinking them a body of Union troops. Yet there has probably never been a better body of troops than these veterans, schooled under Stonewall Jackson and inured to all the hardships and perils of war by four years of constant campaigning.

The character of the ground and the great numerical superiority of Early's forces enabled him to avoid the necessity of a direct attack upon Wallace's defensive works, by a flank attack. Leaving Rodes and Ramseur to deal with Wallace's skirmishers, he sent Gordon, preceded by McCausland's cavalry, down the river to a ford a mile below Wallace's left flank. This movement was covered by a fierce artillery fire which speedily silenced Wallace's pitiful little battery of one howitzer and three rifles.

When Ricketts discovered the approach of the Confederates upon his flank he quickly changed front to meet it. But this maneuver, though it enabled him to offer a more strenuous resistance to his immediate assailants, exposed his whole line to an enfilading fire. Nevertheless he beat back the first attack, which was made by McCausland's cavalry, and was only driven from his position when Gordon's troops crossed the river and joined their forces to the dismounted cavalrymen. Three of Ricketts's regiments had not yet come up, having halted some miles in the rear. No orders could be sent them in season to do any good, for Wallace's telegraph operator, and the railroad agent, with both trains, had run away. Hoping that the delayed troops would make their appearance before long, he fought stubbornly to gain time. After having repulsed the Confederates twice he could have retired easily with all his men, but he chose rather to hold his ground. But when four o'clock came, with no sign of the missing regiments, it became evident to the Union commander that, if he wished to save his troops for still further use against Early's column of invasion, he must withdraw them. Ricketts was accordingly ordered to begin the retreat, which he did by way of the Baltimore pike, the Confederates pressing hotly upon his rear-guard. Unfortunately the topography of the field was such that a bridge over the Monocacy in Tyler's front had to be held against the enemy until the last of Ricketts's men had reached the pike. The bridge was of stone, and therefore could not be destroyed. The result was, the troops holding it were caught between Rodes and Gordon and several hundred of them were captured. Contented with this achievement the Confederates rested on their arms, and the retreat of the little Union army went on without further molestation.

"Think I have had the best little battle of the war," wrote General Wallace, as the sun was sinking behind South Mountain. His enthusiasm was not without reason, though at the moment he did not know how completely he had accomplished that for which he had been fighting—the salvation of the National capital. He had gone forward to meet the enemy, knowing that nothing but defeat could be in store for him. He had disposed and fought his men well. With a force largely made up of raw recruits he had held a veteran and vastly superior enemy in check for a whole day. His own loss had been heavy, 1880 in all, but it was chiefly due to the straggling of his half-disciplined troops. The loss of the enemy, according to General Early's own statement, was between 600 and 700. Yet the importance of the battle is to be measured neither by the numbers of the troops engaged nor by the extent of the losses. "General Wallace contributed on this occasion, by the defeat of the troops under him," writes General Grant, "a greater benefit to the cause than often falls to the lot of a commander of an equal force to render by means of a victory."

Wallace fell back to Ellicott's Mills, where he covered the road to Baltimore, but left that to Washington open. Only a detachment of Early's force, the cavalry under Johnson, went toward Baltimore, tearing up thirty miles of the track of the Baltimore and Ohio Railroad, cutting telegraph-wires, burning bridges, seizing cattle and horses, and spreading alarm throughout the country. The main body of the Confederates went straight down the road toward Washington. In the capital there was excitement and terror. From the War Department messages went speeding over the wires to Grant at Petersburg. In the streets the companies of armed clerks and civilians, hastily mustered in, were marching toward the intrenchments. The wide circle of forts that surrounded the city needed a whole army for its defense, and even of the ill-disciplined troops in the capital there were not enough to garrison so extended a line. Every one in the threatened city knew that, if it was to be saved, the means for its salvation must come from without. Help, however, was already on the way. Wallace had scarcely begun to fall back from the line of the Monocacy when the news was flashed over the wires to Grant. The remaining division of the Sixth Corps was quickly withdrawn from the trenches and marched with all possible speed to City Point, on the James River. There they embarked on swift steamers that were in waiting, and sped down the James, around the point at Fortress Monroe, and up Chesapeake Bay and the Potomac to Washington. They arrived in the very nick of time. President Lincoln's tall figure, towering above the crowd that had gathered to meet them at the dock, told how anxiously they had been expected, while the booming of the big guns at Fort Stevens, which was already engaged with the enemy in the outskirts of the city, gave the most convincing evidence of the timeliness of the arrival.

Early's troops had come within sight of the promised land, but they were not destined to enter it. From the fields in which they halted on that hot July morning they could see the great unfinished dome of the National Capitol, dazzling white against the blue summer sky. The spectacle made enthusiasm conquer, for the moment, the sufferings to which long and arduous service had made them a prey. They had been marching and fighting continuously for thirty days. The weather had been burning hot; no rain had fallen, and the dust rose in clouds, to choke the men in the marching columns. Even the creeks and smaller rivers had run dry, and it was difficult for the men to find water while on the march. The very morning which brought the invaders within view of the Capitol had been excessively hot, and the men were completely exhausted, throwing themselves upon the ground in attitudes showing the utmost weariness, whenever a halt was ordered. Yet Early determined to attack. He could not turn

MASSACRE AT FORT PILLOW.

his back upon Washington while he knew that city to be defended only by a slender force of half-disciplined militia and wholly undisciplined clerks. In imagination he saw himself master of the Federal capital, and Grant turning away from his campaign against Richmond to rush to the defense of the cities of the North. Foreign intervention—that illusive hope which buoyed up the Confederacy when all chance of conquering the North by Southern arms alone had vanished—would surely follow. With these bright dreams playing through his mind, Early began making his dispositions for the attack, when a prodigious cheering from the Union lines told him that his golden opportunity had vanished. He knew too well that enthusiasm proclaimed the arrival of re-enforcements, and that even if he should be able to fight his way into Washington he would in all probability be hemmed in and unable to get out again. Men were too precious then in the Confederacy for him to think for a moment of exchanging his army for the brief pleasure of unfurling the Stars and Bars above the Capitol at Washington. Countermanding his order for the attack, Early held his ground and waited for the Federals to strike first.

The blow was delivered the next morning, when, after the great guns of Fort Stevens had pounded away at the Confederates for a time, one brigade of the Sixth Corps pushed back the Confederate pickets for a mile or more. The battle, which was a fiercely contested one, was viewed by a nmuber of ladies and Cabinet officers from sheltered points in Fort Stevens, while on the parapet of that work stood President Lincoln himself, his tall form making him a conspicuous target for the enemy's sharpshooters, to whose bullets he paid no heed until they killed an officer within three feet of him, when, yielding to the protests of his companions, the President retired. It was no petty and bloodless battle that he had witnessed. The whole field was spread out before him, and the President and the civilians and ladies who accompanied him saw men fall before the bullet and the shell, heard the shouts of the victors and the shrieks of the wounded, and could see the litter-bearers bringing their pitiful burdens to suffer the merciful tortures of the surgeon's knife.

Foiled thus in his attempt to enter Washington, Early began falling back toward the Shenandoah Valley. His bands of cavalry scoured the country for miles around, gathering up cattle and provisions of every kind to take back into the famished land of the Confederacy. Driving before them a vast herd of lowing beeves, and with a prodigious train of wagons heavy laden with corn, flour, cloth, and shoes, the little invading army made its way out of Maryland. Its exploits had been notable, even though it had not marched in triumph through the streets of Washington, and the chief regret of its commander was not that he had failed to enter the capital city, but that the panic caused by his demonstration had not induced General Grant to send more than a single army corps away from the trenches at Petersburg.

In the valley Early found the troops of General Crook, who had returned after his hasty retreat down the Kanawha Valley. A sudden attack threw this force into confusion and Crook was driven into Maryland with a loss of 1200 men. Early was thus freed from any immediate danger, and determined to send his cavalry upon a raiding expedition into Pennsylvania to add to the plentiful store of cattle and horses that he had brought from Maryland. Twenty-nine hundred men, headed by General McCausland, rode their horses across the ford of the Potomac at Williamsport. On the 30th of July they were at Chambersburg. The reports of three cannon from the hills, and three shells bursting in the streets of the city, first gave notice to the people that they were in the hands of a hostile force. Soon after, McCausland, with 500 of his troopers, rode into the town. His orderlies went right and left through the streets of the city and arrested and brought before their chief forty of the leading citizens. Stern and bitter were the words that McCausland spoke to his captives. He was ordered to burn their town, he said, in retaliation for the destruction of several houses in the Shenandoah Valley by Hunter. In one way only could the people save their houses, stores, and goods. General Early had instructed him to accept a ransom of $500,000, if paid in paper money. If the inhabitants had gold, $100,000 in that metal would suffice. But if this payment should be refused, McCausland declared, every house in the town should be laid in ashes.

"But," cried out the spokesman of the citizens, "you have set us an impossible task. There is no gold in our city, and as for our paying you $500,000, there is probably not $50,000 in currency in the town."

The Confederate commander was implacable. His scouts had told him that the Federal cavalryman Averill was pushing forward to the relief of the city with all possible speed. Perhaps the thought that the people were relying upon the arrival of this succor in season to save them the payment of the tribute, occurred to him. At any rate he showed no sign of relenting, but answered shortly:

"Choose your own course—I am going to breakfast. Be ready to pay me the money when I am through or prepare to see your town in flames."

Helplessly the unhappy people of Chambersburg waited for the destruction of their property to begin. They knew that the money demanded could not be raised, and the time given them too short to make it worth while for them to attempt to remove any of their household goods to places of safety. The women and children sought the open fields, while the men thronged about the hotel, perhaps a little incredulous that the man so quietly eating his breakfast within could really intend to put the whole town to the torch. Nevertheless McCausland carried out his threat to the letter. His breakfast finished, he asked if the money had yet been paid, and upon learning that it had not ordered the work of destruction to begin. Colonel Gilmor was assigned the cruel duty of carrying the harsh order into effect, and has left on record the sensations he experienced while discharging it.

"Deeply regretting that such a duty had been assigned me," he writes, "I had only to obey. I felt more like weeping over Chambersburg, although the people covered me with reproaches, which all who know me will readily believe I felt hard to digest; yet my pity was highly excited in behalf of those poor unfortunates, who were made to suffer for acts perpetrated by the officers of their own government. The day was bright and intensely hot. The conflagration seemed to spring from one vast building. Dense clouds of smoke rose to the zenith and lowered over the dark plain. At night it would have been a grand but terrible object to behold. How piteous the sight of those beautiful green meadows—groups of women and children exposed to the rays of a burning sun, hovering over the few articles they had saved, most of them wringing their hands and with wild gesticulations bemoaning their ruined homes."

Leaving Chambersburg still aflame, McCausland turned his steps toward the Valley again. The hue and cry was now out for him, and a superior force of Federals followed fast upon his track. So hotly did they press upon him that he was obliged to abandon his purpose of burning the little town of Hancock, which had failed to pay him the ransom of $30,000 which he had demanded. Before he regained the safer region of the Valley he was surprised by Averill, who captured every cannon the Confederates had with them, all their caissons but one, nearly all their wagons, over 400 horses, three battle-flags, and 420 prisoners, including 38 officers. This crushing disaster quenched effectually all the enthusiasm which had been aroused in the hearts of the Confederates by their exploits in Pennsylvania and Maryland, and they rejoined Early sorely demoralized and much depressed.

CHAPTER XII.

EARLY HOLDS HIS GROUND IN THE VALLEY—SHERIDAN SENT AGAINST HIM—THE VALLEY TO BE RAVAGED—THE BATTLE OF WINCHESTER—ROUT OF THE CONFEDERATES—SHERIDAN PURSUES—BATTLE OF TUMBLING RUN—DESOLATION IN THE VALLEY—THE CAVALRY FIGHT—A MYSTERIOUS MESSAGE—SHERIDAN VISITS WASHINGTON—BATTLE OF CEDAR CREEK—THE SURPRISE—SHERIDAN TO THE RESCUE—THE FEDERALS RALLY.

GENERAL GRANT now expected that Early would return to aid in the defense of Petersburg. Washington was by this time fully garrisoned, and heavy detachments of Union cavalry were now north of the Potomac, making any future raids into the Union border States an impossibility. But Early showed his disposition to hold his ground in the Valley. He knew, no doubt, that his presence there was a constant menace to Washington, forcing the Federals to keep a heavy garrison in the capital city, thus decreasing Grant's force before Petersburg. The harvest time was now at hand, too, and Early's presence in that land which was so fertile as to be called the granary of the Confederacy, gave assurance that the crops would be harvested and stored away to help to feed Lee's regiments.

Little did the people of the Valley suspect the nature of the plan which had been slowly taking form in the brain of the silent man who now wielded as a unit the whole military force of the North. Though their bright and smiling country had been from the very opening of the war a veritable parade ground for both armies; though they had become used to seeing the Confederates pass their cabins in the morning, and the Federals at nightfall, until they had learned to distinguish the various commands in the respective armies and even to recognize individual officers, the people of the Valley, for all their familiarity with the ways of war, had not as yet suffered much from wanton destruction of property. Their surplus they gave cheerily enough to the Confederacy, with which nine-tenths of them were in hearty sympathy. What the Union troops needed was paid for. Seldom had a region, so wholly in the pathway of hostile armies, suffered so little.

Grant was now about to change all this. When Early was first driven from Maryland the Union general had written Halleck that "he should have upon his heels veterans, militiamen, men on horseback, everything that can be got to follow, to eat out Virginia clear and clean as far as they go, so that crows flying over it for the balance of this season will have to carry their food with them." It had become clear to Grant that he could stop the use of the Valley as a pathway for flying raids by stripping it of everything eatable. An army that has to drag about with it an interminable train of wagons is not fitted for swift and adventurous action, and much of the success of the rapid marches of Stonewall Jackson and Early had been due to the fact that the Valley through which they marched had always furnished them ample subsistence. To deprive the enemy of this notable advantage Grant put Sheridan in command of all the forces in the Shenandoah Valley with these instructions:

In pushing up the Shenandoah Valley, as it is expected you will have to go, first or last, it is desirable that nothing should be left to invite the enemy to return. Take all provisions, forage, and stock wanted for the use of your command; such as cannot be consumed, destroy. It is not desirable that buildings should be destroyed—they should rather be protected; but the people should be informed that so long as an army can subsist among them, recurrences of these raids must be expected, and we are determined to stop them at all hazards.

To carry a burning torch through the Valley, applying it to hay-ricks and corn-cribs and stacks of fodder; to drive off the milch cows and the fat beeves from the farms; to take the farmer's oxen, his plow-horse, and his family nag, these were the cruel duties intrusted to Sheridan. Cruel though they were, they were justified by the military situation. War is always cruel, and sometimes an effort to soften its hardships adds to its cruelties by increasing its duration. It was Grant's duty to eliminate the Shenandoah Valley as a factor in the Confederate power. This he could do either by making it untenable for troops of any kind, or by filling it with Union regiments in such numbers that the Confederates could not hope to make any headway against them. The latter course would draw troops from the campaign against Lee, and thus greatly prolong the war. The former would occupy two corps for but a few weeks, after which the Valley would be—so far as its strategic features were concerned—as though it never existed.

Sheridan entered upon his new duties with alacrity and enthusiasm. There had been some opposition to his appointment to so responsible a command on the score of his youth, and he was now fired with a determination to show that though young in years, he was old in the qualities that go to make up the successful soldier. He soon had the fields in the lower part of the Valley smoking with fumes of burning wheat and corn and hay. He made guerrilla warfare perilous, for once, when one of his lieutenants was shot down by bushwhackers, as it was supposed, Sheridan avenged the act by burning every house within five miles of the spot. Horses, cattle, and negroes—live-stock, all alike, in that day— were gathered up and driven into the Federal lines. Early in September Sheridan was able to write to Grant that he had "destroyed everything eatable south of Winchester, and they will have to haul supplies from well up toward Staunton."

This work was attended with but little heavy fighting. Sheridan was not inclined to risk a pitched battle with Early, who had now been re-enforced by Anderson's division. He knew well enough that Grant's operations before Petersburg would before long compel Anderson's return to Lee's lines. Then, and not till then, Sheridan would be able to attack Early with the certainty of success. He could not afford to take any risks, for if his army were swept out of the way, nothing would stand between Early and Maryland. If once again a Confederate force should cross the Potomac, the detachment of the troops necessary to follow it would put an end to the campaign against Richmond. Therefore it behooved Sheridan to be prudent.

Prudent he was—so prudent the civilians in the North began to accuse him of being a laggard in war. But Grant stood nobly by him, guarding him from the intemperate condemnation of politicians. On the 15th of September, at Sheridan's request, Grant went to the Shenandoah Valley to consult with his lieutenant. The general-in-chief carried with him a map of the Valley, with a plan of battle sketched upon it. But he found Sheridan brimful of a plan of his own. By means of an old negro trader, he had managed to get a note to a young woman of Northern sympathies living in Winchester, within the Confederate lines. Sheridan had asked her for information concerning the enemy's troops, and had received word that Anderson's troops had been sent away. Then Sheridan determined to give battle to Early, and when he laid his plans before Grant, that general kept his own plan in his pocket, and contented himself with giving the terse command, "Go in!"

The Confederates were holding Winchester. It had been the fate of that unhappy town to be held now by one army and then by the other ever since the war began. There were both Union and Confederate people in the town, and each had their brief periods of triumph. Seventy times, it is said, the place thus changed hands during the war.

When Sheridan laid his plans for the impending battle, the Confederate forces were scattered, though the greater part of Early's troops were at Winchester. Two divisions were marching northward toward Martinsburg, but these were hastily recalled when Early learned that Grant had been to Charlestown to consult with Sheridan. In war the general must be alert to tell from straws which way the wind is blowing, to read the significance of apparently trivial things. We have seen that the capture of one of

Hood's men, in a place where none of Hood's men was to be expected, saved the Federals a disaster at Peach Tree Creek. Now the mere fact that his spies reported Grant and Sheridan in consultation, put Early on his guard, and impelled him to concentrate his army around Winchester.

Soon after midnight on the morning of the 19th of September Sheridan's men were stirring in their camps. A hasty breakfast was prepared, and the underdone bacon and scalding coffee gulped down while preparations for the coming battle were being pushed forward. The cava.ry was first on the road, and went forward through the Berryville gorge at a gallop. At daybreak the horsemen came suddenly upon a Confederate earthwork at the mouth of the gorge. Dismounting, and leaving their horses in charge of a detachment, the troopers charged, taking the enemy completely by surprise. The breastwork was carried, and many of its occupants only awoke to find themselves prisoners. Though the Confederates tried to retake the work, their efforts resulted only in the useless sacrifice of men. The success of the Union cavalry, however, proved to be somewhat in the nature of a misfortune for Sheridan. It gave the Confederates early warning of the battle, while the main attack did not follow for several hours, owing to the difficulties encountered by the Union infantry in moving to the front along a single narrow road through a difficult and rugged country. This delay gave opportunity for Early to concentrate his scattered troops, and when the main body of Sheridan's army went into action the enemy was united, well posted, and perfectly ready for the battle. Sheridan was disappointed, for he had expected to give battle to a dismembered army; yet he had come to fight, and fight he did.

It was nearly noon when the Union infantry deployed in long lines across the fields and began advancing toward the woods in which the Confederates were stationed. There was a long march in the very face of a rapid and deadly artillery fire. When the woods were gained the fighting was fierce and bloody. There were no breastworks. The enemies stood face to face and bared their breasts to the flying scud of bullets. On the right flank General Grover's division went into action with a rush that swept everything before it. Charging with fixed bayonets on the double-quick, Grover's men drove the enemy in confusion from the woods. The brigade commanders, though ordered by Grover to check the advance when the further side of the woods should be reached, were unable to hold their men. So rapid and impetuous was the charge, so excited the soldiers at the spectacle of the enemy in full retreat before them, they pressed on through the timber and out into the clearing beyond. It was upon Evans's brigade of Gordon's infantry that this blow had fallen. "It was forced back through the woods from which it had advanced," wrote General Early, "the enemy following to the very rear of the woods, and to within musket-range of seven pieces of Braxton's artillery, which were without support. This caused a pause in our advance, and the position was most critical, for it was apparent that, unless this force was driven back, the day was lost. Braxton's guns, in which now was our only hope, resolutely stood their ground."

But Grover's advance had been so much more rapid than that of the Union troops on his left that a gap appeared on that flank. Braxton's guns held the Federals in check now, and while they were trying to close up this gap a fresh brigade of Confederates, Battles's brigade of Rodes's division, came up and drove headlong into this weak point on the Union lines. The remainder of Rodes's troops and all of Gordon's seconded the blow, and the Federals were suddenly changed from pursuers to pursued. They began to fall back through the woods and their lines showed signs of going to pieces before this fierce assault. At this critical juncture Russell's division of the Sixth Corps came up in gallant style and struck the exultant Confederates in the flank. At the same time the Fifth Maine Battery opened an enfilading fire upon the foe, tearing great gaps in his crowded masses with grape-shot and canister. This attack changed the fortune of the day once again. The Confederates began to retreat. The Federals regained confidence, pursued them, and took up once again their advanced line in the woods. Unhappily, in the hour of his triumph the brave Russell fell. A bullet struck him in the breast, but this wound, though severe, he concealed from his associates and sat firmly in his saddle, cheering on his men. A few minutes later a shell exploded directly before him, and one jagged piece cut through his heart, killing him instantly.

There now came a lull over the battle. Sheridan employed it in hurrying the army of West Virginia into position to participate in the battle. When the fight grew fierce again Crook and Torbert came down fiercely on the Confederate flanks and rear. The veterans of Early's army changed front to meet this attack, without waiting for any command from their officers. Swift though their action was, and stubborn as was their stand, they were unable long to hold their ground. The Union charges were repeated and irresistible. Their blows fell both on the Confederates' front and on their flank. A Federal officer, who was unhorsed and captured in the course of one of these charges, thus describes the scene he witnessed as he was being taken to the rear:

"The confusion, disorder, and actual rout produced by the successive charges of Merritt's division would appear incredible did not the writer actually witness them. To the right a battery, with guns disabled and caissons shattered, was trying to make to the rear, the men and horses impeded by broken regiments of cavalry and infantry; to the left the dead and wounded in confused masses around their field hospitals—many of the wounded in great excitement seeking shelter in Winchester; directly in front an ambulance, the driver nervously clutching the reins, while six men in great alarm were carrying to it the body of General Rodes."

The destruction of the Confederate lines, thus begun by the flank attack of Crook and Merritt, was continued and completed by attacks in front, and soon the whole Union force was advancing in unison like an irresistible wave. Everywhere the Confederate battle-flags were going down before the fury of the charges, or being borne in panic to the rear. On the roads and fields were crowds of stragglers ever growing larger and more demoralized. Even Early had to admit to himself that the battle was lost. At half-past one he had declared it a noble victory for the South. Now he sadly gave the order for retreat, and the jaded and despondent columns were soon plodding through Winchester. "I never saw our troops in such confusion before," wrote a captured Confederate. "Night found Sheridan's hosts in full and exultant possession of much-abused, beloved Winchester. The hotel hospital was pretty full of desperately wounded and dying Confederates. The entire building was shrouded in darkness during the dreadful night. Sleep was impossible, as the groans, sighs, shrieks, prayers, and oaths of the wretched sufferers, combined with my own severe pain, banished all thought of rest. . . . . Our scattered troops, closely followed by the large army of pursuers, retreated rapidly and in disorder through the city. It was a sad, humiliating sight."

The battle which had ended thus disastrously for the Southern arms is known, diversely, as the battle of Winchester, and the battle of the Opequan. The loss upon each side was heavy. That of Early was about 4000, and among his dead were Generals Rodes and Godwin. Moreover, he left in the hands of the Federals five pieces of artillery and nine battle flags. The Union loss was heavier, closely approximating 5000 men. Yet the news of one victory to break the long list of Confederate triumphs in the Valley, was so grateful to the country that, save in the homes bereaved by the enemy's bullets, there went up from the whole nation a great shout of joy when Sheridan announced his triumph in this ringing dispatch:

> We have just sent them whirling through Winchester and we are after them to-morrow. This army behaved splendidly.

True to his promise, Sheridan was "after them" the next morning. At daybreak his troops were on the march. Early was soon discovered holding a strongly intrenched position. One flank was guarded by the Shenandoah River. In his front flowed a creek called Tumbling Run, between which and his lines were abatis and slashed timber. Seeing that the position could not be successfully assaulted in front, Sheridan sent General Crook to turn the unprotected flank. The movement was executed with a secrecy and celerity worthy of Stonewall Jackson. The flanking force reached the enemy's rear by a circuitous path. Deploying in the forests they advanced silently to the edge of the timber. They could see before them the men of Pegram's and Ramseur's divisions. The Confederates were peering out over their breastworks to the front, all unconscious of this heavy force of men with loaded rifles and sharp bayonets stealing stealthily up behind them. A volley poured into their backs, a ringing cheer, and a sudden and furious charge into their trenches was the first warning the Confederates received of the impending calamity. "Had the heavens opened," writes one officer, "and we been seen descending from the clouds, no greater consternation would have been created."

There was no defense. Thrown into inextricable confusion the enemy retreated. By this time the Union force in their front had waded Tumbling Run and was charging into their midst, adding to the panic. Sheridan rode first in the charge. "Forward!" he cried. "Forward everything! Go on! Fire on them! Yell! Give them no rest!" The pursuit was continued until ended by the approach of night. The Confederates had lost 1400 men to Sheridan's 400, and they had lost 16 cannon and a great part of their wagon train. Worst of all, however, was the moral effect upon Early's men of so complete and disastrous a defeat.

After following Early for some days, Sheridan concluded to turn and march northward again toward his base of supplies. He was now but little troubled by the enemy, and his attention was turned to carrying out General Grant's orders for the devastation of the Valley. His scouting parties branched out from the army on every side, leaving ruin and desolation in their wake. Great pillars of smoke by day and the lurid glare of the flames by night told of the widespread desolation. Early, completely demoralized by his two defeats, was unable to interpose to check this work of ruin, but his cavalry, under General Rosser, hung on Sheridan's rear, harassing his column by constant attacks.

"Go back and whip that fellow or get beaten yourself," said Sheridan to General Torbert. "I shall ride up to Round Top Mountain and see the fight."

Torbert turned and struck ferociously at Rosser. The Union cavalrymen, Custer and Merritt, were fierce with the fight. The Confederates recoiled before their attacks and fled. A running fight was kept up for twenty-six miles, in the course of which the Federals captured eleven pieces of artillery with their caissons, all the wagons and ambulances the enemy had, and three hundred prisoners. One gun without a caisson was the only thing on wheels left to the Confederates. The pursuit ended near Woodstock, and the running fight was given the name of the "Woodstock races."

The campaign in the Valley ended with a battle which in many ways exceeded in interest any meeting of the hostile armies during the war. It was a battle skillfully planned on the part of the assailants, and of which the result long hung trembling in the balance. In no combat perhaps, during the Civil War, did chance have so much to do with determining the result; in but few battles was the result so greatly affected by individual valor and example.

When Sheridan began his northward march after the battle of Fisher's Hill, he thought that he left behind a wrecked and demoralized army. He had no idea that, after the defeats sustained at Winchester and Fisher's Hill, Early would be able to take the offensive again. So far from dreading an attack, Sheridan fairly invited it by making preparations to send the Sixth Corps back to Grant at Petersburg. But after the Sixth Corps had begun its march, Sheridan's officers were startled by a huge shell which suddenly dropped and exploded by the side of one of their mess tables as they sat at dinner. They sprang to their feet in surprise and terror, for none of them had suspected that any enemy was in the vicinity. Only the day before the cavalry had scoured the country without discovering a sign of a Confederate soldier or a hostile flag. The scouting parties that were sent out to discover whence came the mysterious shell brought back a very different report. They found the woods full of Confederates, while the clouds of dust and of smoke that rose above the tops showed that Early was present in force. This discovery led Sheridan to hastily send off couriers in pursuit of the Sixth Corps, and to bring that body of men back to the neighborhood of the rest of the enemy.

Still Sheridan did not much believe that Early actually meant to fight, and accordingly when Grant ordered him to send one division of cavalry out of the Valley to threaten the Virginia Central railway, he cheerfully complied. As he desired to go to Washington to consult with General Halleck, Sheridan accompanied the cavalry—Merritt's division—as far as Front Royal. Here a courier overtook him with startling news. The Union signal officers had seen flags waving from the Confederate signal stations. Being possessed of the enemy's signal code they had intercepted the message, which read:

TO LIEUTENANT-GENERAL EARLY:
Be ready to move as soon as my forces join you, and we will crush Sheridan.
LONGSTREET, *Lieut.-General.*

Put thus upon his guard, Sheridan ordered back the division of cavalry which he had intended to move from the Valley. Yet he was so little alarmed that he concluded not to abandon his visit to Washington, and accordingly proceeded thither without delay.

The intercepted dispatch which thus warned the Union commander is one of the mysterious and hitherto unexplained incidents of the war. Longstreet was not coming to Early's aid, and had sent him no troops. We shall see later that Early sustained a crushing defeat in a battle which there is every reason to believe would have resulted favorably to him, but for the dispatch which had put the Federals upon their guard.

On the 18th of October the Federal troops in the Valley were posted along the eastern bank of Cedar Creek, near its junction with the Shenandoah. Owing to the protracted dry weather both streams were very low and could easily be waded at any point. The ground was very rugged and the bank of the creek was steep, affording a natural defense for the Union front. The Army of West Virginia, Crook's corps, was on the Union left flank, with one division intrenched and the other posted along the crest of a steep and lofty hill, but with no defensive works. Crook's men were resting quietly in their trenches and their tents that pleasant October afternoon, for a reconnoissance made the day before had developed no sign of the enemy, and the opinion was general in the Union army that Early was falling back again toward the head of the Valley.

Very different indeed were the plans of the Confederate commander. His army was beginning to feel the effects of the famine that Sheridan's unrelenting torches had spread through the Valley. He had either to retreat or to attack, that was certain. But while the Federals thought him retreating he was in fact preparing to give them battle. From the lofty eyrie on Three Top, whence the Confederate signal-flags had waved out the message which so discomposed Sheridan, General Early and his chief engineer studied the Federal position, which lay spread out before them like a map. They could trace the course of every road, mark each intrenchment, tell where the Union lines were most vulnerable, and where the troops stood thickest. They saw clearly that the Federal position was a strong one, and that to attack it at any point would be hazardous. But a narrow road, winding along the base of Three Top Mountain, seemed to offer a way to Crook's flank and rear, and Early determined to essay it. So narrow was the road that no artillery could accompany the column, and the Shenandoah had to be crossed in two places.

The ground once mapped out, preparations for the attack went speedily forward. The divisions of Gordon, Ramseur, and Pegram were designated to constitute the flanking force, together with Payne's brigade of cavalry. The horsemen, however, were not to join in the attack upon Crook, but were directed to ride their hardest to Belle Grove, Sheridan's headquarters. General Early did not know that Sheridan was away, and he had set his heart upon capturing the commander, who had already inflicted upon him two mortifying defeats. The divisions of Kershaw and Wharton were to move directly down the turnpike and attack Crook in front, when the noise of the firing on his flank should tell them that the blow had fallen.

Soon after dark the flanking column was on the march. It wound silently along the narrow, crooked path. Commands were given in low tones. The soldiers had stripped off their canteens and their bayonet-sheaths; the officers had left behind their swords, that no clanking noises might betray the approach of the troops to the watchful enemy. A bright moon made marching easy. By midnight, when Crook's unsuspecting soldiers were sleeping in their tents, there were drawing near to their picket line Stonewall Jackson's old corps, another corps of infantry, and a brigade of cavalry. In the shadows of the forests, along the banks of the creek, were

MORGAN'S ESCAPE.

other divisions ready to spring upon their slumbering prey, while forty guns, limbered up, and with the battery horses champing the bits impatiently, were in line on the turnpike, ready to dash into the conflict as soon as the first shots rang out upon the still air of midnight.

A ripple of musketry comes from the direction of the fords where Gordon is crossing. It is not loud enough to spread the alarm in the Union camp, but it reaches the alert ear of Early, and tells him that the first step in the battle has been taken. He orders Kershaw and Wharton forward, and listens for the louder firing which shall tell that Gordon has actually sprung upon Crook. It comes in a moment.

The dawn had come on but slowly, and a dense fog covered the earth, through which Kershaw's force advanced without fear of detection. A burst of musketry is the first intimation that the men of Thoburn's division, upon whom the blow falls first, have of the calamity that has come upon them. They wake and spring from their tents, only to find the enemy swarming over their breastworks and turning their own guns upon them. Many were only half-clothed; few had a chance to catch up their arms. Bewildered by their sudden call from heavy sleep, scarcely able to tell friend from enemy in that faint light and heavy fog, dazed by the sight of hostile men right in their midst, plying pistol and bayonet with frightful effect, the men of Crook's corps were unable to offer any serious resistance to Kershaw's rapid advance. A few determined and quick-witted men leaped over the breastworks on the farther side of the camp, and tried to hold them in reverse against the advancing Confederates, but even this show of resistance was quickly ended by the arrival of the Confederate artillery, which added its thunder to that of the guns already captured. In fifteen minutes from the time when the alarm was sounded the whole of Crook's command, shattered, disorganized, and demoralized, was in disorderly flight toward the rear, spreading panic in the camp of the Nineteenth Corps, through which the fugitives passed.

General Emory had had a brief space of time in which to prepare for attack. He had been roused by the first volley discharged at Crook, and had hastened to his command. He found one brigade already under arms, for it had been ordered the night before to be prepared for an early reconnoissance. Hurrying this brigade into the fight, he sent forward the remainder of his corps as fast as the regiments could be formed, and soon had a line of defense that, under ordinary circumstances, might have held Kershaw in check. But all this time the long lines of Gordon's and Pegram's divisions were moving forward through the fog unseen and their presence unexpected. Now they burst with fresh vigor, all unwearied with fighting, upon the left flank of the Union line, where were the divisions of the Eighth Corps, commanded by Generals Kitchin and Rutherford B. Hayes, the latter in later days President of the United States. The Federals, already demoralized by the crowds of fugitives and stragglers that had been pressing through their lines, could not withstand this flank attack, and melted away as do the edges of a dyke when some crevasse lets a roaring, rushing torrent force its way through.

There now remained only the Sixth Corps, of all the Union army, which still retained its formation. General Wright, its commander, was commander of the whole field in Sheridan's absence. He saw that a great catastrophe had already come upon his army, and that the zeal and vigor with which the enemy pressed the advantage already won threatened the demolition of the whole of the Union force in the Valley. In the camp of the Sixth Corps the drums were rattling out the long roll, and the voices of the soldiers rose quick and sharp as they answered to their names. Veterans they, tried and true; they were the men who had saved Washington when the same Confederate commander who was now thundering in their front stood pounding at its gates. They knew well enough that, if he should win this day, the road to the National capital would again be open to him. It was with a sense of heavy responsibility that the veterans of the Sixth set themselves down firmly across Early's path.

Now for the first time the triumphant progress of the Confederates sustained a check. Though outnumbered and confronted by an enemy flushed with victory, the Sixth held its ground stubbornly and breasted the charges of the foe with magnificent valor. It is a discreditable fact, too—admitted by Early in his official report—that at this critical moment, when victory was within their very grasp, the Confederates in great numbers left their ranks to plunder the captured camps of the Eighth and Nineteenth corps. The Federals for their part were wholly on the alert. Their cavalry in the rear were halting the stragglers, and forming them into lines, ready to make a stand at some effective point; their wagons were making good their escape along the road to Harper's Ferry, and all the time the men of the Sixth Corps were fighting stubbornly for time. When one position became untenable they would retire, in good order, to another, and there maintain the unequal struggle. They knew, and their commander knew, that they could not long hold the enemy back, but they hoped that the time they won might enable those in the rear to rally the fugitives, or that some unexpected event might occur to save the army from the annihilation that seemed to be in store for it.

The unexpected happened, and the happening of it gave to the annals of the civil war their most dramatic incident.

Let us turn from the battle-field on which the Army of the Shenandoah was fighting for its life, and follow the footsteps of its absent commander. Sheridan had reached Martinsburg, on his return from Washington, on the 18th, and, receiving no word of anything unusual at the front, journeyed leisurely on toward Winchester, which he reached the same night. Early the next morning there came an officer from the picket line outside of Winchester, with a report that he could hear artillery firing at Cedar Creek.

"It's only the reconniossance in force which I ordered for to-day," said Sheridan, and went back to bed to try to sleep a little longer. But despite his confident words to the officer he felt nervous, and after tossing about on his bed awhile, he rose and dressed and went out into the streets. The heavy concussions of the artillery still made the air tremble, but Sheridan still thought that it did not indicate that a pitched battle was in progress. After breakfast he mounted his horse and with his escort of twenty troopers rode out of Winchester. By this time the noise of battle had so increased that the commander no longer doubted that the army was engaged, and spurred his steed to a swifter pace. The demeanor of the people of Winchester convinced him that they had received news from the battle-field and that the fight was going against the Federals. When the little party of horsemen swung into the road leading to Cedar Creek, stragglers began to be met, now singly, then in groups, and last in squads and whole regiments, and wagons, ambulances, the caissons of captured cannon, men riding horses with dangling traces, showing that the animals had been hastily cut loose from a gun-carriage to bear some panic-stricken driver to a place of safety—all this driftwood of a beaten and demoralized army so crowded the road that Sheridan and his followers had to take to the fields to make any progress.

"My first halt was made just north of Newtown," writes Sheridan, in telling of his famous ride, "where I met a chaplain digging his heels into the sides of his jaded horse and making for the rear with all possible speed. I drew up for an instant and inquired of him how matters were going at the front. He replied ' Everything is lost ; but all will be right when you get there '; yet notwithstanding this expression of confidence in me, the parson at once resumed his breathless pace to the rear. At Newtown I was obliged to make a circuit to the left to get around the village. I could not pass through it, the streets were so crowded."

"My God, General, I am glad to see you!" cried General Torbert, when Sheridan came galloping up to the point where his cavalry and the Sixth Corps were acting as a rear-guard for the retreating. A few questions told the newly arrived commander all that the stream of fugitives had left untold. He listened to the recital impatiently, then threw himself into the midst of the drifting tide.

"Turn the other way, boys, turn the other way! We'll beat them yet! We are going to sleep in our old lines to-night," he cried, and the men, catching his enthusiasm, cheered and began to halt, and to face again to the enemy.

"When they saw me," writes Sheridan, "they abandoned their coffee, threw up their hats, shouldered their muskets, and as I passed along turned to follow, with enthusiasm and cheers. To acknowledge this exhibition of feeling I took off my hat, and with Forsythe and O'Keefe rode some distance in advance of my escort, while every mounted officer who saw me galloped out on either side of the pike to tell the men at a distance that I had come back. In this way the news was spread to the stragglers off the road, when they too turned their faces to the front and marched toward the enemy, changing in a moment from the depths of depression to the extreme of enthusiasm. . . . . I said nothing, except to remark as I rode along the road, ' If I had been here with you this morning this would not have happened. We must face the other way. We will go back and recover our camp.' "

Wonderful is the effect of a controlling mind upon a disorganized and panic-stricken body of men. The soldiers were soon shouldering their muskets and falling into line. Order was beginning to appear where all had been confusion. The tide of men that had been flowing toward Winchester now turned and rolled toward the front. The troops still engaged with the enemy heard the cheers, and wondered what could have caused them on that day so heavy laden with sorrow and disaster for the Union cause. Then the word passed down the lines that Sheridan was coming, that he was even then rallying the fugitives, and would soon be on the line of battle. Then the men in the front cheered in their turn, and sent their ramrods home with renewed spirit.

Reaching the front, Sheridan leaped his great black horse over the line of rails and rode along the crest of the hill, hat in hand, where all might see him. A thundering shout rang out from the Union lines, as the men sprang to their feet and cheered and cheered again. All the color-bearers of Crook's stampeded army had formed a line, and their standards rose suddenly before Sheridan's eyes and waved frantically.

Early's next attack was repulsed, and the Confederate commander then abandoned his attempt to destroy the Union army, and bent his energies to the task of getting his prisoners and his long train of captured wagons and artillery back to Fisher's Hill. But it was now Sheridan's turn to assume the offensive. He had a promise to redeem. His assurance to his soldiers, that they should sleep again that night in the lines from which they had been driven in the morning, was no idle boast. At the head of his cavalry he led a charge which pierced the Confederate lines at a vital point, sheltered though they were by stone walls. Into this breach he poured his rallied forces, until the rout that had seized upon the Federals in the morning was paralleled among the Confederates in the afternoon. Broken, demoralized, and panic-stricken, Early's well-ordered divisions were swept away. The twenty-four guns captured by the Confederates were recovered, and twenty-four more guns taken from them. All the ambulances lost in the morning were retaken, together with fifty-six belonging to Early. All over the field the smoke was rising from wagons and ambulances, to which the fugitives had set the torch rather than permit them to be retaken.

Sweeping and complete was the victory that Sheridan thus in the afternoon snatched from the defeat of the morning. Yet the loss in men fell heaviest on the Federals—nearly 4000 of Sheridan's gallant fellows were shot down, while 1770 were captured. Early's loss was slightly in excess of 3000.

There was but little further serious resistance offered to Sheridan in the Valley as he pursued his work of devastation. The figures presented in his report of the destruction done between August 8, 1864, and the first of the following year, almost defy comprehension. Among other things which he destroyed or captured were 157,076 bushels of corn, 460,072 bushels of wheat, 51,380 tons of hay, 16,438 beef cattle, 17,837 sheep, 16,141 swine, 12,000 pounds of bacon, and 140 flour-mills. He found the Valley a smiling and fertile dale; he left it a smoking and barren wilderness.

CHAPTER XIII.

EXPELLING THE CITIZENS FROM ATLANTA—SAVING ALLATOONA—"HOLD THE FORT"—HOOD MOVING NORTHWARD—PLANNING THE MARCH TO THE SEA—DIFFICULTY OF GETTING PERMISSION—THE GREAT MARCH BEGUN—HAVOC DONE IN ATLANTA—FORAGING—THE NEGROES FOLLOW THE COLUMN—DESTROYING THE RAILROADS—TORPEDOES IN THE ROAD—STORMING FORT M'ALLISTER—SHERMAN VISITS THE FLEET—SAVANNAH TAKEN.

WE left Sherman's army making its triumphal entry into Atlanta, whence the Confederates had just taken a hasty and stealthy departure. After being in possession of the town one week, the Union commander determined upon a course of action that brought down upon him the execration of the whole Confederacy. The expansive works with which the enemy had surrounded Atlanta required an army of far greater size than Sherman's to properly garrison them. He determined to contract them until they should barely inclose the city. Within the lines thus diminished there would not be room for the army and citizens both, so Sherman issued a formal proclamation announcing to the people of Atlanta that they must leave their homes and abandon the captured city to its conquerors. He purposed making of the town simply a vast fortified camp, a depot for supplies, and a base whence to conduct expeditions into the enemy's territory. To such of the inhabitants as wished to go into the Confederacy he offered a safe-conduct to the enemy's lines. For those who wanted to go North he had transportation provided. Every assistance was to be given the unfortunate people in their emigration, but in some way or other, go they must.

"War is war, and not popularity seeking. If you want peace you must stop the war," was the tenor of Sherman's reply to the Southerners who made an outcry against his Atlanta order. Nothing swerved him from his chosen course, and for days the railroad leading northward was crowded with the people of Atlanta who wished to go in that direction, while over the roads to the South interminable caravans of wagons, and trudging parties of men in civilians' garb, told of the exodus. The city was deserted by all save the soldiers. The shops were closed and barred. The factories were dismantled. Schools and churches were used for hospitals and barracks. Not a woman was to be seen in the town, nor any man not clad in the blue uniform of the Union soldiers.

Meantime Hood had rallied somewhat from the effects of his repeated defeats and began to threaten Sherman's rear. The Confederate cavalryman Forrest was already in Tennessee, in the immediate vicinity of Sherman's communications, and speeches which Jefferson Davis made in several cities of the South warned Sherman that Hood would soon take the field in the same region. To meet this danger General Thomas was sent to Chattanooga, the Twentieth Corps was left to hold Atlanta, and Sherman, with the rest of the army, went up the railroad to meet and give battle to the enemy.

Soon after Hood had put his army in motion Sherman was convinced that it was the intention of the Confederate commander to place his army at Allatoona. Sherman could not for a moment think of permitting so strong and commanding a position to fall into the hands of the enemy. The Union garrison then on the ground numbered but 800, and the scouts brought in word that three divisions had been sent by Hood for its capture. To rescue Allatoona and its garrison General John M. Corse was sent forward with all possible speed. Corse reached the threatened point just as the Confederate advance was opening fire, but his arrival delayed the attack for a time.

Sherman meantime from a distant signal station had been eagerly looking through his field-glass toward Allatoona. The day before the signal-flags had waved messages back and forth between the two points. "Hold the fort. Help is coming," was the last message that Sherman had sent, and now that the help should be on the ground, he could discern no sign of life about the imperiled position. At last the faint flutter of a flag caught his eye. His signal officer after some study made out these letters: "C," "R," "S," "E," "H," "E," "R." What did it mean?

"Corse is here!" cried Sherman exultantly, as its meaning flashed over him, and he knew that Allatoona was safe. His confidence was well founded, for that afternoon the flags waved again, sending the message that the enemy's attack had been repulsed. The next morning a courier came into camp with a letter from General Corse, announcing his victory, and saying, "I am shot; a cheek-bone and an ear; but am able to whip them yet!"

It was a gallant defense that General Corse had made. The Confederates were greatly superior to him in point of numbers, and tried at first to frighten him into a surrender. "I have placed the forces under my command in such positions that you are surrounded, and to avoid a needless effusion of blood, I call on you to surrender your forces at once and unconditionally," wrote General French, who commanded the attacking force. "Five minutes will be allowed you to decide. Should you accede to this, you will be treated in the most honorable manner as prisoners of war."

Corse did not avail himself of the proffered five minutes, but replied immediately: "Your communication demanding surrender of my command I acknowledge receipt of, and respectfully reply that we are prepared for the 'needless effusion of blood' whenever it is agreeable to you."

The assaults that followed fast upon this sharp note of defiance were manfully met and repulsed. General Corse was wounded by a musket-ball which cut a deep gash across his ear and cheek. Colonel Tourtellotte, his second in command, was shot through the hips, but remained on the field, seated in an arm-chair, delivering his orders in a firm voice. At last the enemy withdrew, leaving 231 of his dead upon the field, and 411 prisoners, 800 muskets, and three stands of colors in the hands of the victors. Then it was that Corse sent his triumphant message to Sherman; but that commander, while full of enthusiasm for the noble victory, was inclined to make light of his subordinate's wound, and is reported to have said to him on first seeing it, " Why, Corse, they came mighty near missing you, didn't they?"

Hood continued his march northward, tearing up railroads and burning bridges as he went, but Sherman did not long pursue him. The mind of the Union commander was now fixed upon that audacious and masterful project of marching through Georgia to the coast, which, when carried into effect, placed him at once among the great captains of history. He began to strip his army as an athlete is stripped for the wrestle. The sick and wounded and the regiments whose term of service had nearly expired, and who could not, therefore, be depended upon, were sent to the rear. Officers, who thought they had reduced their campaigning outfit to the smallest possible dimensions when they started South from Chattanooga, were surprised to find how much more was lopped off by this exacting commander. Atlanta was emptied of everything not vitally necessary.

But while thus quietly pressing forward his preparations for the great march of invasion, Sherman found difficulty in getting permission to undertake the movement he so ardently desired to make. On the 9th of October, four days after the battle of Allatoona, he telegraphed to Grant:

I propose that we break up the railroad from Chattanooga forward, and that we strike out with our wagons for Milledgeville, Millen, and Savannah. Until we can repopulate Georgia it is useless for us to occupy it, but the utter destruction of its roads, houses, and people will cripple their military resources. . . . . I can make this march and make Georgia howl.

There came no favorable answer to the suggestion, and another dispatch to the same effect, two days later, met with the same reception. But on the 16th there came word that the authorities at Washington regarded the proposition with favor, and would have a fleet at Ossabau Sound, south of

Savannah. Toward the latter part of the month, however, Hood's maneuvers in Tennessee became so threatening, and the public clamor concerning his presence there so violent, that for a time General Grant showed an inclination to rescind his former decision and order Sherman to give chase to Hood.

"Do you not think it advisable, now that Hood has gone so far north, to entirely ruin him before starting on your proposed campaign?" asked Grant, in a dispatch on November 1. "With Hood's army destroyed, you can go where you please, with impunity."

But Sherman protested vigorously. "No single army can catch Hood," said he, "and I am convinced the best results will follow from our defeating Jeff Davis's cherished plan of making me leave Georgia by maneuvering." And in a later dispatch, "If I turn back the whole effect of my campaign will be lost. . . . . I am clearly of the opinion that the best results will follow my contemplated movement through Georgia."

A few hours later the response came:

I do not see that you can withdraw from where you are to follow Hood without giving up all that we have gained in territory. I say, then, go on as you have proposed.

U. S. GRANT, *Lieutenant-General.*

Sherman was then at Kingston, the most northerly point he had reached in his brief pursuit of the Confederates. That very night he put his army on the march for Atlanta, which lay to the southward. As the troops plodded along the road by the side of the railroad, train after train went rushing by them, bound north, carrying disabled soldiers, superfluous provisions, and everything that could be dispensed with by an army making a swift march through the country of an enemy. On the 12th of the month Sherman may be said to have taken the critical step that marked the beginning of his great and historical exploit, for on that day he sent his last dispatch to General Thomas at Nashville, and then ordered a bridge burnt in his rear which cut him off from all communication with the North. For the following month Sherman and his gallant army were destined to be as completely shut out from the sight and knowledge of their friends as though they had plunged into some vast cavern and were making a march of a thousand miles in the mysterious chambers of the earth.

The extraordinary spectacle was now presented of two hostile armies which had been almost constantly engaged for several months, suddenly turning their backs upon each other and marching straight in opposite directions. But though Hood and Sherman had each adopted the same strategy, there was a decided difference in the conditions that confronted them. Sherman had nothing in his path save the Georgia Militia. Hood, on the contrary, was confronted by a force almost equal to his own. Thomas was at Nashville, and the original force which Sherman had left him was so rapidly augmented by recruiting, and by the consolidation of garrisons in scattered posts, that, by the time the two armies came in contact, there were no less than 55,000 men in the Union lines.

A pall of smoke hung heavy over Atlanta on the day when the columns of Sherman's army marched out of the southern side of the city and turned to the eastward. Fire and explosives had been busy in the hapless town for many hours. Every structure of a public nature had been wrecked beyond possibility of repair. Roofless buildings, through the empty window casings of which the dreary piles of charred and blackened timbers within could be seen, were on every street. Where the railroad tracks had been were now the smoldering remains of cars and ties; engines toppled over into the ditch and blown to pieces by charges of gunpowder; rails that had been heated and then twisted into fantastic shapes, forever ruining them. One of the railway machine-shops had been used by the Confederates as an arsenal, and was stored full of shot and shell. When the flames reached the latter there were repeated explosions, and the flying bits of iron whizzed through the air in perilous proximity to the house in which General Sherman had his lodgings. The flames, which had been started in the railway stations and shops, spread to the main part of the town, and many dwellings and blocks of stores were blazing. There were but few of the people of Atlanta on the ground, however, to mourn over the destruction of their city, for all the civilian population had been expelled weeks before.

The army which turned its back upon this ruined town and plunged boldly into the enemy's country was a remarkable one. Herculean efforts had been made to purge it of all non-combatants. Invalids, sutlers, servants, war correspondents, and all the host of camp followers that hang upon the skirts of a great army had been relentlessly ordered to the rear. In all there were in line 62,204 men, all able-bodied veterans, ready to do and dare all that their leader might direct. In their cartridge-boxes were forty rounds apiece; in the ammunition wagons was enough powder and ball to make up 200 rounds for each soldier. Stripped to its lightest, as it was, the wagon train of this army was formidable. Twenty-five hundred wagons dragged by teams of six mules each, six hundred ambulances with two horses apiece, and sixty-five cannon, to each of which were harnessed eight animals, made up a column that, if extended along a single road, would have been over twenty miles long. As the army advanced by four nearly parallel roads, however, this train was broken up, and in each column a procession of wagons about five miles long held the center of the road, while the troops trudged along on either side. Herds of cattle were driven along to furnish food for the army. The wagons held some quantity of food,— 1,200,000 rations, or enough for twenty days, Sherman says,—but the chief reliance for food and forage for the horses and mules was to be placed upon the country, on which the leaders of the different columns were instructed to forage liberally.

Though not a holiday jaunt exactly, the march through Georgia was still so easy a task that, when the heads of the columns entered Savannah, the men were actually more robust and in better spirits than when they left Atlanta. The armed resistance that was offered to the progress of the columns was so slight as to afford only amusement to these grizzled veterans. Sherman had had a clear idea of what he had to expect, when, before starting from Atlanta, he had told an officer whom he was sending back to join Thomas at Nashville, "If there is going to be any fighting at all you will have it to do." Indeed the fierce words of the proclamations of Confederate governors, senators, and members of Congress were the principal weapons which the startled and demoralized people of Georgia employed against the invaders.

It was a cheerful and confident army that undertook the great march to the sea. General Sherman describes for us the scene upon the first day.

About 7 A. M. of November 16 we rode out of Atlanta by the Decatur road, filled by the marching troops and wagons of the Fourteenth Corps, and reaching the hill just outside of the old Rebel works, we naturally paused to look back upon the scene of our past battles. We stood upon the very ground whereon was fought the bloody battle of July 22, and could see the copse of wood where McPherson fell. Behind us lay Atlanta, smoldering and in ruins, the black smoke rising high in air and hanging like a pall over the ruined city. Away off in the distance, on the McDonough road, was the rear of Howard's column, the gun-barrels glistening in the sun, the white-topped wagons stretching away to the south ; and right before us the Fourteenth Corps marching steadily and rapidly, with a cheery look and steady pace that made light of the thousand miles that lay between us and Richmond. Some band, by accident, struck up the anthem of "John Brown's soul goes marching on;" the men caught up the strain, and never before or since have I heard the chorus of "Glory, glory, hallelujah!" given with more spirit or in better harmony of time and place.

Then we turned our horses' heads to the east ; Atlanta was soon lost behind the screen of trees and became a thing of the past. . . . . The day was extremely beautiful, clear sunlight with bracing air, and an unusual feeling of exhilaration seemed to pervade all minds—a feeling of something to come, vague and undefined, still full of venture and intense interest. Even the common soldiers caught the inspiration, and many a group called out to me as I worked my way past them, "Uncle Billy, I guess Grant is waiting for us at Richmond!"

Two tasks occupied the attention of the soldiers while on the march—foraging and tearing up railroads. The work of scouring the country for provisions was soon reduced to a science. The twenty days' rations that were in the wagons when the army left Atlanta were held as a reserve store, only to be touched in case of dire need. Scarcely was the second day's march begun before the foragers had begun their work. About one-twentieth of each regiment was detailed upon this duty. The men scattered over the country in every direction, taking care to keep near enough together to be able to protect themselves against a sudden dash of the enemy's cavalry which hovered about the flank of the marching army. They started out at daybreak on foot, and returned at nightfall mounted on horses and mules, or driving wagons, carts, family carriages, or buggies heavy-laden with all kinds of provisions. It was a sorry moment for a Georgia plantation when a party of Sherman's "bummers," as the foragers came to be called, descended upon it. It is greatly to the honor of the army that cases of any personal violence to the people of the plantations were very rare, but the rights of property were not so strictly respected. Everything was seized by the insatiate marauders. The barns and the coach-houses were first raided and every beast of burden and every vehicle seized—the barn-yards received early attention, and the "bummers" soon became expert in running down and capturing chickens, ducks, and pigs. When everything eatable, and frequently a good many things that were not eatable, but which caught the fancy of some unscrupulous soldier, had been secured, the foragers would make their way back to the route of the main army and await the arrival of the wagons, into which their booty was poured.

"Often would I pass these foraging parties at the roadside waiting for their wagons to come up," writes General Sherman, "and was amused at their strange collections—mules, horses, even cattle packed with old saddles and loaded with hams, bacon, bags of corn meal, and poultry of every character and description."

Sometimes the foragers would appear clad in the gorgeous uniform of the Georgia militia, taken from trunks in some plundered plantation. Occasionally an old revolutionary Continental uniform, after over half a century of fairly religious care and preservation, would be thus rudely dragged forth to bedeck the person of a "bummer." On one occasion several parties of foragers joined together and captured a town. The usual pillaging followed, and when the van of the main column came up the soldiers were astonished to be greeted by a procession of their comrades clad in Continental blue and buff. In the midst of the cavalcade there progressed at a dignified pace a much-battered family carriage, laden with hams, sweet-potatoes and other provisions, and drawn by two horses, a mule and a cow, the two latter ridden by postilions.

Sometimes the foragers had to fight for their plunder, for the Confederate cavalry hung close on the flanks of the Union column, ready to snatch up any unwary stragglers who might stray too far away. But in the pursuit of their adventurous calling the "bummers" soon learned to rally at the first note of danger, and to fight stubbornly while falling back slowly to the main line. In this way they not only protected themselves, but interposed an impenetrable shield between the flank of the marching column and the enemy's forces. And though the duty of the foragers was more perilous than that of those who stayed with the main column, it had its compensations. More than one garden yielded up its buried treasures to their persuasive bayonets. Guided by the sly hints of slaves they extracted jewelry and money from their hiding-places beneath cellar floors and behind oak wainscots. They lived on the fat of the land. Before the fruits of their foraging were turned over to their respective commands the cravings of their own appetites were fully assuaged. General Sherman tells of meeting one soldier who bore a ham impaled upon his bayonet, a jug of sorghum molasses under his arm, and a big piece of honey in his hand, which he was voraciously devouring. "Forage liberally on the country," remarked the soldier, quoting meaningly from the general orders as he caught a reproving glance from Sherman. But the general stopped him to explain that foraging was not for the sole gratification of the foragers, but that the provisions thus obtained must be turned over to the regular commissaries. Instances of wanton or irregular plundering of plantations, however, were comparatively rare, and the Georgia newspapers, published at the time of the invasion, afford ample evidence that the planters suffered quite as much from the rapacity of Wheeler's Confederate cavalrymen as they did from Sherman and his foragers.

Before the invading column had penetrated very far into Georgia the immense concourse of negroes that gathered in its rear and followed it upon the march had become a source of serious annoyance. Despite the efforts of planters the news of emancipation had spread among the slaves. To them the men in blue were saviors and protectors, all-wise and all-powerful, come to lead them from slavery into a better land and a better

THE REWARD OF TREACHERY.

life. Their childish nature saw nothing to fear in the future. They did not trouble themselves about details, nor with problems of life, but simply caught up their scanty goods and chattels and followed the soldiers in great throngs. "Ise gwine whar youse gwine, Massa," was their invariable response to the soldier who asked them where they were going. Some of the able-bodied colored men were employed by Sherman as pioneers and road builders, but the greater number hung on the skirts of the army, begging their food of the soldiers and retarding the progress of the column.

The destruction of railroads soon became an exact science with the men of Sherman's army. It was a work to which their commander gave his personal attention, for he had determined to leave no line of communication between the eastern and western parts of the Confederacy. Tools had been provided—many of them invented for this especial purpose—but the inventive genius of the men themselves soon conceived a method of destruction which, for effectiveness and expedition, challenges admiration. Several hundred men would form in two parallel lines along the track, facing it. At the word of command all would stoop, and each grasping the end of a tie would lift it breast high. A piece of track several hundred feet long would thus be torn from the ground. Then, at the commander's order all would spring back, throwing the track heavily down. The shock loosened bolts and rivets, and it was an easy task then to wrench off rails, which were used as levers to detach others which were still bolted to the ties. The sleepers then were piled up like log houses and set on fire, the rails being laid across the top. When the middle of the rails became red-hot they were seized with huge nippers, and twisted like corkscrews, wound around trees, or bent and interlaced so that they could hardly be packed on a flat car. Only by being made over in a rolling mill could they ever be used again.

Besides tearing up the track, every station, warehouse, water tank and roundhouse was destroyed. Mills and machine shops were burned almost invariably. The track of the army was a broad zone of desolation and smoking ruins. Sherman appealed to a negro for information as to the work of the wing of the army that had marched through the little town of

Tenille. "Why, Massa," responded the freedman, "first there came along some cavalrymen and they burned the depot; then came along some infantrymen and they tore up the track; then came some fellows and they sot fire to the well." And incredible as the negro's last statement seems, it was literally true, for the well had a timber casing and steps leading down to it, all of which the soldiers had torn to pieces and burned.

So onward through the very center of the fertile State of Georgia the army marched, its four columns keeping nearly abreast of each other on the parallel roads along which they advanced. Well fed, in high spirits, with little fighting to do, the men stepped along, doing their fifteen or twenty miles a day with ease. Roads had to be "corduroyed," bridges to be built, obstructions cleared away, besides the work of destroying the railroads and public buildings, but all was done cheerily and rapidly. The tidings of the swift and seemingly irresistible progress of the Federals spread all over the Confederacy, and the people, long buoyed up by false hopes, began to understand that the military power of their government must indeed be at a low ebb if no resistance could be offered to so audacious an invasion.

Early in December the invaders reached the vicinity of Savannah. There the Confederates had rallied a handful of troops and thrown up defensive works, with the determination to hold the town against the Federals. General Hardee commanded the defenses. About 18,000 men were enrolled under him, and besides formidable earthworks, covering all the roads leading into the city, the Confederate flag waved over Fort McAllister, a very powerful work with lofty and ponderous bastions, spacious bomb-proofs, and deep ditches. Its fifteen cannon commanded the Ogeechee River, so that communication with the city by water was cut off.

Sherman pressed his way onward toward the city with all possible speed. For the last 100 miles of his march forage was scarce, and it was essential that he should reach the coast, where well-laden supply ships were awaiting him, without delay. Besides, he knew that every day of delay was advantageous to Hardee, to whom recruits were flocking. "You-uns will have some fighting to do before you get into Savannah," said a Georgian, to whom a soldier was boasting of the ease with which the march from Atlanta had been made.

When within a few miles of the city General Sherman, while riding along the road, noticed a group of officers and men standing about a prostrate soldier by the wayside. Stopping to inquire the meaning of the delay, the general found that a young lieutenant had been seriously wounded by a torpedo which the Confederates had planted in the road. Though weak with loss of blood and agony, the officer was able to speak. " I was riding with the brigade staff of the Seventeenth Corps," said he, in response to Sherman's inquiry, "when suddenly there came a roar, and a great shock directly beneath me. My horse and I were thrown to the ground, and when I recovered my senses I found my horse dead and my leg torn to pieces." He was then waiting for the surgeon to amputate the mutilated limb.

Sherman was very angry. Upon investigation he discovered that the Confederates had planted 8-inch shells in the road, equipping them with friction matches so that they would explode when trodden upon. There was no resistance being made at that point. Not a Confederate was to be seen. No battle was in progress, and the only guns to be heard were far in the rear, where Wheeler and Kilpatrick were still skirmishing. Under these circumstances the employment of torpedoes was not legitimate warfare, but wanton butchery. Sherman determined to let whatever suffering was to result fall upon the Confederates themselves, and bringing up a party of prisoners, provided them with picks and shovels, and ordered them to go first and either explode their own torpedoes or dig them up. " I could hardly help laughing," he writes, " at their stepping so gingerly along the road, where it was supposed sunken torpedoes might explode at each step, but they found no other torpedoes until near Fort McAllister."

The army was now drawing near to Savannah. The low, sandy character of the soil, and the many sluggish tidal streams with which the country was cut up, told of the proximity of the seashore, while the multiplying roads and railroads gave the surest evidence that a great city was not far off. On the 9th and 10th of December the different wings of the army came up against the Confederate defenses and their further advance was checked for a time. While reconnoitering these works General Sherman walked into a railroad cut about eight miles from Savannah. Down the track about 800 yards he saw a Confederate redoubt, the gunners in which were about to discharge a cannon. A word of warning from Sherman caused his officers to scatter, and he himself kept a sharp eye on the gun and stepped aside out of the track of its ball. But an unfortunate negro, heedless of the warning, stepped directly into the path of the projectile, which struck him under the jaw, literally carrying away his head.

Sherman first turned his attention to Fort McAllister. With that work in his hands the problem of fixing a base of supplies on the seacoast would be solved, for vessels could ascend the Ogeechee to his lines, whether Savannah were taken or not. He knew that the vessels were lying at anchor out beyond the reedy marshes, the tortuous bayous and lagoons, and the gloomy and dismal swamps that intervened between him and the open sea. He knew, too, that the men of the navy were expecting him, for the negroes told him that every night for a week past rockets had been sent up from the fleet, as though to attract the attention of friends on shore.

Sherman sent General Hazen with his division to march down the right bank of the Ogeechee and carry Fort McAllister by assault. Though strong on its river front, the fort was weak to landward, and the Union commander believed it could be carried without heavy loss to the attacking force. He himself went down the opposite bank of the river to a point about three miles from the fort, where the Union signal officers had built a platform on the ridge-pole of a rice mill. Sherman clambered up to this lofty eyrie and through his glass watched eagerly the progress of the column down the other side of the river. Occasionally, too, he cast an anxious glance out to sea, and his gaze in this direction was at last rewarded by the discovery of a faint cloud of smoke on the horizon and a small object which, as it rapidly approached, took on the form of a gunboat flying the Stars and Stripes.

"Who are you?" was the signal waved from the deck of the vessel when she came within signaling distance.

"General Sherman," was the response, and then the signal officers began sending the order to Hazen, who was out of sight of the gunboat, to attack at once.

"Is Fort McAllister taken yet?" was the next impatient inquiry from the gunboat.

"No; but it will be in a minute," was the confident reply, for just at that instant Sherman saw Hazen's troops burst out of the fringe of woods before the fort, their colors flying, their lines regular, and the pace at which they advanced firm, even, and rapid. Then the great guns of Fort McAllister began to flash and to spout smoke and flame. The lines pressed sturdily on. Now the soldiers plunged into the midst of the lowering clouds of sulphurous smoke. Their forms could be seen but faintly, but the colors floating in the clear air above were plainly visible. One flag went down, but soon reappeared. Then the cannon flashes became less regular and rapid. The garrison was plainly weakening. The smoke was wafted away on the ocean breeze, and the eager watchers across the river could see the men in blue swarming over the parapet, waving their colors, firing their muskets in the air, and cheering for a quickly won and important victory.

That night Sherman entered a skiff and was pulled down the river to the gunboat with which he had been exchanging signals during the afternoon. He stopped on the way at Fort McAllister, where he found that Hazen had won his victory with a loss of but 24 of his gallant fellows killed and 110 wounded. The torpedoes, which the Confederates had planted thickly in the ground before the fort, did more execution than the great guns of the work itself, and while Sherman was there one poor fellow was blown to pieces by one of them while seeking for a comrade among the dead upon the battle-field.

"Look out for torpedoes!" was the warning cry of those on shore when, after a short stay at the fort, Sherman pushed his craft out into the black channel of the river and started down stream again. The night was clear and cold, and the stars sparkled with midwinter brilliancy. The tide was rushing in swiftly, and the oarsmen had hard work of it, as they bent to their task and propelled the boat along the tortuous course of the stream.

No torpedoes or other obstructions of any kind were encountered, and after a six-mile pull, and just as Sherman had concluded that the vessel had steamed out to sea again, the lights of the gun-boat were seen gleaming through the darkness. A few more tugs at the oars and the hoarse hail, " Boat ahoy! what boat's that?" came floating over the water. Sherman was soon clambering over the bulwarks of the vessel, and enjoying a hearty greeting. He learned that the military situation had not changed materially since he started from Atlanta. Grant was still besieging Lee at Petersburg and Thomas was at Nashville preparing to fall upon Hood. After sending off dispatches to the authorities at Washington, in which he declared that he regarded Savannah as already taken, Sherman returned to his army to press forward the siege.

Though it was evident that Savannah must ultimately fall into their hands, the National forces had some hard work to do before they could in fact enter the city. The immense advantage, in point of numbers, which Sherman enjoyed, and his possession of heavy siege guns with which he could compel a surrender under penalty of bombarding the city, gave him ample assurance of ultimate success. Yet the enemy's defensive works were too strong to be lightly walked over. The country thereabouts, too, was ill suited for campaigning. The land lay low, and when a high tide and an east wind sent the salt water into rivers and lagoons it was all awash. Most of the fields were used for the culture of rice, which necessitate the frequent flooding of the land. The flood gates and sluices provided for this purpose had been opened by the Confederates, and water a foot deep, with mud beneath as deep again, extended in every direction before the Federals. Under such conditions the siege progressed but slowly. Sherman, however, had a double purpose in view. To take Savannah was not enough; he wished to capture Hardee and his men as well. To accomplish this he was gradually extending his lines, so as to cover every road leading out of Savannah. On the 17th of the month he called upon Hardee to surrender, accompanying the summons with a threat to bombard the city unless the demand were complied with. Hardee, however, contemptuously refused compliance, and Sherman, disliking equally to bombard a city full of helpless women and children, or to attack a fortified position, renewed his efforts to starve the Confederates into subjection. One road was still uncovered—an old plank road leading into South Carolina, with which Hardee had established connection by means of a pontoon bridge. Sherman had no troops available to cover this point and complete his investment of the town, but he knew of a division at Hilton Head which he thought might be moved to that vital point; thither he went, accordingly, in a swift vessel supplied by Admiral Dahlgren, but just as he was completing his arrangements for the transportation of the troops, there came a dispatch boat from Savannah saying that Hardee had evacuated the city and had moved, horse, foot, and dragoons, over the pontoon bridge, blowing up his iron-clads and the navy yard, and was then in full retreat into South Carolina.

Sherman lost no time in moving into the evacuated town, and speedily sent off to President Lincoln this dispatch, which reached the White House on Christmas Eve:

To His Excellency, President Lincoln, Washington, D. C.:

I beg leave to present you as a Christmas gift the city of Savannah, with one hundred and fifty heavy guns and plenty of ammunition. Also about twenty-five thousand bales of cotton.

W. T. SHERMAN, *Major-General.*

CHAPTER XIV.

INCIDENTS OF THE WAR—THE STOLEN LOCOMOTIVE—PLAN OF THE RAID—UNEXPECTED DIFFICULTIES — THE BLOCK AT KINGSTON — THE PURSUIT — TENACITY OF THE PURSUERS — TRYING TO BURN A BRIDGE—THE ENGINE ABANDONED—SAD FATE OF THE RAIDERS — GENERAL JOHN MORGAN—REFUSED PERMISSION TO CROSS THE OHIO—HIS DISOBEDIENCE—CROSSING THE OHIO — MORGAN CAPTURED AND HIS COMMAND DISPERSED — THE ESCAPE— THE NEW YORK DRAFT RIOTS—FIGHTING IN THE STREETS.

E may for a time turn aside from the direct course of the narrative of the decisive military operations of the war to read of some minor operations, of an irregular character, which, though having little or no effect in determining the outcome of that gigantic struggle, are yet full of interest because of their romantic or adventurous nature. There were two sides to the war. Besides the ponderous movements of the great armies, there was a constant succession of lesser events in which irregular forces played the chief parts. What is known as the "war on the border"; that series of pitched battles, midnight massacres, and cowardly murders in which neighbor was arrayed against neighbor, and brother against brother, in what seemed destined to be a war of extermination, is an example of the secondary and useless warfare which went on while the great results of the struggle were being determined in Georgia and around Richmond.

The exploits of the Confederate guerrillas and "partisan" horsemen make an interesting chapter of history. Such dashing troopers as Shelby, the cavalier of the Southwest, who led a force into Mexico when the Confederacy finally tottered and fell into ruins; Morgan, the fearless Kentuckian, who carried the war into Ohio and could not be held a captive by iron bars and walls of masonry; Mosby, the Virginia lawyer, who was pitched into the saddle and rode like a centaur and fought like a Paladin—all these were the products of that restless daring and intolerance of restraint and discipline that pervaded the men of the South.

The North produced no such men. War was a grim business with those who followed the Stars and Stripes. They tolerated no irregular forces. Guerrillas and partisan rangers were unknown among them. Discipline was everywhere, and the chain of responsibility was unbroken from the humblest private up to the commander-in-chief. Nevertheless, the undaunted pluck and recklessness of danger characteristic of Americans animated the men of the North equally with their Southern brethren.

Not least notable among the many daring and dramatic exploits of the war was the desperate dash of a party of Ohio soldiers on a stolen locomotive into the heart of Georgia, at that time, April, 1863, swarming with Confederate troops.

The expedition had its origin in the mind of a Union spy named James J. Andrews. Under pretense of carrying on a traffic in quinine, this man had several times made his way through the Confederate lines, but had failed to bring out any information of importance. Once he had been sent with eight men, all carefully disguised, to burn the railway bridges west of Chattanooga, but in this too he had failed. The adventure which ended in his falling into the hands of the enemy and being executed, with seven of his comrades, as a spy, was undertaken for a like purpose.

In the early part of April, 1862, twenty-four soldiers in the brigade of General J. W. Sill were quietly notified that they were needed for secret and very dangerous service. Not a man quailed, though all must have known that they were embarked upon an enterprise which was almost certain to end in death. They were told to discard their uniforms and don citizens' garb. The muskets that they had so long shouldered were taken away, and a revolver given to each. When, after these preparations, they were told that the field for their future operations lay within the enemy's lines, they realized at once the desperate character of their mission—for a soldier out of uniform captured within hostile lines, is a spy, and, in default of extenuating circumstances, is speedily hanged by sentence of a drum-head court-martial.

Clad in the homely butternut-gray homespun cloth and slouch hats which commonly constituted the apparel of the Southerner of that day, the raiders met Andrews near Shelbyville, Ky. In a few brief words he outlined the plan of the raid. In groups of two and three they were to enter Confederate territory and make their way southward by rail to Marietta, Ga. To any who questioned them they should declare that they were Kentuckians going to join the Confederate army. At Marietta they were to meet and all take a train northward. Eight miles out of the town the train would stop to enable passengers to breakfast. Here, while the trainmen were eating their meal, the raiders were to slip into one of the forward cars, uncoupling the rest of the train. Two locomotive engineers, who were with the party, would seize the engine and pull out, leaving the passengers and crew in the lurch. With the captured train they would then make for Chattanooga, burning the bridges behind them, and thus destroying the only road by which the Confederates could send troops to that city, which was threatened by the Union forces under General Mitchel. It was a romantic and adventurous project, and appealed strongly to the daring spirits who had been chosen to participate in it.

Three days later a train steamed out of Marietta, carrying twenty of the raiders. Two had been forced into the Confederate army while making their way to the rendezvous, and two more were belated. The twenty who started knew that their enterprise was even more hazardous than had been anticipated. The road was crowded with trains hurrying troops to the front, and the station at which the capture was to be effected had been made the site of a Confederate camp, so that the exploit would have to be performed in full view of a whole brigade of the enemy. Frankly pointing out to his men these new and unexpected obstacles, Andrews gave to any one or to all of them full permission to abandon the attempt. Not one flinched, and with undaunted courage, but with hearts beating fast, they took their seats in the train.

After a run of eight miles the station of Big Shanty was reached. The passengers leaped from the train and ran to the lunch counter. The conductor, engineer, and other train hands followed. In the general scramble for food nobody noticed the soldierly looking fellows in civilians' clothes who left the passenger coaches and strolled forward toward the locomotive. One of them slipped in between the cars and pulled out a coupling-pin, breaking the train in two. Three box-cars remained attached to the engine. Into the last one of these the raiders sprung with all possible dispatch. The Confederate recruits in their tents, not twenty yards away, looked on with languid interest. It never struck them that there could be a hostile force at work in the very heart of the Confederacy. Not a dozen feet from the engine stood a Confederate sentry, loaded rifle in hand. He looked on while Andrews walked up, nodded to the engineer, swung himself into the cab, and pulled the throttle wide open. Not until he saw the locomotive's wheels whiz around before catching the track, and then discovered that half of the train had started at full speed, leaving the remainder and all the passengers behind, did the sentinel suspect anything wrong and raise the alarm.

Under a full head of steam the locomotive sped up the track. Andrews and his comrades were exhilarated with hopes of success. They believed that in capturing the train and getting away before the very eyes of the enemy's troops, they had met and overcome the only great obstacle to their project. Occasionally they stopped, once to tear up the track and cut the telegraph-wires, and several times to take on wood and water. When any question was asked Andrews coolly said that he was taking a train-load of powder to General Beauregard, and he pointed to the box-cars behind the closed doors of which were sixteen of his companions, who, in their moving prison, could only vaguely guess at the scenes that were being enacted outside.

For a few hours all went well, but the raiders little knew that they were being pursued, while the road ahead was blocked with trains that would prevent their escape. Had the attempt been made the day before there is every reason to believe it would have been successful in every respect. But this day the road was blocked. The first intelligence of this came to Andrews when he reached Kingston, thirty miles from his starting place. Here he waited, as he had planned, to allow a local freight to pass him. Once that train was out of the way he expected to have a clear track to Chattanooga. But to his dismay, the freight train upon arriving displayed from the last car a red flag, signifying that another train was following close behind. Andrews, greatly disquieted, sought for an explanation.

"What does it mean," said he boldly to the conductor, "that the road is blocked in this manner when I have orders to take this powder to Beauregard without a moment's delay?"

"Mitchel has captured Huntsville and is said to be coming to Chattanooga," was the answer. "We are getting everything out of there as quickly as possible."

This was serious news. It appeared that the expedition which was to co-operate with Andrews was likely to be the chief factor in his defeat. To add to the strain on the minds of the raiders the next train also bore a red flag. For over an hour the adventurers were held at the station, those in the box-car fairly holding their breath lest some noise should betray the fact that they were not gunpowder for Beauregard, while those without had to simulate an air of easy indifference to deceive the station men, who were beginning to manifest some suspicion of this mysterious train manned by strangers and running without orders.

At last, the blockade was broken and the raiders' train pulled out of Kingston. The adventurers all drew a deep breath of relief. The track was now clear to Chattanooga and they expected no pursuit. Just to make certain that nothing need be feared from the rear, however, they stopped to tear up a rail or two, which would effectually block a pursuer's progress.

BATTLE-FIELDS AND VICTORY.

While engaged in this work, they suddenly heard the shrill whistle of a locomotive. They gazed at each other in dismay. The alarm, then, had been given! The Confederates were really upon the track, and close at their heels. Catching up their tools, they redoubled their efforts to lift the rail. It began to bend. A few minutes' work only was needed to tear it from its place. But this time, brief though it was, could not be had. Another whistle was heard close at hand, and in a moment a locomotive crowded with armed men, appeared but a short distance down the road. There was nothing left for the raiders but to spring to their engine and make a race for their lives.

If the coolness, ingenuity, and daring of Andrews and his companions up to this time had been worthy of admiration, none the less so were the quick decision and dogged persistence of the two men who were now heading the pursuing party. When the stolen train pulled out of Big Shanty station it left behind a panic-stricken and bewildered throng of Confederates. Two men only, of all those who crowded about the track, maintained their presence of mind. Conductor Fuller, of the dismembered train, and a railroad mechanic named Murphy, determined to foil Andrews in his daring plan. They could not intercept him by telegraph, for the wires were cut. No engine was at hand to bear them in chase of the fugitives, but they started off down the track as fast as their legs would carry them. It seemed a hopeless, indeed almost a ridiculous task, for two men on foot to attempt to overtake a locomotive that had several miles the start of them, but Fuller knew of the tangle of extra trains ahead and hoped that Andrews would be blockaded. A short distance down the track the pursuers found a handcar, with the aid of which their progress was greatly hastened until they came suddenly upon a broken rail, which sent the car and its crew flying into the ditch. Picking themselves up and finding no bones broken, they pushed on, rather more cautiously now, until they reached Etowah. There an engine was found with steam up. Now the pursuers felt sure of their prey. Loading their locomotive with soldiers, they continued the chase. Kingston was reached. Here Fuller had felt confident he would overtake the fugitives, for he knew of the special trains that blocked the road at that point and did not believe that Andrews could by any possibility get by them. Though greatly disappointed to find his birds flown he did not lose heart, but pressed on in swift pursuit. It was the whistle of this locomotive that startled the raiders at their work of breaking the line.

It was a fair race now and both engines thundered down the track at frightful speed. Andrews and his companions knew that, if caught, their lives would pay the penalty. They could not stop and give battle to their pursuers, for they could see, by the crowd of men clinging to the engine and tender, that they were outnumbered. If they could but gain a little time to tear up a rail or burn a bridge, escape might yet be possible. The last car of the raiders' train was uncoupled, in the hope that the pursuers would crash into it and be thrown from the track, but the keen eye of the Confederate engineer discerned the danger in season, and he slowed up his locomotive and pushed the car ahead of him. The same attempt was made with a second car, but was similarly defeated, and the pursuers soon rid themselves of the two cars at a switch at Resaca station. It was there that the first bridge stood which the raiders were to destroy, but so hot was the pursuit that they were obliged to dash across it without stopping.

In point of speed it soon became evident that the two engines were about evenly matched, and there was but little likelihood of the second one overhauling the first. But the plan of the pursuers was to keep so close behind Andrews that he would have time, neither to do any damage to the track or bridges, nor to take on wood and water. But Andrews's men, by knocking out the end of their box-car and dropping the ties with which it was loaded upon the track, managed to delay the pursuers long enough to supply their engine with its food.

Thus sped on pursuers and pursued, mile after mile, along a rough and winding road. So great was the rate of speed that it is strange that both of the engines were not wrecked. The escapes of the men in the second train seem, indeed, miraculous. At one place Andrews stopped and placed a loose rail upon the track, on a curve, in such a position that the pursuers could not see it. Fuller's engine, thundering along the track, ran upon the rail at full speed. There was a terrible jolt, and the engine

LOSS OF "THE CRICKET."

sprang from the track, but lighted again upon the rails and continued the pursuit.

The raiders now became desperate. Nothing that they could do seemed to shake the dogged inflexibility of the pursuit. Some wished to spring from the engine, reverse its valves and let it demolish the enemy. Others suggested stopping and fighting a desperate battle for their lives. But Andrews still hoped to complete the work which he had set out to do. He knew that a few miles farther along the road was a covered bridge. He began building a fire in the one box-car that remained attached to his engine. Wood was piled up on its floor, and ignited with coals from the locomotive furnace. The sharp draft from the rapid rush of the train through the air fanned the flames into fury. By the time the bridge was reached, the whole car was a roaring mass of fire.

Slowing up upon the bridge, Andrews uncoupled the blazing car and left it there. The flames curled among the rafters of the structure, and the whole dark tunnel-like shed was filled with smoke. This was the raiders' last hope of success, and they watched the progress of the fire anxiously. If the bridge caught fire and the path of the pursuers was blocked, they were safe. But their high hopes were doomed to disappointment. The heavy rains had so soaked the canopy of the bridge that it caught but slowly, and the pursuers were able to run into the midst of the smoke and flame, couple on to the blazing car, and push it out on the other side.

This sealed the fate of the raiders. The enemy was close upon their heels. They had no longer any ties with which to obstruct the track. No wood was in the tender, and steam was going down rapidly. Leaping from the engine, they reversed it and fled in all directions. But the steam was by this time so low that the collision that followed did no damage, and Fuller and his men were soon running through the fields in pursuit.

Though not far from the Union lines, the members of Andrews's party were unable to elude their determined pursuers. The alarm was spread far and wide, and the whole neighborhood turned out to hunt for the reckless Yankees who thus invaded Confederate territory. Several were captured on the very first day of the hunt. Others avoided detection for a time by hiding in the woods and gloomy swamps, living on roots and berries, and moving only by night. But at the expiration of a week two only were still at large, and these were captured a few days later when they thought themselves out of danger. A court-martial followed, and Andrews and seven of his comrades were condemned to death and hanged. Their graves may now be seen, side by side, in the military cemetery at Chattanooga.

One of the picturesque and romantic figures of the Confederate Army was General John Morgan, the cavalryman. His dashing charges and brilliant forays have been the theme of many a song and story; and his marriage, almost on the battle-field, with the Confederate soldier priest, General Polk, officiating, and surrounded by the officers of Bragg's army in their campaigning garb, lent a spice of romance to his career. Morgan was a born cavalryman. He rode like a centaur, and his frame of iron seemed never to yield to fatigue. Relentless of purpose, swift of action, fertile in expedient, he was at his best when at the head of an independent column, operating in hostile territory and away from the, to him, galling control of a superior officer.

In the summer of 1863 General Morgan was given an opportunity to display in the most striking manner those soldierly characteristics that made him renowned. Vicksburg was then sturdily standing out against Grant's besieging forces, and Bragg, who was at Tullahoma, had sent a liberal detachment of troops to attempt to raise the siege. This left him exposed to an attack on his flank and rear, and he ordered Morgan to make a raid into Kentucky, with a view to checking the re-enforcement of Rosecrans.

"Let me go into Indiana and Ohio," pleaded Morgan. "That will be far more effective, for the Federals will be alarmed at the thought of our men in their home territory. I will threaten Cincinnati and draw after me every loose bluecoat west of the Alleghanys."

"You will be captured, sure as fate," responded Bragg, "and I shall lose the flower of my cavalry."

"Suppose I am captured," replied the trooper. "It will be but a loss to you of about 2000 men, and I will guarantee that the benefit you will derive from our raid will more than offset the sacrifice."

Still Bragg was not to be convinced. To threaten Louisville, he thought, would alarm the enemy as much as to undertake the perilous adventure of entering the outskirts of Cincinnati. And so, when he gave Morgan his orders for the raid, he added a peremptory injunction that on no account should he cross the Ohio River.

Morgan began at once his preparations for the raid. It is characteristic of the man that his first step was in the direction of disobeying his commander. He had argued long to win permission to cross into Northern territory, and that permission having been denied him he determined to undertake the adventure in flagrant disregard of orders. Trusted men were sent out to examine the fords of the upper Ohio, and Morgan told one of his lieutenants that he proposed making the raid despite Bragg's commands.

"It is the only way that I can give any substantial aid to Bragg's army," said he, "and my determination is fixed. I shall take about 2500 men and four light guns. We will cross the Cumberland at Burkesville, and the Ohio at Brandenburg. This route will take us so close to Louisville that the enemy will feel certain that that city is our destination. Once in Indiana we will ride straight to the eastward, passing through the suburbs of Cincinnati. General Lee may be in Pennsylvania at that time, and in that event we shall try to join him. Perhaps we may be captured; in fact, I think we shall, but we'll tear a piece out of the Yankee territory, and draw all their troops away from Bragg."

The morning of the 8th of July found Morgan and his men on the south bank of the Ohio River, at Brandenburg. They had not reached that point without hard fighting and some loss. A detachment that had been sent to make a demonstration before Louisville had failed to make its way back to the main column, so that the Confederate leader found his force less, by at least 400 men, when he reached the banks of the turbid stream that marked the southern boundary of the loyal States of the North.

The day before the arrival of Morgan's main column at the river two companies, sent in advance, had reached Brandenburg. They found two steamers lying at the levee. One had steam up, and her captain pushed out into the stream when he heard shouts and shots from the town announcing the arrival of a hostile force. But the raiders rushed on board the second craft, forced the engineer to get up steam, and soon overhauled the fugitive and brought her back to the dock in triumph. When Morgan arrived the boats were tied to the bank, with steam up, ready to ferry him and his command across.

The Confederates soon found that crossing the river was no easy task. On the Indiana shore a battalion of home guards was assembled, and began a spirited fire as soon as the first boat-load of Confederates left Kentucky. The range was too great for the musketry to do any serious hurt, but the militiamen soon ran a field-piece into position, which threw shells across the river with deadly aim. But the raw, undisciplined volunteers were no match for Morgan's battle-tempered veterans, who soon landed and drove their antagonists away from the river's bank, capturing the cannon.

Two regiments had now been ferried across, and the steamers were loading for another trip, when a serious interruption occurred. A Union gun-boat, the *Elk*, evidently attracted to the scene by the sound of the firing, came swiftly around a point of land up the river, and took up a position fairly athwart the ferry. Her captain was a man of action, and his guns were soon flashing from both batteries.

Matters now began to look critical for Morgan. He dared not continue the work of ferrying his troops, for one shell from the gun-boat would have sent either of his frail river steamboats to the bottom, with all on board. Yet to leave the two regiments that had already crossed alone was to offer an easy prize to the Indiana militia, who could swoop down upon them in overwhelming numbers. The knowledge, too, that the Union cavalry was hot upon his trail, made Morgan anxious to get his whole force across the river with as little delay as possible. The four guns that he had with him were therefore run into battery on the river's brink, and opened fire upon the gun-boat. The commander of that craft was a plucky sailor, with a full comprehension of the trouble he was making for the Confederates, and he held manfully to his position. His guns flashed fast, and their shells burst right among the Confederate cannoneers, while occasionally he dropped

HAND-TO-HAND FIGHTING AT ATLANTA.

one among the raiders on the Indiana shore, as though to warn them that he would attend to them later. But after two hours of vigorous work the gun-boat was driven off, and the crossing of the stream was continued.

Once in Indiana, the Confederates pressed forward at a rapid rate. The stories of their endurance of fatigue and ready responsiveness to the demands of their leader challenge our admiration. "We were habitually twenty-one hours out of the twenty-four in the saddle, very frequently not halting at night or going into camp at all," writes one of them. They had but little fighting to do. Here and there the militia made a stand, as at Corydon, where Morgan lost sixteen men before a redoubt of rails too high for his horses to leap, but as a rule the militia rallied about the chief towns, which Morgan did not attack, but only threatened and passed on. The farmhouses he passed on the way were deserted save by the women. "The men hev all gone to the rally," the farm-wives would say meaningly; "you'll see them soon."

Provisions they found in plenty. To the half-starved soldiers, long accustomed to the meager larders of the war-swept Confederacy, the bountiful supply of food of all kinds was a constant delight. Many of the farm people were afraid to await in person the coming of the raiders and fled, leaving the tables covered with food to propitiate the hungry cavalrymen. At first this silent hospitality was regarded with suspicion by the Confederates. "Maybe them Yanks hez put pisen in the pies," said a trooper doubtfully to one of his officers, who inquired why a whole squad of them stood hesitating before a table covered with pastry. The officer by way of reply devoured a pie, and the men soon cleared the table.

General Morgan did not cherish those scrupulous ideas concerning the sanctity of private property that were enunciated by Lee when he led an invading column. Morgan's men were allowed to take about whatever they wanted, and they looted stores and dwellings with the utmost enthusiasm. Whatever they saw that met their fancy, they carried off, often throwing it away after a few hours and replacing it with something else. Their thefts did not appear to be based on any principles of common sense. One man hung seven pairs of skates around his neck and carried them for three days, over dusty roads, under a burning July sun, while another trooper rode at his side loaded down with sleigh-bells. Calico was a staple article, and baby shoes were next in appealing to the covetousness of the soldiers. A large chafing-dish, a medium-sized Dutch clock, a green glass decanter with goblets to match, a bag of horn buttons, a chandelier, and a bird-cage containing three canaries, are some of the articles which an officer remembers to have seen carried by these men who were marching twenty-one hours out of the twenty-four. It is little wonder that a Northern eye-witness describes Morgan's command as resembling a circus with an unusual number of clowns.

When Ohio was reached, the invaders began to find the obstacles in their path increasing. They were now in a densely populated State. The crowds of able-bodied men they saw amazed them. Every man in the South was in the army, and the North had still larger armies in the field; yet its farms and cities were well filled with masculine defenders. The militia was well organized and efficient. From a holiday march the raid became a succession of sharp encounters. The ranks of the raiders were thinning fast. The militia felled trees across the roads, and from the forests adjoining shot down the axmen who tried to clear the way. Rapid and uninterrupted marching had sorely wearied the invaders. Their bodies were weak and their spirits drooping. Their cartridge-boxes, too, were almost empty, for they had had no chance to replenish their store of ammunition since crossing the Ohio. Their Parrott guns had become so clogged with dust as to be almost useless. This, however, was a misfortune which did not long occupy Morgan's attention, for the four pieces, together with a large part of the Kentucky regiment to which they were attached, were, before long, taken by the Federals. If anything was needed to complete the depression of the Confederates, it was supplied when the news reached them that Vicksburg had fallen, and that Lee, whom they hoped to join in Pennsylvania, had suffered a bloody repulse at Gettysburg and was falling back across the Potomac.

The heavy blow that hastened the breaking up of Morgan's column fell on the 18th of July. The Confederates were attacked near Chester by a force of Ohio and Michigan troops under General Judah, aided by two gun-boats which could throw their shells into the Confederate lines. Morgan at once began a retreat which speedily degenerated into a tumultuous rout. The only way of escape lay through a narrow valley, and at the entrance to this the demoralized Confederates crowded upon each other, pushing and struggling for precedence. The whole crowd surged backward and forward, crying out with a mighty shout of fear when the Union shells began to drop in among them. The gun boats steamed up within easy range and turned their guns, shotted with grape, upon the writhing mass. The Federal infantry dashed into the mob and cut out hundreds of prisoners. Not less than 700 Confederates were captured here, and the killed and wounded numbered 120.

With the remnant of his force, amounting to perhaps 1000 men, Morgan continued his flight, running with the untiring endurance of a wolf, and twisting and turning upon his pursuers like a fox. His only hope now was to get out of Ohio. At a point about three miles above Buffington he reached the river, but found it too deep to ford. About 300 of the men crossed by swimming, the commander among them, but, many were drowned in the attempt. At this moment the two gun-boats made their appearance, steaming up the river in pursuit. There was no longer any hope of getting the entire command across, and General Morgan manfully returned to share the perils and sufferings of the men on the Ohio shore. Again the retreat commenced, but after exerting to the utmost his ingenuity, energy, and daring, Morgan confessed himself outdone, and surrendered the pitiable remnant of his command. Three hundred and sixty-four were all that now remained of the two thousand who with light hearts and high hopes had crossed into Ohio.

A few days later Morgan and sixty-nine of his officers found themselves confined in the Ohio penitentiary at Columbus. A part of the prison had been boarded off for their use, that it might not be said that prisoners of war had been forced to associate with robbers and murderers. They were kept under the strictest surveillance. No newspapers were permitted to reach them. Their letters were read by the warden before reaching their hands. Two sets of guards, civil and military, watched over them, and there seemed to be no possible precaution against their escape neglected.

Yet it was a restless party of men whom the State of Ohio had locked in its great strong-box, and no precautions could be too great. Scarcely were they in before they began planning an escape. One project after another was suggested in their daily consultations, and one after another was rejected. At last Captain Hines suggested one that all hailed as feasible. The plan involved cutting a flag-stone out of a cell floor, tunneling under the jail proper into the yard, then scaling the outer wall, dodging the sentries, and escaping through a densely populated State to the Ohio River and thence southward to the Confederate lines. For tools they had two small knives, purloined from the prison hospital.

This is not the place to recount in detail the progress of the work, the subterfuges adopted to conceal from the guards what was being done, or the astute plots by which the warden of the prison was made, all unwittingly, to give material aid to the conspirators. A single illustration must suffice.

It was essential that the prisoners should get a glimpse of the outside wall which they had to scale, in order that they might know the most advantageous point at which to approach it. But the only windows in the prison were high in air, and though a long ladder was leaning against the inner wall, the prisoners dared not climb up to the windows lest they should arouse suspicion. A clever trick solved the difficulty. One afternoon, when the warden of the prison was chatting pleasantly with the prisoners, they began boasting of the great physical strength of Captain Taylor, one of their number. Taylor was of diminutive stature and the warden rather laughed at his pretensions.

"Well," said Taylor, "you see that fifty-foot ladder leaning against the wall? If you will permit me I will go up that ladder hand-over-hand on the under side and come down the same way."

The warden acquiesced and the wiry soldier made the ascent. At the top he stopped a moment to rest, and occupied the time in staring furtively out of the window. When he descended he brought a vivid mental photograph of the wall, which he lost no time in transferring to paper.

The days passed until, by the 20th of November, there was a loose flagstone in the floor of each of six cells, beneath which the builders of the prison had left a large air passage. From this passage ran a tunnel which had been dug almost to the surface of the earth in the jail-yard. It was on this night that the prisoners had determined to make their escape, and at the given signal each descended into the air chamber, Captain Hines leaving behind him in his cell the following note.

CASTLE MERION, CELL NO. 20, November 27, 1863.—Commencement, November 4, 1863; Conclusion, November 24, 1863; number of hours per day, five; tools, two small knives. *La patience est amère, mais son fruit est doux.* By order of my six honorable Confederates.
THOMAS H. HINES, *Captain, C. S. A.*

A few minutes later the ground in the jail-yard heaved and shook a little in a certain spot near the wall, and then parted, and the disheveled head of a man burst through. Out of the hole in the ground the seven Confederates crawled, one after the other, each springing quickly into the dark shadow of the wall, where he awaited the arrival of the others. The dirt with which their clothes were plentifully besmeared was brushed away, the wall scaled, and a descent made upon the other side, within sixty yards of the spot where a number of sentinels were sitting around a camp-fire and conversing. But the soldiers did not see the seven ghostly forms swiftly vanish in the surrounding shadows.

Once out of sight of the prison the fugitives scattered. Morgan and Hines went to the railway station and purchased tickets for Cincinnati. Entering the car Morgan coolly chose a seat by the side of a Federal major in full uniform, with whom he soon began a friendly conversation. The train passed near the penitentiary from which the fugitives had just escaped, and when it came in sight of the building the Union soldier pointed to it, saying: "There is where the rebel General Morgan and his officers are put for safe keeping."

"I hope they will keep him as safe as he is now," replied Morgan unconcernedly.

A series of narrow escapes was in store for the fugitives. General Morgan succeeded in avoiding recapture, but Hines fell into the hands of the same party of Federals that captured three of his comrades. All four, however, managed to escape again and finally, after much suffering and many privations, made their way back to the Confederate lines. Their expedition had brought heavy loss upon the Confederacy, while exerting scarcely any appreciable influence upon the course of the struggle between Bragg and Rosecrans.

Another of the minor events of the great war, yet one which at the time caused wide-spread anxiety and was thought by many to be portentous of a reign of anarchy in the North, was the great New York draft riot of 1863. In the levy of 300,000 men ordered by President Lincoln, New York City had failed to supply its full quota of volunteers, and a draft was ordered. Never more than half-hearted in its support of the war, New York was goaded to fury by this action. The more orderly people openly condemned the draft; the disorderly and criminal classes threatened to resist it with violence. In many of the newspapers the draft was declared unconstitutional and despotic, and the quota demanded excessive. The next day was Sunday, and in the Sunday papers the people read the long list of names of those whom the fateful chance of the provost marshal's wheel had chosen to serve the nation in the ranks. In all the bar-rooms of the city the draft was the topic of the day. In the groggeries of the Five Points and the purlieus of the water front the idle and vicious element of a great city's population denounced the draft and determined to resist it on the morrow. They knew well that, save for its police force, the city was defenseless. Most of the troops had been sent hurriedly into Pensylvania to meet Lee's invading forces.

Monday morning, July 13, a great crowd surged about the building at the corner of Third Avenue and Thirty-Sixth Street, in which the provost-marshal's wheel was turning. Sixty policemen guarded the building, but in the street were thousands of yelling, cursing, struggling men, who had come there for trouble, and were not to be held in check. When the blow was struck it was resistless. With a fierce, hungry yell the mob poured down upon the building as though to level it at one blow. The policemen, plying their clubs fiercely, cracking a skull with each stroke, were forced back. The crowd surged into the office, breaking in the windows, smashing furniture and doors, and driving the officials away. The hated wheel was stamped upon, ground to pieces, pulverized. Then the building was fired, and when the engines came the rioters blocked the pathway of the firemen and refused to permit any water to be thrown upon the flames. The superintendent of police, coming to the scene of the trouble, was recognized by some of the rioters—many of whom indeed had ample reasons to recognize a man whose profession was the detection and punishment of criminals—and was set upon, clubbed, stoned, beaten into insensibility, and then thrown, face down, into a puddle, where his assailants hoped that he would drown. When rescued he was so bruised and mutilated as to be unrecognizable.

Meantime the riot had spread to other parts of the city. A whole block of buildings on Broadway was blazing. Two blocks further down Third Avenue there was a pitched battle between the rioters and the police, in which the latter were badly worsted. One policeman suffered so brutal a beating that his comrades thought him dead and laid his inanimate form away in the dead-house of a neighboring hospital. His wife, coming thither to mourn by the side of her dead husband, discovered that his heart was still beating, and prompt measures brought him back to health, after a long and critical illness.

Women fought by the side of men in that ferocious mob. One officer received a cruel thrust in the side from a knife wielded by one of the enraged viragos. Boys brandished clubs, threw stones, and yelled out curses upon the police and the soldiers as fiercely as the most hardened criminal among them.

Throughout the day the rioters held complete possession of those parts of the city in which they gathered. The police were slow to awaken to the gravity of the outbreak, but toward evening they began in earnest the work of repressing the disorder. Crazed by their success, and many of them maddened by liquor, the rioters fancied themselves invincible. Some thousands of them formed in a great procession and marched down Broadway. They bore banners displaying inflammatory mottoes; muskets, clubs, and pitchforks were openly carried, and there was scarcely a man that had not a pistol in his pocket. The roll of their drums and their cries of "Down with the draft!" "Down with Lincoln!" alarmed the whole city.

Up the street came a platoon of 200 policemen, marching to meet the rioters. At their head was Inspector Carpenter, to whom the command had fallen when his chief was beaten into insensibility by the mob.

"Hit for their heads, men," said Carpenter; "hit quick and hard. We don't want any prisoners."

The blue-coats charged into the crowd in a solid body. Carpenter struck the first blow, and a burly rioter went down before the stroke of his locust club. The undisciplined mob made but a feeble effort at resistance. A few pistols cracked, but there was no one to lead them, and the rioters were soon flying in every direction with no thought save to escape from the terrible clubs. The street was left covered with the dead and dying.

The next day the fury of the now thoroughly enraged populace took the form of murderous assaults upon every negro who was to be seen. They looked upon the negroes as the cause of the war, and swore vengeance against the entire race. Black men were hanged to trees in the streets. The Colored Orphan Asylum was sacked and burned, and it was only by the most superhuman exertions that the two hundred helpless children whom it sheltered were saved from the violence of the mob. At another point three negroes having taken refuge on the roof of a house, the rioters, inhumanly set fire to the building, and the unhappy blacks were forced to drop to almost certain death to avoid being burned alive.

Several times during this fearful day the police and the rioters came into fierce collision. The police were everywhere victorious. Their heavy clubs proved to be formidable weapons. Their blows were aimed at their adversaries' heads, and each one that went to the mark smashed a skull. A surgeon, who attended twenty-one wounded men, reported that each had sustained a fracture of the skull, and all were past recovery.

CADETS AT NEWMARKET.

The Eleventh New York Volunteers fired a volley of rifle-balls point-blank into a mob, which speedily dispersed, carrying away its dead and wounded. An hour or two later the colonel of the regiment, Colonel Henry O'Brien, returned to the scene of the skirmish alone, fearing no trouble. But he was recognized by some rioters, who sprang upon him, knocked him down, beat and stamped upon him until he was insensible, and then, putting a rope about his neck, dragged him through the streets, until at last some frenzied women beat out his poor struggling life with clubs.

In the tenement house district of Second Avenue the scene was like the sack of a city. There the rioters fired from windows and housetops upon the militia and the police, who were fighting side by side.

Enraged by this flank attack, the defenders of the law battered in the doors of the houses, rushed from room to room, bayoneting or clubbing their skulking assailants wherever found. Some they threw from the windows, others they cast over the railings of the stairways, or over the cornices of the roofs. No heed was paid to the prayers or imprecations of the women with whom the houses were filled. It was grim, bloody work; fiercer and more cruel even than any soldiers at the front were ever called upon to do. But the militiamen and the police were dealing with a desperate class of men, enrolled under no banner save that of outlawry.

Three days of hard fighting brought the rioters under control. The results of the pitched battles show strikingly the difference in effectiveness between a well-disciplined body of men, though small, and an undisciplined mob. Only three policemen were killed, and but fifty in all were hurt. Against this trivial loss, the number killed alone among the insurgents was over 1200. How many there were of their wounded cannot be told.

There was sorrow in the South when the news came that the people of New York had put down the great riot. The leaders of the Confederacy had seen in this outbreak a fire in the rear of their adversaries that might exert a decisive influence upon the course of the war. But the North found the air all the clearer for the storm that was past, and its armies pressed onward, confident of victory.

CHAPTER XV.

REPELLING HOOD'S INVASION OF TENNESSEE—BATTLE OF FRANKLIN—THE UNION WORKS CARRIED—GOOD WORK OF THE RESERVES—GENERAL THOMAS DELIBERATE—CLAMOR OF THE COUNTRY—BATTLE OF NASHVILLE—A GREAT CONFEDERATE DISASTER—HOOD'S ARMY DISPERSED—FORT FISHER—ITS VALUE TO THE CONFEDERACY—BUTLER'S POWDER SHIP—THE NAVAL BOMBARDMENT—GENERAL TERRY'S SUCCESSFUL ASSAULT—SHERMAN LEAVES SAVANNAH—HIS NORTHWARD MARCH—BURNING OF COLUMBIA—CHARLESTON EVACUATED.

IT will be remembered that when Sherman set the torch to Atlanta, cut his last telegraph wire, and set the heads of his columns upon the roads to Savannah, he left in his rear a very considerable Confederate force under the command of the audacious General Hood. To General Thomas, "the Rock of Chickamauga," had been intrusted the task of dealing with Hood. The situation was one that taxed to the utmost the military sagacity and energy of this eminent general. His antagonist had 54,000 men, 13,000 of them cavalrymen. This army was compact, well-disciplined, and made up largely of Tennesseeans familiar with the country in which they were to operate. To oppose to this veteran force, General Thomas had, at the outset, but 25,000 men. This was the number left him by Sherman, and it must be remembered that the flower of Sherman's army went with him upon the march through Georgia, so that these troops that he left behind could not have ranked first in point of discipline or efficiency. Scattered among the isolated forts and barracks of Kentucky and Tennessee were several thousand available troops, and in Missouri, where by this time the war had degenerated into a cruel and cowardly neighborhood vendetta, there were two divisions which could be added to his forces. When these widely dispersed troops could be consolidated into one army, Thomas would have a command numerically equal at least, to that of his adversary, although he would still be at a disadvantage because of the large number of new recruits in his ranks.

To gather together these scattered regiments and brigades required time. But Hood, who had now learned that he could neither lure Sherman out of Georgia, nor overtake him upon his flying march to tidewater, was pushing forward into Tennessee with the celerity and dash typical of his character. His cavalry, under the brilliant leadership of Forrest, was opening the way for him, saving and holding an important bridge here, capturing a Union gun-boat and fleet of transports there, and driving Federal garrisons from one strategic point after another. Lack of provisions for a time delayed the Confederate advance, but by the last of November this obstacle was removed and Hood's campaign was well under way. The course laid down for him by his superior officer, General Beauregard, was this: "You will take the offensive at the earliest practicable moment, and deal the enemy rapid and vigorous blows, striking him while thus dispersed, and by this means distract Sherman's advance into Georgia."

Thomas was in Nashville personally pushing the work of building up his army. Schofield with 18,000 men was in Hood's front, striving to delay that commander's advance to the uttermost possible minute. He imitated the tactics of Johnston before Atlanta. One fortified position after another he held stubbornly, until Hood turned his flank, which the Confederates with their vastly greater force could readily do, then falling back to another stopping place. At Spring Hill, however, Schofield narrowly escaped destruction, for in obedience to the commands of Thomas he held to his position too long, exposing his retreating column to a flank attack. The attack did not come. Hood says it was ordered, but that the order was disobeyed by the officer to whom it was given. Others declare that its failure was due to a most untimely excess of caution upon the part of Hood himself, to whom caution was commonly a stranger. Be that as it may, the Confederates missed such a chance to demolish the Union army as was never again offered them.

The little town of Franklin, Tenn., stands on the southern bank of the Harpeth River. Through this town and across this stream lay Schofield's line of retreat, and his army turned thither when it faced away from the enemy at Spring Hill. To cross the river pontoon bridges were necessary, and Schofield galloped on ahead of his columns to see whether the pontoons, for which he had telegraphed, had yet arrived. To his dismay he found that none had appeared. A deep, wide river was in front of his troops, and a powerful enemy only a few hours behind. Schofield saw that he must turn and give battle, and he at once examined the surrounding country to find the most advantageous place for his lines.

Early in the morning Schofield and his staff rode up to the farm-house of a man named Carter, which stood upon a slight hill just south of the town. He could see that the Harpeth River curved around the town so that a line of works built across the farm would extend from the river's bank southeast of Franklin to its bank southwest of the city. With his flanks thus protected Schofield hoped to be able to withstand Hood's onslaught.

The soldiers were soon busily at work building the works. Ten thousand men plied spades and pickaxes. Buildings were torn down and the lumber used in backing up the earthworks. The work of an army tells quickly. It was not long before a line of frowning breastworks stretched across the hillside, with the apple and foliage trees in front cut down, making a rough road for an attacking force to travel. In the rear of the city, too, the men were hard at work, cutting down the banks of the river to afford approaches to the ford, and in building bridges out of old lumber obtained by tearing down buildings. As fast the wagon trains came up they were hurried across the ford to the north bank of the river, where they would have at least a chance of escape in case of disaster. Much of the artillery crossed also, the guns being posted where they could be used against the enemy beyond the stream. All this work was done by men who had been marching without intermission for twenty-four hours. The soldiers, as soon as relieved from active toil, flung themselves down upon the ground and dropped to sleep almost instantly. The trenches were filled with slumbering men. The new recruits, who brought up the rear of Schofield's column, which was by this time entering the works, were totally exhausted. Their officers had been compelled to cut the knapsacks from their shoulders and to drive them along at the point of the bayonet to prevent their falling by the roadside to become the prey of the pursuing enemy.

The hour of noon had now passed. No sign of an offensive movement had been given by the enemy, and the weary Federals began to hope that they were to be allowed that afternoon and the coming night to rest. Vain hope. About two o'clock word came into the trenches from General Wagner, who was holding an advanced line of observation, that he could see Confederate signal flags waving on the hills a mile or so away, and that there were signs of suspicious activity among the enemy in his front. In a few minutes the Confederate line of battle with bayonets gleaming and bright flags flaunting in the November breeze came sweeping forward. Wagner's two cannon gave them a shot and galloped back to the intrenchments. The infantry should have followed, but by some great error Wagner with his two brigades, and not a shadow of a defensive work, tried to hold his ground and beat back the resistless rush of two divisions. This the scene that followed, as described by Colonel Stone of the staff officers of General Thomas:

"The first shock came, of course, upon the two misplaced brigades of Wagner's division which, through some one's blunder, had remained in their false position until too late to retire without disaster. They had no tools to throw up works, and when struck by the resistless sweep of Cleburne's and Brown's divisions they had only to make their way, as best they could, back to the works. In that wild rush in which friend and foe were intermingled, and the piercing 'Rebel yell' rose high above the 'Yankee cheer,' nearly seven hundred were made prisoners. But, worst of all for the Union side, the men of Reilly's and Strickland's brigades dared not fire lest they should shoot down their own comrades, and the guns, loaded with grape and canister, stood silent in the embrasures. With loud shouts of 'Let's go into the works with them!' the triumphant Confederates, now more like a wild, howling mob than an organized army, swept on to the very works with hardly a check from any quarter. So fierce was the rush that a number of the fleeing soldiers, officers and men, dropped exhausted into the ditch and lay there while the terrific contest raged over their heads till, under cover of darkness, they could crawl safely inside the intrenchments."

The day began to look dark for the men of the North. A raw regiment, still unaccustomed to the scenes of battle, was panic-stricken by the fury of the enemy's attack, and broke and fled to the rear. Others followed. The panic spread even to veteran troops, and the roads leading to the bridges over the Harpeth were jammed with fugitives. A gap the width of two regiments was left in the Union line. Into this the Confederates poured with triumphant yells, seized the abandoned cannon, and began to break down the Federal flank.

But now, when all seemed lost, the Union reserves plunged into the fiercest of the fray and carried all before them. A brigade of Wagner's division under Colonel Emerson Opdycke, and two Kentucky regiments, had been sheltered thus far from the storm of bullets, and they now rushed into the fight with the enthusiasm of fresh troops on a hard-fought field. It was hand to hand fighting. The enemy was already within the works and must be expelled. The clubbed musket, the bayonet, the saber, and the pistol were the weapons available at such close quarters.

Opdycke's horse was shot beneath him. General Stanley was severely wounded. Officers and men fell fast, but in the end the enemy sullenly retreated step by step, until he was without the earthworks and the Union line showed no gap nor weakness.

In no wise daunted by having the advantage they had so easily gained wrested from them, the Confederates returned time and again to the assault. The wind had gone down and the dense clouds of gunpowder smoke hung heavily over the field. Through this dense yellow curtain the Confederates charged again and again. Their valor was indomitable. Their color bearers and their brigade commanders marched straight to the redoubt only to be shot down. General John Adams leaped his horse over the ditch and mounted the parapet, where his horse was killed bestriding it and he himself pitched headlong into the works mortally wounded. Cleburne, the hero of a hundred fights, fell at the ditch. General Stahl stood in that dismal excavation, directing the efforts of his men, so many of whom fell around him that when he received his death wound he remained in an erect posture —a dead man propped up by corpses.

So all through the afternoon and far into the night the fighting continued. It were useless to try to catalogue the deeds of valor done on both sides that day. A desperate attack stubbornly resisted, an attack in which 6300 men were sacrificed, and to repulse which cost Schofield 3226 men, such is the story of the battle of Franklin briefly told. Late at night, when the Confederates at last ceased their furious assaults, the Union troops were withdrawn across the river, the bridges were burned, and the retreat to Nashville continued.

A sorrowful experience was that of the Carter family, whose farm-house stood within the Union lines just where the battle was fiercest. So suddenly burst the storm of war, the people in the household had no time to flee, but took refuge in the cellar, where they crouched trembling while the shot and shell crashed through the timbers over their heads, and the din of the battle reverberated outside. When returning quiet gave assurance that the fight was ended, two of the women, bent on a merciful errand, came up from the cellar to give aid to the wounded. When they threw open the door, they found, lying across the step, their own brother, who was a staff officer in the Union army, and who lay there with his life's blood ebbing away through a ghastly and mortal wound in his breast.

Troops were now coming in fast to Thomas at Nashville. From Missouri, from Kentucky, and even from Ohio, the gallant regiments of blue-clad men came marching. The gaze of the country was directed thither.

The complete and crushing defeat of Hood was, at that moment, the most important task of the whole military problem. Unmindful of popular clamor, General Thomas made his preparations with deliberation and thoroughness. Many of his troops were new recruits. He would take time to drill and discipline them. His cavalrymen were short of horses. He calmly waited until his requisitions were filled. His wagon train was incomplete, and his stores insufficient. Very well, then, he would wait until the needs of his army had been fully provided for. So he delayed attacking the enemy, but worked with unremitting energy meanwhile, bringing up troops and munitions of war.

The people, not fully understanding the situation, set up the cry, "Why doesn't Thomas attack?" The impatience of the populace spread to the War Department and to the tent of the commander-in-chief before Petersburg. Strenuous telegrams urging an immediate attack began to reach Thomas. "Attack him before he fortifies," was Grant's first order, but Hood was already intrenched on the hills before Nashville when this order was received. Then daily for two weeks came telegrams from the commander-in-chief, now positive orders which could by no possibility be obeyed, then complaints and stinging rebukes or expressions of dissatisfaction, which to the experienced mind of Thomas offered certain indications that he was to be relieved. Grant was a thousand miles away, and could by no possibility know the circumstances which impeded the movements of his lieutenant at Nashville. On the very day that Grant wrote out an order relieving Thomas from command, and turning the army over to General Schofield, a driving storm of rain and sleet was falling on the camp at Nashville. The whole country thereabouts was an ocean of mud with a thin frozen crust above, not thick enough to bear the weight of a man. The natives declared that the Yankees had brought their weather as well as their army with them. To have attempted to take the field at such a time would have been sheer madness.

The order relieving Thomas from command never reached him. Before it was telegraphed Grant recalled it, and issued another, giving the command of Thomas's troops to Logan. With this order in his pocket, to be delivered personally, Logan started westward as fast as express trains could carry him. A few hours later Grant concluded that perhaps it might be as well for him also to go to Nashville, so he boarded a steamer at City Point and started for Washington, there to take the train for the West. But before either of these officers had proceeded very far on his journey, news was received that made them both stop short.

The 14th of December, the day Sherman reached the sea, dawned clear and sunny at Nashville. The sunshine dissipated the depression in the Union army as it did the clouds in the sky. This was what all had been waiting for. The soldiers scarcely needed any orders to tell them that, if the weather held, a battle would be fought within twenty-four hours. The orders came, however, and at the same time a telegram went speeding over the wires to Washington, " The ice having melted away to-day, the enemy will be attacked to-morrow morning."

Long before dawn the Union camps were all astir. The men were giving the last touches to their equipments, eating a hasty breakfast, and chatting of the chances of the fight. There were many raw recruits in the ranks, and they listened with respect to the veterans' stories of battles lost and won. It was a warm, moist morning, and a heavy curtain of fog hung over the field, under cover of which the Federal troops moved out to their positions unperceived by the enemy. By nine o'clock, however, the mist cleared away, and heavy bodies of blue troops could be seen advancing at all points of the field. The Confederate cannon quickly burst forth with a full-throated roar, and the yellow gunpowder smoke filled the air, from which the fog had vanished. There was hot skirmishing and a fierce exchange of cannon-shot for some hours. The advance of the Federals was slow but uninterrupted. The enemy was driven everywhere. Now a stone wall, then a lightly fortified line that he attempted to hold, was wrested from him. Three four-gun redoubts were taken by storm. The troops of General Chalmers were driven so fast that his headquarters train with all his baggage and papers was captured.

This is the story of the taking of one redoubt, as told by Colonel Stone, an eye-witness: " Post's brigade, of Wood's old division, which lay at the foot of Montgomery Hill, full of dash and spirit, had since morning been regarding the works at the summit with covetous eyes. At Post's suggestion it was determined to see which party wanted them most. Accordingly a charge was ordered, and in a moment the brigade was swarming up the hillside straight for the enemy's advanced works. For almost the first time since the grand assault on Missionary Ridge, a year before, here was an open field where everything could be seen. From General Thomas's headquarters everybody looked on with breathless suspense as the blue line, broken and irregular, but with steady persistence, made its way up the steep hillside against a fierce storm of musketry and artillery. Most of the shots, however, passed over the men's heads. It was a struggle to keep up with the colors, and as they neared the top only the strongest were at the front. Without a moment's pause the color-bearers and those who had kept up with them, Post himself at the head, leaped over the parapet. As the colors waved from the summit, the whole line swept forward and was over the works in a twinkling, gathering in prisoners and guns. Indeed, so large was the mass of the prisoners that a few minutes later was seen heading toward our own lines, that a number of officers at General Thomas's headquarters feared the assault had failed, and the prisoners were Confederate reserves who had rallied and retaken the works. But the fear was only momentary; for the wild outburst of cheers that rang across the valley told the story of complete success."

The triumph of Post's men was imitated to a greater or less degree in all parts of the field. From every quarter came lusty cheers, celebrating Federal successes. One point still invited attack—the salient of the Confederate line, which reared its frowning head upon a lofty hill, overlooking a valley across which the attacking force would have to advance. Aids rode forth with the order for the attack. "You don't mean to say that we have got to go in here and attack the works on that hill?" exclaimed the first brigade commander whom the orders reached.

"Those are the orders."

"Why, it would be suicide, sir; perfect suicide."

"Nevertheless those are the orders," was the cool response, as the aid rode on. But the brigadier, for all his protests, was a gallant officer trained to obey. Before the messenger from General Thomas had returned to headquarters the salient had been carried, and the enemy was streaming backward, leaving guns, colors, and many prisoners in the hands of the victorious Federals.

It was now night. Everywhere the Confederates had suffered heavily. Their lines had been pierced in many places, and many of their men were captives in the hands of Thomas's troops. They had been forced back by successive assaults until, at night, they intrenched a line two miles in the rear of that which they had held in the morning. All night they had worked with their intrenching tools, and the early dawn was ushered in by the opening roar of the Union cannon heralding another day of battle.

Shattered and disheartened though they were, the Confederates fought gallantly on this second day of the fight. They beat back a desperate assault led by the dashing Colonel Post, who fell sorely wounded at the head of his men. They shot down and drove off three regiments of colored soldiers who hazarded a daring assault. But there came at last a charge which the men of the South could not withstand. McMillen's brigade swept up the steep and rocky hillside before Bates's division, just as two cannon which some dismounted cavalrymen had with infinite labor dragged to the crest of a high hill opened a galling fire upon the Confederate rear. The double attack disconcerted the defenders of the redoubt, and they broke and fled ingloriously. McMillen's men, who had reached the redoubt without firing a shot, now poured deadly volleys into their backs. Hatch's dismounted cavalry came dashing in with more volleys. In an incredibly short space of time the green hillside was covered with frantic men fleeing for their lives. Cannon were abandoned, muskets and colors thrown aside, artillerists cut the traces and galloped away on the battery horses, the prayers and entreaties of officers were unheard. Hood no longer had an army; it had become an undisciplined and affrighted mob.

The Union troops pressed remorselessly upon their stricken antagonists. Post's brigade charged again over the ground where it had once suffered a repulse, and captured 14 guns and 1000 prisoners. Steedman's negro soldiers also won their share of trophies. The Confederate General Johnson and nearly all his division were captured. Night brought the retreating Confederates no relief. The Union cavalry still cut and slashed their trains and their straggling columns. In the morning the main body, taking up the pursuit, found the road littered with burnt and wrecked wagons, discarded arms, wounded, dying, and dead Confederates, and all the débris of a wrecked and despairing army. The pursuit was pressed to the banks of the Tennessee River. When it ended General Thomas had in his hands 4500 prisoners, including four general officers, and 53 pieces of captured artillery. His loss amounted to 3057 men, of whom less than 400 were killed. The extent of Hood's loss has never been known. Greatly as his army suffered from the casualties of battle, it suffered still more from wholesale desertions; for during that disorderly retreat hundreds and even thousands of the soldiers concluded that the life of that army and the fortunes of the Confederacy were at an end, and they dispersed to their homes, never again to be forced to take up arms.

It was the news of this great victory that met Logan at Louisville on his way to relieve Thomas from command. He stopped short in his journey and tore up his orders, for the nation was shouting again for Thomas, as in the time when he saved the day at Chickamauga.

On a long, narrow, sandy spit, on the coast of North Carolina, between the Cape Fear River and the ocean, stood Fort Fisher. It was the strongest fortification in the Confederacy. There were heavy bastions, traverses, and redoubts of sand, in which round shot would bury themselves and shells explode harmlessly. Bomb-proofs sheltered the gunners who worked the fifty or more heavy rifled guns. In front of the parapet on the landward side was a stockade of lofty, sharpened piles. Beyond the stockade mines and torpedoes were planted, so arranged that when an attacking force should be directly over them they could be exploded by an electric flash carried on wires from the fort.

It would seem at first sight strange that so formidable a fortification

WINTER SPORTS IN LEE'S ARMY.

should have been erected on that barren sandbar, far from any populous country. But the Cape Fear River was a famous harbor for blockade-runners. Twenty-eight miles from its mouth was the town of Wilmington, whence railroads ran to all parts of the Confederacy. If the blockade-runner could but elude the vigilance of the fleet of blockaders that steamed ever up and down before the harbor's mouth, she could find a safe refuge under the guns of Fort Fisher, and then steam up the river to Wilmington secure from any pursuit. And very many of the adventurous craft accomplished this, bringing in cannon for the Confederate armies, and taking out heavy cargoes of cotton of enormous value.

In the latter part of 1864 two ports only, Wilmington and Charleston, remained to the Confederates. Farragut closed the harbor of Mobile when he took the forts at its mouth, though the Confederates still held the town. Sherman held Savannah, and the one luckless blockade-runner that steamed into that harbor, in ignorance of the change in ownership, was speedily made a prize. The northward march of Sherman would cut off Charleston, too, so that the Confederates would have to abandon it. The National government now desired to complete its work by capturing Fort Fisher, and thus finally shutting off the Confederacy from all communication with the foreign world. The accomplishment of this task was in no wise easy. The garrison of Fort Fisher stood by their guns as though the war had just begun, and the star of the Confederacy were in the ascendant, instead of being, as was now too clearly evident, about to be extinguished forever.

The army and navy co-operated in the attempts to reduce Fort Fisher. There were more than fifty men-of-war tossing on the waves before the lowering sea-front of the work. Six thousand five hundred men were in the military force. They were in command of General B. F. Butler, whom we saw last in New Orleans. The general's active and ingenious mind conceived a plan for destroying the fort without sacrificing a single Federal soldier. He procured an old gun-boat, painted it white and otherwise disguised it, so as to look like a blockade-runner, stored two hundred and fifty tons of gunpowder in its hold with fuses penetrating every part, ran the craft in within fifteen hundred feet of the works and exploded it. Butler expected that the shock would demolish the seaward face of the fort altogether, and perhaps bury the guns under great masses of sand, but in this he was mistaken, for the heavy bastions, were not in the least disturbed by the shock, the guns peered as viciously as ever through the embrasures, and the flag flaunted as defiantly from its staff.

"Oh, it was terrible!" said one of the Confederates sarcastically. "It woke us all up!"

The navy then took its turn, and for some hours the heavy vessels of Admiral Porter's fleet poured so rapid and well aimed a fire upon the work that the garrison were driven from their guns, and only the occasional report of a heavy cannon told that the fort was still tenanted. But secure in their heavy bomb-proofs, the garrison minded the storm of shells and solid shot no more than the well-housed farmer heeds a hailstorm. It was very clear that Fort Fisher could not be taken at long range. If that flag that floated so saucily through all the bombardment was to come down, it must be pulled down by a storming party. The original plan had contemplated an assault as soon as the fire of the fleet should have silenced the guns of the fort, and in pursuance of this 700 men had been landed from the army transports. But the weather was too rough to permit of landing more troops that day, and the next morning General Butler concluded that Fort Fisher was impregnable, withdrew his men already landed, and sailed away, greatly to the disgust of the navy.

This was on the 25th of December, 1864. The chagrin of the whole North over the failure of the expedition was so great that it was speedily determined to renew the attempt. January 13th saw a new Federal force, this time under command of General A. H. Terry, landing on the shore of the sandy neck of land above the fort. The disembarkation went on rapidly and methodically, and, as fast as landed, the troops began throwing up earthworks and mounting fieldpieces bearing on the fort. The garrison saw clearly that this new commander had come to stay.

Within the fort there was the depression bred of the knowledge of impending defeat. Colonel Lamb, who was in command, was insufficiently provided with ammunition. His appeals for aid and re-enforcements received but scant attention from General Bragg, who was now in command at Wilmington. When at last General Whiting came with 700 men, he entered the fort with the remark, "Lamb, my boy, I have come to share your fate. You and your garrison are to be sacrificed."

In the military force landed above the fort were about 8500 men. They were scarcely fairly installed on the shore before they began working their way forward, nearer and nearer to the threatened work. The sea was calm and the aim of the naval gunners, who maintained a constant fire upon the fort, was deadly. Many of the ships' batteries were trained upon the palisade before the fort, and the heavy balls cut away the timbers and made great gaps in this important part of the Confederate system of defense.

At early dawn of the 15th the attack was begun. The ships, arranged in a great semicircle, poured their fire upon the fort, dismantling guns; driving the garrison to the bomb-proofs, and mowing down the stockade. A line of sharpshooters, each carrying a shovel in one hand and a gun in the other, spring out from Terry's most advanced lines, rush forward to within 175 yards of the fort and dig pits for their protection before the Confederates can attack them. Then the sharpshooters and the navy occupy the attention of the enemy, while Curtis's brigade dashes forward and digs a trench within 500 yards of the fort. By this time too a party of 2000 sailors and marines has been landed from the fleet. They are to storm the sea-wall of the fort while the army attacks its landward face.

Suddenly the thunder of the naval artillery is stilled. There is a moment of silence, and then the shrill scream of the whistles rises from every steamer in the fleet. It is the signal for the assault. The sailors on the beach spring to their feet and dash forward at a rapid run; they fire no shot, for they carry no guns. Cutlasses and pistols, the blue-jackets' traditional weapons, are their only arms. Toward the other side of the fort came Terry's troops, in line after line like the waves of the sea, roaring forward to fall on the sands of the beach.

The fate of the naval column is quickly determined. Upon it is concentrated the fire of the heaviest Confederate batteries, Napoleon guns, Columbiads, and rifles shotted with grape and canister. The blue-jackets, unable to reply to this murderous fire, and seeing their companions falling fast around them, waver, halt, and fall back to the beach, throwing themselves upon the ground to escape the enemy's missiles. But though repulsed they have contributed largely to the capture of the fort. While the chief attention of the Confederates has been directed toward them, the troops have been carrying all before them on the other front. Colonel Lamb turns from his direction of the defense against the naval column to see three Union flags waving over other portions of the work. General Whiting rushes to tear them down but falls, shot through the hip. Lamb goes to the electric button which should explode the mines before the fort over which the Federals are now advancing in great numbers, but though he presses again and again there is no explosion. The fire of the fleet has cut the wires. More Federals come to join those who have already effected a lodgment. The fort is full of blue uniforms; they fight their way from traverse to traverse and turn the captured guns on the gallant but fated garrison. The Confederates were determined, even desperate. Long after the fort was virtually in the hands of its captors they stubbornly clung to a bomb-proof. Finally they retreated to Battery Buchanan and there maintained themselves stoutly until late at night when, all hope being at an end, they surrendered themselves, and the National victory was complete.

We left Sherman in Savannah. Notable though his success had been in making his way from Atlanta to the sea, his work was only half done. Savannah in itself was no objective point. His part in the grand strategy of the closing months of the war was to put his army shoulder to shoulder with Grant's troops, who were remorsely grinding Lee into powder. How was this to be done? The original plan had been for the troops to embark at Savannah upon swift transports, steam along the coast and up the James River, and then disembark and take their places in the lines before Petersburg. But Sherman conceived a more ambitious plan. This was nothing less than to march northward through the Carolinas as he had through Georgia, spreading desolation in his path. The part that South Carolina had taken in fomenting the war had greatly embittered the Northern troops, and the soldiers were anxious to visit upon that State some of the horrors that had fallen to the lot of less guilty commonwealths. There were those in the South who felt much the same. "If you will march in this way through South Carolina," said a Georgian, whose farm had been ravaged by Sherman's columns, "and make the State that did most to bring on the war feel its dreadful results, we can more easily forgive you for this."

There were more difficulties in the path of an army marching north from Savannah than had attended the march from Atlanta. Though it was unlikely that the enemy could rally any very great force to combat it, yet it was possible that Hood's troops might be brought on from the West and united with the force that Hardee had led out of Savannah. The topography of the country was well fitted for defense. The rivers all ran across Sherman's path, and a handful of cavalry could burn a bridge which would delay the advancing column for hours. There was danger, too, that Lee might slip out from his trenches at Petersburg, effect a junction with the other Confederate troops and crush Sherman. But of this peril Grant told Sherman to have no dread, promising that he would hold the great leader of the waning forces of the Confederacy secure within his lines.

Sherman moved out of Savannah on the last day of January, 1865. The month had been one of unprecedented moisture. Day after day the rain had fallen in sheets. The low, marshy country around Savannah, and the banks of the sluggish rivers of South Carolina were swamps waist deep in water. The water-logged condition of the country gave the Confederates a false sense of security. General Hardee reported certain swamps to be absolutely impassable at the very moment when the Union soldiers were trudging through them at the rate of ten or twelve miles a day, building corduroy roads all the way for the wagon trains. Sometimes the troops advanced through water that reached to their arm-pits, forcing the soldiers to carry their cartridge-boxes strapped about their necks and their muskets on their heads. The pertinacity with which the Federal soldiers adhered to their arduous task, and the ingenuity of the countless expedients they employed to lighten it, were causes of continual astonishment to the Confederates. "There has been no such army since the days of Julius Cæsar!" said General Johnston, on hearing the story of the great march.

In addition to their mistaken idea that Sherman could not pass the swamps, another notion interfered with the concentration of troops by the Confederates for the defense of South Carolina. Such a concentration would have necessitated the withdrawal of the troops from Charleston ; and Jefferson Davis, and the authorities other than military, could not bring themselves to consent to the evacuation of that city, which they regarded as the cradle of the Confederacy. For a time the military officers represented in vain that the direction of Sherman's march was such that Charleston must inevitably be surrendered in any event, and that it would be better to lose the city and save the garrison rather than to lose garrison and city both. The reluctance of the Richmond authorities to yield to the inevitable was so great that, in combination with other causes, it so delayed the concentration of troops that Sherman entered Columbia, the capital of South Carolina, having accomplished the most difficult and perilous portion of his march, with no more serious fighting than an occasional skirmish at a bridge-head.

With Columbia is connected an incident of the famous march of Sherman's army which has been the theme of almost interminable controversy. The city suffered severely from a conflagration which broke out shortly after the entrance of the Union troops. Who was responsible for it? Did Wade Hampton, who commanded the Confederate troops that fled before Sherman's advance, fire it, as the Russians burned Moscow, in order that it might furnish no shelter to the hated invader? Or was the town sacrificed to satisfy the malice and lust for destruction of the men of the Union army?

When the invaders entered the town they found the two railroad stations and all the cotton already in flames, having been fired by the retreating Confederates. The citizens were trying to quench the flames with water thrown from buckets and by a rickety hand-engine. The advance-guard of the army of occupation immediately set to work to assist in the subjugation of the fire and were thus engaged when Sherman rode up. The general gave every assurance to the mayor of the town that all private property, colleges, and libraries would be respected, and only arsenals and public workshops destroyed.

Despite the best efforts of the citizens and the soldiers the fire which had begun before the entry of the Federals could not be checked and began to spread. And then some foolish townspeople, thinking to ingratiate themselves with the soldiers, brought out whisky by bottles and even by pailfuls, and gave it to the soldiers to drink. Discipline had been the only thing that held the rougher instincts of the men in check, and with drunkenness all discipline vanished. They ceased their efforts to extinguish the flames and many of them even slyly set new fires in parts of the town as yet unthreatened by the conflagration. Every effort was made by the Union officers to check the progress of the flames and to repress the disorder that was spreading in the Federal ranks. But a fresh wind that sprung up carried the fire to all parts of the town. The bits of blazing cotton, caught up by the wind, were carried high over the housetops and started new conflagrations in other quarters. General Hazen thus tells the story of the fire :

"At sundown a fire broke out in several places in a clump of isolated wooden building, a little north of the principal hotel. A few men could easily have torn down the buildings. I met Colonel W. B. Woods, who was provost-marshal, and suggested that he take his guard and pull the buildings down. He told me that he could not get men enough together to do any good. This seemed to annoy him very much. I then rode to General Sherman's headquarters. He saw the darkness lit up with the lurid hue of the conflagration. He remarked regretfully, ' They have brought it upon themselves.' I mounted my horse and hurried to the city. The houses in the main street were now burning in many places along nearly its whole length. The fire could not have been communicated from the clump of houses I first saw burning. It was evident that incendiaries had been actively at work. The buildings were mainly of wood, and the wind sent large sheets of blazing siding and shingles high into the air, landing them hundreds of yards away on the roofs of buildings. All over the eastern part of the city the wind now set in with great force, much increased by the fire itself. Any general effort to stop the conflagration would have been useless."

It was long after midnight when the flames were extinguished, and the breaking of dawn showed a half a city full of homeless people shivering in the streets and open squares. The very heart of the town had been burned out. The old State House, several churches, and a great number of stores and dwellings had gone down before the flames. The people were bitter in their denunciations of Sherman, yet nothing has ever been more clearly proved than that the Union general was not in the slightest degree responsible for the disaster. Individual Federals did indeed add fuel to the flames, but so far from being encouraged by their officers they were checked in their vandalism and punished when detected.

Meantime the last Confederate posts on the Atlantic coast had fallen into the hands of the Federals, either because of Sherman's march or as the result of co-operating movements of the Union troops. Charleston was evacuated on the 18th of February, the very day that the flames were roaring in Columbia. Then the Union men-of-war that had so long been held at bay by Fort Sumter steamed proudly into the harbor. The smoldering wrecks of three Confederate iron-clads, which had been fired by Hardee, lay smoking at the wharves. Railway stations and cotton presses were blazing in every part of the town. The new bridge to James Island was being licked up by the flames. Much of the town was in ruins from the shells that had been thrown into the city during the long bombardment. Fort Sumter, which had risen so grandly from the waters of the bay when the war began, was now only a shapeless heap of bricks and mortar. The people of the town were impoverished and starving. The war had borne heavily upon Charleston, the cradle of the Confederacy.

Still further up the coast Wilmington had fallen into the hands of the Union forces. Its capture was a forgone conclusion after the fall of Fort

HOT WORK AT COLD HARBOR.

Fisher, but the Confederates made desperate efforts to hold it. General Grant sent Schofield, who had just come from Tennessee, to accomplish the capture of the town. The work was quickly done. The difficulties encountered were rather due to the swampy and water-logged character of the land than to the resistance of the enemy. Once in possession of Wilmington Schofield was in a position from which he could readily effect a juncture with Sherman. It was not long before word was received from that commander asking that Schofield join him at Goldsboro.

Sherman had left Columbia while the ruins were still smoking. There was the usual prolonged struggle with swampy territory and muddy roads, and the exhaustion was beginning to tell upon the soldiers when they entered Fayetteville. Here, however, the troops were greatly cheered by news from home, for a swift tug had been sent up the Cape Fear River, bearing letter-bags crammed full of mail for the soldiers, who for many weeks had been cut off from all tidings of home. The communication thus opened with the coast also enabled Sherman to rid himself of thousands of the negro refugees, who with childish confidence had attached themselves to the marching column, neither asking where it was going nor providing themselves with necessary food. They had become a heavy charge upon Sherman, who was glad to seize this opportunity to send them to the coast.

Only a short stop was made at Fayetteville, and then the march was continued toward Goldsboro. In one respect the perils in Sherman's path had been increased. The political authorities at Richmond could no longer close their eyes to the fact that the Confederacy was now falling to pieces. After having denied Lee supreme command of all the armies of the Confederacy when there were armies to command, they now invested him with the authority of a general-in-chief, when there remained only the pitiful wreck of an army. General Lee's first act was to recall Johnston from the retirement into which Jefferson Davis had forced him, and order him to conduct the opposition to Sherman's advance.

" It is not overstating the truth," writes General Jacob D. Cox, the commander of the Twenty-Third Army Corps, "to say that the news of Johnston's assignment was received throughout Sherman's army as a note of warning to be prepared for more stubborn and well-planned resistance to their progress." Events showed that the forebodings of the Federals were well founded, but they showed also that it was too late for Johnston, or any other man backed only by the waning resources of the dying Confederacy, to check the advance of Sherman's triumphant veterans.

CHAPTER XVI.

THE END NO LONGER IN DOUBT—PRIVATIONS OF THE CONFEDERATES—PEACE NEGOTIATIONS FAIL—LEE DETERMINES TO ATTACK FORT STEDMAN—THE SURPRISE—CONFEDERATES DRIVEN BACK—DINWIDDIE COURT-HOUSE AND FIVE FORKS—LEE'S LINES PIERCED—UNION VICTORIES ALL ALONG THE LINES—PANIC IN RICHMOND—THE CONFEDERATE CAPITAL ABANDONED—WORK OF THE MOB—RETREAT OF LEE'S ARMY—THE SURRENDER AT APPOMATTOX COURT-HOUSE—GENERAL GRANT'S MAGNANIMITY—THE END OF THE WAR.

THERE now remained but one thing to be done to complete the triumph of the Union arms and the repression of the great uprising. The end of the war was no longer in doubt. The defeat of Hood in Tennessee had annihilated the power of the Confederacy in the West. Sherman's march had demonstrated that there was neither defensive nor offensive power left in Georgia, Alabama, or the Carolinas. There was no man in the Confederate ranks so blind as not to see that the end was near at hand. The soldiers were dropping out by scores daily and returning to their homes. The officers from General Lee down were well aware of the futility of further resistance, but it was their duty to maintain the contest until forced into an actual surrender, or until the civil authorities at Richmond should direct the abandonment of a hopeless cause.

All winter the army of General Lee had remained pent up within the works at Petersburg, confronted by the confident and patient forces of the nation. The sufferings of the Confederate soldiers in their bleak winter camps were extreme. They were half-clad and not half-fed. In a secret session of the Confederate Congress it was officially declared that there was not enough meat in all the South to feed the armies which the Confederacy then had in the field. In addition to this general scarcity of provisions the difficulty of feeding the men in the Petersburg trenches was vastly increased by the broken condition of the Confederate railway connections. Both because of their long, hard service without repairs, and as the result of the frequent raids ordered by Grant, the railroads were so weakened that the greater part of the provisions had to be hauled in wagons.

It was sorely against General Lee's desire and judgment that the Confederate army was held at Petersburg to be slowly starved into subjection. He believed that the only course to pursue in this desperate state of the Confederacy was to abandon Richmond, effect a juncture with the shattered remnant of Hood's army, and take refuge in the craggy fastnesses of the mountains, there to fight a defensive war which might be prolonged for years. But Jefferson Davis would not listen to the proposition for the abandonment of Richmond, and there was nothing left for the Confederate general to do but to hold his ground with as much tenacity as he might, although he could discern by the gradual extension of Grant's lines that he would soon be completely surrounded, with no possible avenue for retreat.

The winter passed away with but few encounters between the hostile armies beyond an occasional skirmish upon the picket lines, or a fight for a piece of railroad. There had been efforts made by the Confederates during the winter to bring the war to an end upon some kind of a compromise. Commissioners went to Fortress Monroe to meet President Lincoln, and make to him such a proposition. But the President would listen to no overtures for a peace that would not include the entire restoration of the Union, while the Confederate commissioners insisted upon the separation of the two sections. So the negotiations ended in nothing, and the Confederate soldiers awaited only the coming of spring to begin the fighting again.

When the spring came, opening the roads and mitigating the hardships of campaigning, Lee struck the first blow. He wished to get past Grant's left flank and withdraw his whole army from the Petersburg works, proceeding to join Johnston and demolish Sherman. This might have been easily done earlier in the year, but by the time that Jefferson Davis gave his tardy assent to the movement Grant had so extended his lines to the left that it was more than doubtful whether Lee's forces could pass that way. To force the withdrawal of some of the troops from that point Lee determined to attack the Union right flank. The point chosen for attack was Fort Stedman. At that point the hostile lines were scarce forty rods apart, and the ground between was hard and level, a most inviting field for a charge.

The Confederate plan, however, did not contemplate a direct assault. General Gordon, to whom the conduct of the sortie was intrusted, had hit upon a plan for taking the Federals by surprise that in the end proved entirely successful. The Federals had long been employing every conceivable means to induce Confederates to desert. Circulars had been distributed offering to pay each deserter who would come into the Union lines bringing his musket with him. Gordon took a shrewd advantage of this. The pickets before Fort Stedman were not more than fifty yards in his front. He sent forward a number of stragglers with arms in their hands who proclaimed themselves deserters. The pickets allowed them to approach without challenge, and were not enlightened as to the true character of these pretended deserters until they found themselves disarmed and on their way to the Confederate rear. With the pickets thus easily disposed of, the Confederates swept forward and were soon in possession of the coveted fort. But the men in the works to the left of Stedman which were included in

Gordon's plan of attack had taken alarm, and when the Confederates turned to capture that stronghold also, they were met by a heavy and well directed fire that drove them back in confusion. Even Fort Stedman, which they had won fairly, they held but a little time, for, while the Union batteries concentrated a deadly fire upon the fort, the troops of the Ninth Corps attacked and retook it. Lee had lost 4000 men from his already feeble army, and the way around Grant's inflexible left flank still remained closed.

It was now the turn of the Union commander to move. He determined to advance still further to the left and cut the railroads which supplied Richmond with provisions. If this were once accomplished Lee would either have to come out of his works and fight, or retreat. To Sheridan was intrusted the task of directing this movement, which was destined to be so full of moment for the Federal cause. To accomplish his purpose it was necessary to pierce the enemy's lines at Five Forks. Thither Sheridan marched with all possible celerity. There was sharp fighting at Dinwiddie Courthouse, and Sheridan was forced back about two miles, but General Grant sent Warren with the Fifth Corps to his assistance, and he pushed on again. At Five Forks the enemy was heavily intrenched, but Sheridan's troops were no sooner up than he attacked. The general himself was in the very front. He utilized to its fullest extent the rare personal influence which he exercised over every man in his command. His voice seemed to make them forget death and wounds. "You're not hurt a bit," he cried to a man who had fallen, shot through the jugular vein, " pick up your gun, man, and move right on to the front!" And incredible as it may seem, the desperately wounded soldier did stagger to his feet and rush on until he fell dead, a dozen paces nearer the enemy's lines.

The story of the assault and Sheridan's share in it makes the blood leap in the veins of the reader. It is told thus dramatically by General Horace Porter, who was himself in the charge:

"As the troops entered the woods, and moved forward over the boggy ground and struggled through the dense undergrowth, they were staggered by a heavy fire from the angle, and fell back in some confusion. Sheridan now rushed into the midst of the broken lines, and cried out, 'Where is my battle-flag?' As the sergeant who carried it rode up, Sheridan seized the crimson and white standard, waved it above his head, cheered on the men, and made heroic efforts to close up the ranks. Bullets were humming like a swarm of bees. One pierced the battle-flag, another killed the sergeant who had carried it, another wounded Captain A. J. McGonigle in the side, others struck two or three of the staff-officers' horses. All this time, Sheridan was dashing from one point of the line to another, waving his flag, shaking his fist, encouraging, threatening, praying, swearing, the very incarnation of battle. It would be a sorry soldier who could help following such a leader..... Ayres, with drawn saber, rushed forward once more with his veterans, who now behaved as if they had fallen back to get a 'good-ready,' and with fixed bayonets and a rousing cheer, dashed over the earthworks, sweeping everything before them, and killing or capturing every man in their immediate front, whose legs had not saved him.

"Sheridan spurred Rienzi up to the angle, and with a bound the horse carried his rider over the earthworks, and landed in the midst of a line of prisoners, who had thrown down their arms and were crouching close under their breastworks. Some of them called out, 'Whar do you want us-all to go to?' Then Sheridan's rage turned to humor, and he had a running talk with the 'Johnnies' as they filed past. 'Go right over there,' he said to them, pointing to the rear. 'Get right along there, now. Drop your guns; you'll never need them any more. You'll all be safe over there. Are there any more of you? We want every one of you fellows.' Nearly 1500 were captured at the angle.

"An orderly here came up to Sheridan, and said, 'Colonel Forsyth of your staff is killed, sir.' 'It's no such thing,' cried Sheridan. 'I don't believe a word of it. You'll find Forsyth's all right.' Ten minutes after Forsyth rode up. Sheridan did not even seem surprised when he saw him, and only said, 'There, I told you so!'"

It was an important victory that Sheridan had won. At last, those inflexible Confederate lines that had so often buffeted back all assailants were pierced. There was loud rejoicing about General Grant's headquarters when the tidings arrived. Men cheered and danced like madmen;

hats, blankets, and burning brands from the camp-fires were waved madly in air. Only the imperturbable commander-in-chief gave no sign, but entering his tent wrote out a half a dozen brief dispatches, sent them off, and coming out again, to where his staff were still talking of the day's success and its probable results, said quietly, "I have ordered an immediate assault along the lines." After some further consideration, other dispatches were sent out, ordering the attack to be made at four o'clock the next morning, Sunday, April 2. Then General Grant turned into his little camp-bed, and slept as soundly as though the last chapter in the Civil War were not just opening.

When Sherman started south from Atlanta the whole Confederacy was found to be but a shell. It required a little hard work to get through the crust, but when that was once accomplished no further resistance was encountered. Such, on a smaller scale, proved to be the situation at Petersburg; those frowning bastions, these long curves and zigzags of revetted earthwork, well garnished with cannon, that had so long held the Union armies at bay, proved to be but a slight obstacle in the path of the men in blue when once seriously attempted.

It was still dark when the storming parties picked their way forward from the Union lines; the pioneers were in advance with their axes with which to cut away the abatis that barred the path to the enemy's works. The Confederate pickets soon gave the alarm, and there came a storm of bursting shell and whistling grape-shot from the threatened redoubts. Through it all the assailants pressed on. The works were reached and the torrent of blue went pouring over the crest, with irresistible force. Wright, Parke, Ord, and Humphreys carried the enemy's lines in their front, one after the other. Thousands of prisoners were taken. General A. P. Hill, who had fought by Lee's side since the war opened and whose name was last on the lips of the dying "Stonewall" Jackson, was killed. Disaster followed disaster so rapidly that the Confederates were soon in complete rout, drifting aimlessly along toward Appomattox.

There was panic in Richmond that bright April morning. It was Sunday, and the Confederate President, Jefferson Davis, was in church. Through

DEFENDING AN EMBRASURE

the open windows the sound of the cannon booming on Lee's lines came floating in. Though the people in the congregation knew that the day could not be far distant when their city must fall before the tireless energy and boundless resources of the Northern army, they had become so accustomed to looking upon Lee's army as invincible that they felt no present dread of disaster. Though the department clerks and the home guards had been hurriedly summoned to the front, that gave the citizens no concern, for that had happened often before and still no Northern soldier had trodden the city's streets, save as a prisoner. The last news that had come from the front had told of General Lee's sortie and capture of Fort Stedman. The Richmond papers had carefully suppressed the news of the recapture of the work, and the worshipers, who heard that Sunday morning the heavy notes of the cannon rising over the sound of the singing and the preacher's reverent voice, thought that perhaps Lee was making another sortie and winning new laurels for the Confederacy.

In the midst of the service a heavy step caused the congregation to turn to stare at the intruder. Up the middle aisle to President Davis's pew strode a courier, booted and spurred. He handed Mr. Davis a sealed official dispatch. " It is absolutely necessary," so ran the fateful dispatch, " that we should abandon our position to-night, or run the risk of being cut off in the morning."

The Confederate President rose and walked quickly out of the sanctuary. Under his cold and impassive face he hid the knowledge that the day of the fall of Richmond had at last arrived. That terse dispatch from the leader of the Confederate forces told the story of the hopelessness of the situation, and Mr. Davis and other officials high in the Confederate service made hasty preparations for flight.

The news spread fast through the city. Panic seized upon the people. Everybody who had money spent it in securing the means of escape from the town—fleeing from they knew not what. All day long the wagons and carts rumbled through the streets and over the bridge. The railroads were taxed to their utmost, and even the canal was used as an avenue of escape for those who believed that all sorts of atrocities would accompany the entry of the Federal troops to the town. As night came on, knots of ill-visaged men began to come out from the slums of the city. Liquor flowed freely, and robberies were of frequent occurrence. Next day the panic was still wilder. Not one-tenth of the people who had determined upon flight could escape by the railroad, and the roads and lanes leading from the town were jammed by throngs of excited men, tearful women, and crying children. The streets resounded with the crash of glass and the sound of splintering doors, for the mob was at work, and store after store was pilfered. The Confederate troops had gone. Only a rear-guard of cavalry remained, to which was intrusted the work of burning the bridges and the great tobacco warehouses. The Confederate officer whose duty it was to set the torch to the bridge, after the last gray-clad troops had crossed, writes:[1]

"I hurried to my command, and fifteen minutes later occupied Mayo's bridge, at the foot of Fourteenth Street, and made military dispositions to protect it to the last extremity. This done, I had nothing to do but listen for sounds and gaze on the terrible splendors of the scene. And such a scene probably the world has never witnessed. Either incendiaries, or, more probably, fragments of bombs from the arsenals, had fired various buildings, and the two cities, Richmond and Manchester, were like a blaze of day amid the surrounding darkness. Three high-arched bridges were in flames; beneath them the waters sparkled and dashed, and rushed on by the burning city. Every now and then, as a magazine exploded, a column of white smoke rose up as high as the eye could reach, instantaneously followed by a deafening sound. The earth seemed to rock and tremble as with the shock of an earthquake, and immediately afterward hundreds of shells would explode in the air and send their iron spray down far below the bridge. As the immense magazines of cartridges ignited, the rattle as of thousands of musketry would follow, and then all was still for the moment, except the dull roar and crackle of the fast spreading fires. At dawn we heard terrific explosions about "The Rocketts," from the unfinished iron-clads down the river.

---

[1] Captain Clement Sullivan, in " Battles and Leaders of the Civil War."

"By daylight on the 3d a mob of men, women, and children, to the number of several thousands, had gathered at the corner of Fourteenth and Cary streets, and other outlets, in front of the bridge, attracted by the vast commissary depot at that point; for it must be remembered that in 1865 Richmond was a half-starved city, and the Confederate Government had that morning removed its guards and abandoned the removal of the provisions, which was impossible for the want of transportation. The depot doors were forced open and a demoniacal struggle for the countless barrels of hams, bacon, whisky, flour, sugar, coffee, etc., etc., raged about the buildings among the hungry mob. The gutters ran whisky, and it was lapped as it flowed down the streets, while all fought for a share of the plunder. The flames came nearer and nearer, and at last caught in the commissariat itself.

"At daylight the approach of the Union forces could be plainly discerned. After a little came the clatter of horses' hoofs galloping up Main Street. My infantry guard stood to arms, the picket across the canal was withdrawn, and the engineer officer lighted a torch of fat pine. By the direction of the Engineer Department, barrels of tar, surrounded by pine-knots, had been placed at intervals on the bridge, with kerosene at hand, and a lieutenant of engineers had reported for the duty of firing them at my order. The noisy train proved to be Gary's ambulances, sent forward preparatory to his final rush for the bridge. The muleteers galloped their animals about half-way down, when they were stopped by the dense mass of human beings. Rapidly communicating to Captain Mayo my instructions from General Ewell, I ordered that officer to stand firm at his post until Gary got up. I rode forward into the mob and cleared a lane. The ambulances were galloped down to the bridge, I retired to my post, and the mob closed in after me and resumed its wild struggle for plunder. A few minutes later, a long line of cavalry, in gray, turned into Fourteenth Street, and, sword in hand, galloped straight down to the river. Gary had come. The mob scattered right and left before the armed horsemen, who reined up at the canal. Presently a single company of cavalry appeared in sight, and rode at headlong speed to the bridge. 'My rear-guard,' explained Gary.

Touching his hat to me, he called out, 'All over, good-by; blow her to h—ll,' and trotted over the bridge. That was the first and last I ever saw of General Gary, of South Carolina.

"In less than sixty seconds Captain Mayo was in column of march, and as he reached the little island about half-way across the bridge, the single piece of artillery, loaded with grape-shot, that had occupied the spot, arrived on the Manchester side of the river. The engineer officer, Dr. Lyons, and I walked leisurely to the island, setting fire to the provided combustible matter as we passed along, and leaving the north section of Mayo's bridge wrapped in flame and smoke. At the island we stopped to take a view of the situation north of the river, and saw a line of blue-coated horsemen galloping in furious haste up Main Street. Across Fourteenth Street they stopped, and then dashed down Fourteenth Street to the flaming bridge. They fired a few random shots at us three on the island, and we retreated to Manchester."

The people of Richmond who remained in the city to confront its conquerors soon discovered that they had to fear no violence either to their persons or property. The men of the North treated the people of this captured city, for which they had fought for four long and bloody years, with consideration, even with kindness. A sort of sense of poetic justice impelled the Federals to send a brigade of colored troops first to take possession of the town. The citizens looked askance at these dark-faced blue-clad men, lately their slaves now their conquerors, but their countenances changed when they saw these blacks join heartily in the work of extinguishing the flames which the retreating Confederates had left behind them. This was no easy task, and a great part of the city was sacrificed. Soon after the occupation of Richmond, President Lincoln came to see the city for which the armies of the nation had so long striven. It was his only taste of triumph, for before the last army of the Confederacy had surrendered, and a free flag waved again over a single nation from Maine to the Rio Grande, the President was dead, struck down by the cowardly hand of a frantic assassin.

Meantime Lee was still retreating, closely pursued by Grant, who hung remorselessly upon the skirts of his antagonist's army, never losing an opportunity to strike a blow, and fairly wearing out the Confederates by the merciless pertinacity of his pursuit. Lee's army was fast going to pieces because of its own internal weakness. The men knew well enough that the end was nigh, and desertions were of hourly occurrence. Worn out by fatigue, and weak because of insufficient food, hundreds of stragglers lagged behind the column and were cut off by Grant's alert cavalrymen. Sheridan's troopers made many dashes into the Confederate column, cutting out prisoners and guns and burning wagons. Every hour was a reverse for the men who followed Lee; every day a dire disaster.

The line of the retreat lay to the westward, Lee naturally trying to effect a juncture with Johnston's army at Danville. This it was the effort of Grant to prevent, and the two armies marched in parallel lines. There were occasional collisions when the lines came in contact, some of which rose to the dignity of actual battles, like that at Sailor's Creek, where Custer broke the Confederate lines, capturing 400 wagons, 16 guns, and many prisoners. Custer's success was scarcely won when the Sixth Corps came up and supplemented it by taking prisoners the whole of Ewell's corps, together with the commanding officer himself and four other general officers. Yet both armies understood that the fate of this campaign was to be settled chiefly by the walking powers of the contestants. If Grant could bar Lee's path before he reached Johnston, the fate of the Confederacy would be determined then and there. A lucky stroke, by which Sheridan captured a provision train upon which the Confederates had relied, forced them to halt a day to scour the surrounding country for forage. As a result, when, a day or two later, Lee reached Appomattox Court-house, he found his path barred by a long line of dismounted cavalry. The Confederate veterans advanced confidently to sweep these out of their way, but recoiled in dismay when the cavalrymen, falling back, disclosed a solid rank of blue-clad infantry, and the gleaming muzzles of many cannons. The cavalry, which had screened this formidable force, were now seen to be massing on the Confederate flank for a charge. Then a white flag fluttered in front of the tattered gray lines, and the last collision between the gallant but unfortunate Army of Northern Virginia and the no less gallant Army of the Potomac was over. "I had 'em like that," said Sheridan some hours later, clinching up his fist to show how he had held Lee's battle-scarred veterans in his clutches.

The display of a flag of truce, which had checked Sheridan's assault, was followed by a message telling him that General Grant and General Lee were in conference concerning a surrender, and asking for an armistice until the result of that conference could be determined. For two days the two chieftains had been exchanging notes relative to a surrender, and at the very moment when Sheridan brought the Army of Northern Virginia to bay, they sat face to face in a parlor of Colonel McClean's house, in Appomattox Court-house. The results of that meeting were so momentous and its incidents revealed so much true nobility in the character of the Union commander, that the graphic and trustworthy account of an eye-witness, General Horace Porter,[1] may be given in part.

"The contrast between the two commanders was striking, and could not fail to attract marked attention, as they sat ten feet apart, facing each other. General Grant, then nearly forty-three years of age, was five feet eight inches in height, with shoulders slightly stooped. His hair and full beard were a nut-brown, without a trace of gray in them. He had on a single-breasted blouse, made of dark-blue flannel, unbuttoned in front, and showing a waistcoat underneath. He wore an ordinary pair of top-boots, with his trousers inside, and was without spurs. The boots and portions of his clothes were spattered with mud. He had had on a pair of thread gloves, of a dark-yellow color, which he had taken off on entering the room. His felt sugar-loaf, stiff-brimmed hat was thrown on the table beside him. He had no sword, and a pair of shoulder-straps was all there was about him to designate his rank. In fact, aside from these, his uniform was that of a private soldier.

"Lee, on the other hand, was fully six feet in height, and quite erect for one of his age, for he was Grant's senior by sixteen years. His hair and

---

[1] In "Battles and Leaders of the Civil War."

full beard were a silver-gray, and quite thick, except that the hair had become a little thin in front. He wore a new uniform of Confederate gray, buttoned up to the throat, and at his side he carried a sword of exceedingly fine workmanship, the hilt studded with jewels . . . . . His top-boots were new, and seemed to have on them some ornamental stitching of red silk. Like his uniform they were singularly clean and but little travel-stained. On the boots were handsome spurs, with large rowels. A felt hat, which in color matched pretty closely that of his uniform, and a pair of long buckskin gauntlets lay beside him on the table."

The subject of the surrender was brought up and there was some general talk about the prospects of peace. "Lee was evidently anxious to proceed to the formal work of the surrender, and he brought the subject up again by saying:

"'I presume, General Grant, we have both carefully considered the steps to be taken, and I would suggest that you commit to writing the terms you have proposed, so that they may be formally acted upon.'

"'Very well,' replied General Grant, 'I will write them out.' And calling for his manifold order-book, he opened it on the table before him and proceeded to write the terms. The leaves had been so prepared that three impressions of the writing were made. He wrote very rapidly and did not pause until he had finished the sentence ending with 'officers appointed by me to receive them.' Then he looked toward Lee, and his eyes seemed to be resting on the handsome sword that hung at that officer's side. He said afterward that this set him to thinking that it would be an unnecessary humiliation to require the officers to surrender their swords, and a great hardship to deprive them of their personal baggage and horses, and after a short pause he wrote the sentence: 'This will not embrace the side-arms of the officers, nor their private horses and baggage.'"

The letter was as follows:

APPOMATTOX COURT-HOUSE, VA., April 29, 1865.
GENERAL R. E. LEE, COMMANDING C. S. A.

General: In accordance with the substance of my letter to you of the 8th instant, I propose to receive the surrender of the Army of Northern Virginia on the following terms, to wit: Rolls of all the officers and men to be made in duplicate, one copy to be given to an officer to be named by me, the other to be retained by such officer or officers as you may designate. The officers to give their individual paroles not to take up arms against the Government of the United States until properly [exchanged] and each company or regimental commander to sign a like parole for the men of their commands. The arms, artillery, and public property to be parked and stacked, and turned over to the officers appointed by me to receive them. This will not embrace the side-arms of the officers, nor their private horses or baggage. This done, each officer and man will be allowed to return to his home, not to be disturbed by the United States authorities so long as they observe their paroles and the laws in force where they may reside.

U. S. GRANT, *Lieutenant-General.*

"Lee took it and laid it upon the table beside him, while he drew from his pocket a pair of steel-rimmed spectacles and wiped the glasses carefully with his handkerchief. Then he crossed his legs, adjusted the spectacles very slowly and deliberately, took up the draft of the letter and proceeded to read it attentively. . . . . When Lee came to the sentence about the officer's side-arms, private horses and baggage, he showed for the first time during the reading of the letter a slight change of countenance, and was evidently touched by this act of generosity. It was doubtless the condition mentioned to which he particularly alluded when he looked toward General Grant, as he finished reading, and said with some degree of warmth in his manner: 'This will have a very happy effect upon my army.'

"General Grant then said, 'Unless you have some suggestion to make in regard to the form in which I have stated the terms, I will have a copy of the letter made in ink and sign it.'

"'There is one thing I would like to mention,' Lee replied after a short pause. 'The cavalymen and artillerists own their own horses in our army. Its organization in this respect differs from that of the United States.' This expression attracted the notice of our officers present, as showing how firmly the conviction was grounded in his mind that we were two distinct countries. He continued: 'I would like to understand whether these men will be permitted to retain their horses?'

"'You will find that the terms as written do not allow this,' General

THE FIELD HOSPITAL.

Grant replied: 'only the officers are permitted to take their private property.'

"Lee read over the second page of the letter again and then said:

"'No, I see that the terms do not allow it; that is clear.' His face showed plainly that he was quite anxious to have this concession made, and Grant said very promptly and without giving Lee time to make a direct request:

"'Well, the subject is quite new to me. Of course I did not know that any private soldiers owned their animals, but I think this will be the last battle of the war—I sincerely hope so—and that the surrender of this army will be followed soon by that of all the others, and I take it that most of the men in the ranks are small farmers, and as the country has been so raided by the two armies, it is doubtful whether they will be able to put in a crop to carry themselves and their families through the next winter without the aid of the horses they are now riding, and I will arrange it in this way: I will not change the terms as now written, but I will instruct the officers I shall appoint to receive the paroles to let all the men who claim to own a horse or mule take the animals home with them to work their little farms.'

"Lee now looked greatly relieved, and though anything but a demonstrative man, he gave every evidence of his appreciation of this concession, and said, 'This will have the best possible effect upon the men. It will be very gratifying and will do much toward conciliating our people.'

"After this colloquy, General Lee signified his intention of accepting the terms and surrendering his army, and beckoning to his private secretary, Colonel Marshall, he dictated and signed a letter to that effect. There then followed a few moments of general conversation, during which the many Union officers present were introduced to the fallen Confederate chieftain. Lee, however, presently brought the conversation back into business channels by saying:

"'I have a thousand or more of your men as prisoners, General Grant, a number of them officers, whom we have required to march along with us for several days. I shall be glad to send them into your lines as soon as it can be arranged, for I have no provisions for them. I have, indeed, nothing for my own men; they have been living for the last few days principally upon parched corn, and we are badly in need of both rations and forage. I telegraphed to Lynchburg, directing several train loads of rations to be sent on by rail from there, and when they arrive I should be glad to have the present wants of my men supplied from them.'

"At this remark all eyes turned toward Sheridan, for he had captured these trains with his cavalry the night before, near Appomattox station. General Grant replied, 'I should like to have our men sent within our lines as soon as possible. I will take steps at once to have your army supplied with the rations, but I am sorry we have no forage for the animals. We have had to depend upon the country for our supply of forage. Of about how many men does your present force consist?'

"'Indeed, I am not able to say,' Lee answered, after a slight pause. 'My losses in killed and wounded have been exceedingly heavy, and, besides, there have been many stragglers and some deserters. All my reports and public papers, and, indeed, my own private letters, had to be destroyed on the march, to prevent them from falling into the hands of your people. Many companies are entirely without officers, and I have not seen any returns for several days. So that I have no means of ascertaining our present strength.'

"General Grant had taken great pains to have a daily estimate made of the enemy's forces from all the data that could be obtained, and judging it to be about 25,000 at this time, he said: 'Suppose I send over 25,000 rations; do you think that will be a sufficient supply?' 'I think it will be ample,' remarked Lee, and added, with considerable earnestness of manner, 'and it will be a great relief, I assure you.'"

Again the conversation drifted into general topics, Lee joining in but infrequently, and soon rising to take his leave. As he stepped out into the yard and stood waiting for his horse, the Union officers, of whom there were many lounging about, sprang to their feet and doffed their caps respectfully. The higher officers who had been in the council chamber came out on the piazza of the McLean house and, following General Grant's example, lifted their hats in a silent salute, as the white-bearded Confederate, followed by his solitary aid, rode off toward his crushed and sorrowing army.

A strange and unaccustomed quiet hung over the camps of the armies lately hostile that night. The Confederates, depressed and down-hearted, were silent in their tents. They crowded about him who had so long been their leader, and listened respectfully to the few quiet words in which he bade them go to their homes and pursue the vocations of peace " until exchanged." They knew well enough that there would be no exchange ; that their cause was now a lost cause, and that they would never bear arms again. It was quiet, too, in the Union lines. When the news of the surrender became known the men cheered and danced in triumph, and the artillerymen made the country resound with the roar of triumphant salutes. But in the midst of the enthusiasm came an order from General Grant. "The war is over," said he. "The rebels are our countrymen again, and the best sign of rejoicing after the victory will be to abstain from all demonstrations in the field." A noble and a magnanimous heart spoke there !

How swiftly the closing scenes in the great drama of the civil war followed each other. It seemed that the Confederacy was like one of those glass toys of the scientist that crumble to powder if their points be broken. Once Lee's lines were broken all was over. When a report of his army was made it was found that he had left him scarce 8000 men capable of bearing arms. This pitiful force had been all that stood between the Confederacy and collapse. Once it was out of the way the remaining armed forces of the Confederacy were surrendered. Johnston heard the tidings and gave up his army to General Sherman without seeking to prolong the struggle. There then remained but one organized Confederate army in the field—that of General Kirby Smith in the far Southwest. But to Smith, too, came the tidings of the annihilation of the Confederate military strength, and his colors were furled and his guns thrown down. May 27, 1865, saw no longer a single regiment in the field fighting to overturn the National authority.

One man alone remained irreconcilable. Jefferson Davis, as he fled southward from Richmond, spread on every hand appeals for a continuation of the war at whatever odds. His proclamations scorned the very thought of failure. He would have the people of the South carry on a guerrilla warfare. He would have such soldiers as still remained with arms in their hands take to the mountains and there fight a defensive war for years. Blind to the desire of the Southern people for peace, deaf to the protests of his officers, who saw that further resistance was hopeless, he clung to his determination to prolong the conflict. At last he was overtaken in his flight by a detachment of United States Cavalry, and the President of the Confederacy was captured while seeking to escape in the garments of a woman.

It was in the midst of the triumph of the nation, when every day and every mail brought tidings of some fresh victory for the National arms, some new sign that the effort to disrupt the Union was effectually withstood, that the shot was fired by Wilkes Booth which struck down the great and wise leader who had guided the nation through the storm of war. The murder of Abraham Lincoln was a crime that shocked Christendom. It was a deed that revolted even the men against whom his every thought and deed had been directed for more than four years. The South sorrowed for him. The Southern leaders, mindful of the fact that an enraged public sentiment would probably charge them with complicity in the assassination, hastened to declare their abhorrence of the crime. It is well to set down once again the verdict of history which acquits the leaders of the "Lost Cause" and the Southern people, as a people, of all complicity in this execrable assassination.

The long and sanguinary war which covered the country with battle-fields and with soldiers' cemeteries has not been barren of results for the nation. It taught the South that the despised "Yankees" could fight when occasion arose. It taught the North the Southerners were not mere braggarts. It silenced the sneers of Europe by demonstrating that Americans were not merely a "nation of shop-keepers." If it showed that Americans could fight bravely, it showed, too, that they

INCIDENT OF THE RAILWAY RAID.

could forgive nobly. Twenty-five years of peace have healed the wounds of war. No bitterness, no malice remains. Purged of the great evil of slavery, united in every part by social and commercial ties, discharging with unprecedented rapidity the enormous debt which four years of war piled up, the Republic is to-day greater, stronger, and more prosperous than ever. No cloud appears upon its horizon. Those who for base purposes would stir up war-time animosities daily grow fewer. Honored in the congress of nations, seeking no quarrels, and dreading no foe, the United States seem to be entering upon a period during which the triumphs of peace shall fairly outdo the victories won on the battle-fields of the Union.

www.ingramcontent.com/pod-product-compliance
Lightning Source LLC
Chambersburg PA
CBHW022051230426
43672CB00008B/1140